ANNA FREUD

RADCLIFFE BIOGRAPHY SERIES

MARGARET FULLER
*From Transcendentalism
to Revolution*
Paula Blanchard
Foreword by
Carolyn G. Heilbrun

ALVA MYRDAL
A Daughter's Memoir
Sissela Bok

THE THIRD ROSE
Gertrude Stein and Her World
John Malcolm Brinnin
Foreword by John Ashbury

DOROTHY DAY
A Radical Devotion
Robert Coles

ANNA FREUD
The Dream of Psychoanalysis
Robert Coles

SIMONE WEIL
A Modern Pilgrimage
Robert Coles

WOMEN OF CRISIS
Lives of Struggle and Hope
Robert Coles and
Jane Hallowell Coles

WOMEN OF CRISIS II
Lives of Work and Dreams
Robert Coles and
Jane Hallowell Coles

CHARLOTTE MEW AND
HER FRIENDS
Penelope Fitzgerald

MARGARET BOURKE-WHITE
A Biography
Vicki Goldberg
Foreword by Phyllis Rose

MARY CASSATT
Nancy Hale
Foreword by Eleanor Munro

MARIA MONTESSORI
A Biography
Rita Kramer
Foreword by Anna Freud

BALM IN GILEAD
Journey of a Healer
Sara Lawrence Lightfoot

THE ALCHEMY OF SURVIVAL
One Woman's Journey
John E. Mack, M.D.
with Rita S. Rogers, M.D.

A MIND OF HER OWN
The Life of Karen Horney
Susan Quinn
Foreword by Leon Edel

EMILY DICKINSON
Cynthia Griffin Wolff
Foreword by R. W. B. Lewis

RADCLIFFE BIOGRAPHY SERIES

PUBLISHED BY DELACORTE PRESS

BUYING THE NIGHT FLIGHT
Georgie Anne Geyer

HELEN AND TEACHER
*The Story of Helen Keller and
Anne Sullivan Macy*
Joseph P. Lash

ANNA FREUD

115 3464

The Dream of Psychoanalysis

618.92
COL

ROBERT COLES

A Merloyd Lawrence Book

ADDISON-WESLEY PUBLISHING COMPANY, INC.

Reading, Massachusetts   Menlo Park, California   New York
Don Mills, Ontario   Wokingham, England   Amsterdam   Bonn
Sydney   Singapore   Tokyo   Madrid   San Juan
Paris   Seoul   Milan   Mexico City   Taipei

Library of Congress Cataloging-in-Publication Data

Coles, Robert.
    Anna Freud : the dream of psychoanalysis / Robert Coles.
        p.   cm. — (Radcliffe biography series)
    "A Merloyd Lawrence book."
    Includes bibliographical references and index.
    ISBN 0-201-57707-0
    1. Freud, Anna, 1895-   . 2. Child analysis—History.   I. Title.
II. Series.
RC339.52.F73C65   1991
618.92′89′0092—dc20
[B]   91-30542
                                                                      CIP

Jacket design by Diana Coe
Jacket illustration © by Richard Giedd
Text design by Janis Owens
Set in 11-point Weiss by Shepard Poorman Communications Corporation

1 2 3 4 5 6 7 8 9-MA-9594939291
First printing, December 1991

To Jane: Many thanks, much love

B+T 11/92

Contents

The Radcliffe Biography Series   xiii

Preface   xv

I   A Life with Children   1

II   Teacher   29

III   Theorist   55

IV   Healer   79

V   Leader   103

VI   Idealist   129

VII   Writer   155

Appendix   179

The Achievement of Anna Freud   181

Letters from Anna Freud to Robert Coles 7/10/66, 6/1/68, 7/19/69, and 1/20/70   199

Notes   205

Selected Bibliography   211

Index   217

About the Author   221

RADCLIFFE BIOGRAPHY SERIES

On behalf of Radcliffe College, I am pleased to present this volume in the Radcliffe Biography Series.

The series is an expression of the value we see in documenting and understanding the varied lives of women. Exploring the choices and circumstances of these extraordinary women—both famous and unsung—is not merely of interest to the historian, but is central to anyone grappling with what it means to be a woman. The biographies of these women teach us not only about their lives and their worlds, but about ours as well. When women strive to forge their identities, as they do at many points throughout the lifespan, it is crucial to have models to look toward. These women provide such models. We are inspired through their example and are taught by their words.

Radcliffe College's sponsorship of the Radcliffe Biography Series was sparked by the publication in 1972 of *Notable American Women*, a scholarly encyclopedia sponsored by Radcliffe's Schlesinger Library. We became convinced of the importance of expanding the public's awareness of the many significant contributions made by women to America, continuing the commitment to educating people about the lives and work of women that is reflected in much of Radcliffe's work. In addition to commissioning new biographies, we decided to add reprints of distinguished books already published, with introductions written for this series.

It is with great pride and excitement that I present this latest volume.

Linda S. Wilson, President
Radcliffe College
Cambridge, Massachusetts

In 1950, while an undergraduate at Harvard College, I chanced upon a lecture given by Anna Freud. On my way "home" (to my dormitory room) from the organic chemistry laboratory, which for me at the time seemed a parcel of hell's acreage, I met another premedical student who was already interested in psychiatry and psychoanalysis as well. He knew of the scheduled lecture, and suggested we grab a Coke, then hurry for good seats—for there was certain, he said, to be a large audience to hear Miss Freud. I had to confess that I didn't know who Miss Freud was—except that she must be some kin to Sigmund Freud, none of whose books I had read. My friend, on the other hand, knew a great deal about her and her father, and while we had our snack—in Hayes Bickford, a cafeteria long gone—he told me some of what he knew.

I still remember one sentence—the sheer innocence of it, in retrospect!—and I remember becoming more, rather than less, confused for hearing it: "She discovered child psychoanalysis." What did he mean by "discovery"? I asked. (He and I were getting our fill, then, of scientific discoveries—all the laboratory breakthroughs Professor Louis Fieser recounted in his lectures and in his daunting organic chemistry textbook.) My friend was short on details. He didn't know how "she had done it," but she was the one, he asserted, who "brought" psychoanalysis to the nursery. When I asked how in the world such analytic inquiry took place, I was told that if I went to the lecture I'd surely find my answer. By then I had the sense to lose interest, although as I did my friend made one of those cautionary remarks I'd later find familiar: "Don't be scared by what she'll say." I hadn't the slightest idea what that remark meant—or more properly, was meant to mean. I can still remember my puzzled interest in what seemed to me a mix of solicitude and barely concealed condescension. While stifling the urge to pursue the matter, I also put aside the impulse to say goodbye, go study chemistry rather than listen to Miss Freud's lecture. I realized that such a decision, whatever its basis, would be seen only as a confirmation that I was, indeed, a bit frightened. In self-defense, I showed a heightened interest in both Freuds while we made haste to get to the lecture hall early.

We sat fairly close to the front. While we were waiting, we looked around at the others, and noticed that many, indeed most of them, weren't our age, weren't students at all. In the 1950s, the "New Lecture Hall" was much used (it is now in great need of repair). In those days, attendance was taken at the beginning of each class, so I would ordinarily have sat in an assigned seat. It seemed doubly strange, then, to be sitting where I wished, and to be among so many "adults." Quite a few spoke in accents, and I was not always able to fathom the meaning of many words used by those who did speak excellent English. My friend observed my perplexity, hastened to help me out: we were in the midst of the "psychoanalytic community." Again I didn't ask him what he meant for fear of being thought stupid; but I was not at all reassured. I knew next to nothing then about psychiatry or psychoanalysis, only that Sigmund Freud was someone important in twentieth-century cultural or intellectual history, someone who had figured out how the mind works, what dreams meant, and a way of helping people who had gotten into psychological trouble. The phrase "psychoanalytic community," for an instant, at least, conjured in my mind the thought of a somewhat disturbed group of people—maybe "patients" who lived in Cambridge and had been treated by this or that psychiatrist and who now wanted to hear a prominent one speak. Years later, of course, lying on the couch and letting all things come to mind, into words, I would recall my ignorance that afternoon—a twenty-year-old brought up by a devoutly religious mother from an Iowa farm and an English-born scientist father with little interest in or patience for the social sciences, never mind, to use Freud's word, matters "metapsychological." I would also recall the nature of that historical moment—the years immediately after the Second World War, when psychoanalysis was just beginning to have an influence on American culture. But at the time, all I could try to do was to appear as sophisticated as possible— listening to my friend without evident surprise or anxiety as he told me about where "they tended to live," to have their offices, and even their fees: the astonishing sum of ten or fifteen dollars an hour for five visits a week, for years. In the privacy of my mind I wondered who had so much money, and why so many visits each week. Wasn't one good long talk enough to help anyone fathom what ailed him or her?

Soon such thoughts were interrupted by the arrival on the platform of a short, thin, middle-aged lady, accompanied by a taller, somewhat heavyset man. I never did, even back then, catch his name. He introduced Miss Freud briefly, and she wasted no time getting into the heart of her message—an exposition of the important principles of psychoanalysis, its view of mental function, and its clinical method. To my surprise, I followed her line of reasoning rather well. Here was someone who really wanted to teach us; who spoke with conviction and clarity; who did not intimidate or condescend to her audience. I didn't, of course, use such words back then. Less exact psychologically, I simply pronounced the lecture "good," the speaker "persuasive." I admitted to being "interested" in what she had said—and told my friend I intended to go to the library and look up what she had written. Since I was heavily burdened with course work, such a decision was a real commitment.

At the time, I was also involved as a volunteer tutor in what was still called a "settlement house"—a place where children from vulnerable families (psychologically or sociologically speaking) received needed educational or medical assistance. I remember even today the first visit I made to that settlement house after Miss Freud's lecture. I was working with Gerry, a nine- or ten-year-old boy who had severe temper tantrums in school and had been suspended for a week or longer. He and I studied his homework together, and I often brought him a candy bar. I had assumed that his primary problem was medical—he had a "clubfoot" that gave him difficulty as he tried to get to school, play with his friends, keep up with the rhythms of his neighborhood. Although I knew he had a temper, that seemed of little significance: Gerry never mentioned it to me; I had never observed it; and no one else seemed interested in it; whereas his physical difficulty (and the repeated ear infections he had suffered earlier, necessitating surgery in those years before antibiotics) prompted much discussion. He was seen as a physically handicapped child in need of some help in learning, because he'd missed school when younger and was still somewhat incapacitated.

It is hard now to remember Gerry as I knew him, thought of him, back then. Today so many of us—millions, perhaps, without any idea of who Anna Freud was—will meet or learn of a Gerry, and immediately think not of his body, but of his mind. What happens to a boy's head when his leg does not work well—is congenitally short or abnormal with respect to bone formation, muscular or nerve supply? It was less than forty years ago that Gerry and I did our weekly work together, yet my view of him back then would be regarded by a student volunteer today as naive, indeed. Thanks to Miss Freud's lecture, however, I began to have some second thoughts about Gerry, and my own involvement with him. In her lecture, she had mentioned the impact upon children of illness and deformity—the way in which a child whose body doesn't work well takes the defect to heart. As she spoke, Gerry had momentarily crossed my mind. Now, sitting across the table from Gerry, I saw her before me. I wondered what she would think of this boy, who could be so cooperative, even compliant with me—yet, who would strike out angrily at friends at home, classmates at school, swear without restraint, throw rocks, withdraw in sullen resentment and defiance. No doubt, I imagined, she would say something to the boy—be a good teacher in the sense of knowing *le mot juste*.

That afternoon, as I sat with Gerry and helped him with a school composition, I had a fantasy that Miss Freud would arrive, ask the boy to come over to her teacher's desk, sit him down in a chair nearby, put him at ease, tell him some things about himself that would have the clear, convincing ring of truth, then send him off, a changed person. How would he be different? I hadn't really thought the matter out, but I suppose I had in mind the image of an attentive student (Gerry) listening to a compelling teacher (Miss Freud) and, as a consequence, *shaping up*—a phrase my father used to use in an admonishing and exhortative fashion. In no time, however, I was caught up again with the immediate contingencies of tutoring, and Miss Freud slipped out of my memory.

A year later I was in medical school, where I fastened my hopes on pediatric work with children. During an internship and residency in pediatrics and child psychiatry, I became especially interested in the ways children struggle with severe illness—their moods, their hopes and worries, as they lay sick in the hospital. It was then that I had occasion to hear Miss Freud again. She had come back to America, and she was now talking about her work after the Second World War with children who had survived concentration camps. This talk was less "public"; it was given in the seminar room of a Boston hospital. I had been invited to attend by an older physician, a surgeon who had taken an interest in psychoanalysis and, as a matter of fact, had been analyzed by a prominent colleague of Anna Freud's father, yet another "refugee" who had found his way during the late 1930s to the United States.

The small room was crowded, with about forty people, almost all physicians. I was once more struck by the directness of the speaker, her evident command of her subject, her willingness to share her knowledge with us in such an accessible manner. Each sentence seemed a perfectly formed jewel, sparkling and delightful to contemplate. An uncanny mixture of relaxed self-assurance and intense dedication emanated from this small, still thin woman, plainly dressed, her voice strong but not insistent. I still remember the talk, and I still remember a sudden desire, afterward, to ask a question about a girl I had come to know, a patient at Children's Hospital in Boston. This girl had a serious diabetic condition, and yet seemed so resolutely cheerful and confident that all of us—nurses, social workers, doctors—wondered what "really" crossed the child's mind when she was alone, when she was not putting up such a valiant show of outgoing optimism. I didn't expect Miss Freud to say what our young patient was thinking, but all of us at the hospital were worried about her future psychological prospects, and so I did ask about prognosis—about the likelihood of psychopathology developing in a year, two years, or even farther along.

Even now, I can see as well as hear Miss Freud's response. She put her hands on her papers, moved them slowly, deliberately, but with increasing animation. Her message was pointed—and a real challenge for the young doctors in the audience who were accustomed to receiving categorical or specific advice: "Who can ever foretell what a child will be like in the time ahead?"

I wrote the words down, and found them quite unsatisfying— the kind of remark, actually, one of my grandparents would make out of the stoic surrender of old age. I was convinced that *she* was the very one who could with reliability and accuracy do such prophesying. But she persisted, and reminded us, at length, how difficult it can be for even the best-informed observer of any given child to know what tomorrow will bring in the way of psychological adjustment, or the lack thereof. Later that week, when George Gardner, chief of child psychiatry at the Children's Hospital, and a child psychoanalyst, met with us residents, we discussed Miss Freud's lecture, the way in which she answered questions and, especially, her seeming reluctance to make psychological forecasts. His response was brief: "She is genuinely modest." I think some of us took that comment as a reprimand—so heady were we with our newfound (and incomplete) knowledge, and so eager were we to wield it in front of others, colleagues and patients alike.

Soon afterward I began a prolonged period of supervision with Dr. Gardner, who admired both Miss Freud and another child psychoanalyst whose work I was just then getting to know, Erik H. Erikson. Often when I came to my supervisory hour Dr. Gardner would listen to my case presentation, make a comment or two about the child, or the therapy I was trying to do, and then bring up for discussion some aspect of Anna Freud's thinking, or Erik H. Erikson's. During such talks, we tried to connect the writing of those two child analysts to the clinical issues I had brought to Dr. Gardner's attention. He was a great one for the casual remark that was meant to reassure a nervous young doctor—but often unnerved him. For example, after I'd made my initial presentation, he might say: "I can

see why you are concerned, but don't forget your biggest ally: time."
Hearing those words, I was supposed to sit back, stretch my legs, and
swallow the soft drink or coffee he invariably had waiting for his
supervisees.

Dr. Gardner asked me to read carefully Anna Freud's *The Ego
and the Mechanisms of Defense,* as well as her monograph *War and Children.* We discussed her point of view at great length; and in this way,
she became a distinct and continuing presence all through my supervisory experience as a resident in child psychiatry. In the mid-1930s,
she had insisted upon the mind's capacity to respond with energy,
guile, resiliency, and, not least, intelligent resourcefulness in response
to the unconscious yearnings and compulsions that psychoanalytic
theorists had worked so hard to understand. This was so even with
young children, Dr. Gardner reminded me, and I learned to see this
resilience in the boys and girls I was treating—in their often astonishing maneuvers, remarks, deeds, dreams, drawings, as they tried hard
to give their lives shape and purpose, however burdensome their psychological difficulties. "Miss Freud will help you as you work," Dr.
Gardner once told me in a moment of reassurance. Indeed, the sensible directness of her observations on children was a welcome contrast to some of the theoretical writing I was then trying to master in
the psychoanalytic journals. His comment—or prophecy—was
meant to help me make the connection between clinical challenges
and Miss Freud's ideas in such a manner that the children under my
care would benefit. It is not always that articles and books have such
a bearing on the lives of both doctors and patients.

After completing my training in child psychiatry, I went south to
Mississippi under the old doctor's draft law to take charge of a large
U.S. Air Force neuropsychiatric hospital. There, in nearby New
Orleans, I underwent psychoanalysis and took courses at the Psychoanalytic Institute, while also beginning work with the black (and, eventually, white) children caught in the turmoil of school desegregation.
What was to be a two-year stint in Dixie turned into a whole new
professional life—an effort to understand how children of various backgrounds manage under all sorts of social, cultural, and political circumstances. I have described that work in a number of books,[1] and in them I

constantly make reference to Anna Freud. Indeed, in the very first articles I wrote, in the late 1950s and early 1960s, she was very much *there*—helping me understand the young polio patients I came to know at the Children's Hospital,[2] and later, the beleaguered children of Louisiana who faced down daily mobs in order to integrate elementary schools.

By 1965, I was anxious to study her writing at length, and to write about the significance of her ideas for people in my field. I titled the essay "The Achievement of Anna Freud"; it was published in a literary quarterly, *The Massachusetts Review*, in 1966. A month or so later, I received a letter from Miss Freud, thanking me, and saying that I was on target. (An analysand of hers had shown the article to her.) I replied. She replied. We were on our way to a correspondence that lasted for many years, and eventually, to meetings, discussions—many valuable exchanges that helped me in so many ways. Her visits to Yale, for a while an annual occurrence, became an important part of my life—the trip there to meet her, listen to her, learn from her. Child psychoanalysis was far from her only interest. She read broadly, had a lively mind that reached toward the world and its various problems. She was especially interested, during the late 1960s and 1970s, in the social and racial problems with which both the United States and Great Britain were struggling, even as she had responded so brilliantly and passionately to the English children who lived under the threat of Nazi bombers during the Second World War, or to those children who had survived the concentration camps at the end of that war. To talk with her about such matters was always a privilege and moment of important instruction.

To talk with her about other matters—that of religion as children experience it, for instance—was not only a privilege, but also, I now realize, an utter necessity for me as I examined the way the boys and girls I was interviewing saw the world, tried to find meaning in it. Again and again, as I tried to make sense of the research I was doing—the statements I heard, the drawings and paintings I was shown—I thought back to her written remarks, her spoken comments, made as we looked together at a particular child's artwork, read transcripts of the child's declarations, questions, complaints, speculations. We carry with us, emotionally and intellectually, various guardian spirits (or "mentors," as today's language would have it), and for me Anna Freud was one such constant presence.

Still later, when I came to work with, and know, and in time write about Erik H. Erikson, the name of Anna Freud came up: she was his analyst. Then came a friendship with Helen Ross, a child analyst who was close to Miss Freud. Miss Ross and I were on the board of the Field Foundation in the 1970s, and a major interest of that foundation was the training center Miss Freud ran at Hampstead in London. Her reports, her letters, her American visits, meant a lot to us—another chance to learn from her. To read her accounts of how things went at her clinic was to learn not only about a child psychoanalyst's view of the young, but a strong leader's visionary interest in the next generation. So many educators of all kinds (doctors, nurses, social workers, teachers) have taken their training at Hampstead and learned from Miss Freud not only the specifics of psychoanalysis but, more broadly, how to think about the possibilities in children as well as their inevitable times of trial. So many of us have worked with children differently, thought differently, because of her. She was a strong moral and intellectual force in psychoanalysis for a half a century.

During the 1970s, I often thought of writing a biography of Anna Freud, and several times broached the subject with her. She was, indeed, as Dr. Gardner had told us, "genuinely modest." Once, when a mutual friend sent an article I'd written about her, she wrote back to say that I had too high an opinion of her, but that "anyway, it is something to live up to." Instead of a biography, she suggested, "you can do me the honor of using my thoughts in your work." I remember her as she spoke those words in a Yale dormitory: eyes as always alertly focused on the person being addressed, a cup of coffee in her hand, a plate of Viennese cakes nearby. One did not easily take issue with her. On the other hand, she was more than eager to be of help to me as I wrote or considered writing biographical studies of others—Erik Erikson, Simone Weil, Dorothy Day.[3] She even read my essays on William Carlos Williams and Walker Percy, and was intrigued, I think it fair to say, by those two physician-writers.[4] After all, she was the daughter of a predecessor of theirs. Several times, as a matter of fact, she told me how important writing was to her father—

not only the ideas formulated, but also the process of giving the words a proper and inviting shape.

I was working on these biographies of Simone Weil and Dorothy Day when Miss Freud died in London in 1982. That twin project (two books written in tandem) took the form it did because of a suggestion she once made to me: "You can highlight their work; you can show the intellectual directions they took; you can weigh and compare their successes and failures." Anyone who knew her would recognize in those words her characteristic way of putting things—clear, pointed, sparse phrasing—and a certain quality of mind as well. In her advice she showed a keen sense of life's victories, life's defeats, as they come upon us all, as well as a wry skepticism that kept company with personal decency, and reticence, shyness almost. She did not suggest that I do a conventional psychological portrait or biography of those two women. Not that they, or Miss Freud herself, wouldn't be fit candidates for such. She and they lived interesting, provocative, even challenging lives. But for her (as for her two fellow inhabitants of the twentieth century), the significance of a life ought to be judged, ultimately, in this way: "What she [Simone Weil] left us to think about is what we *should* be thinking about! We can safely leave aside her personality with no risk of missing something very important and revealing." Again, a characteristic bit of self-revelation—of the ironic outlook that informed so much of her thinking. She was not one to be startled by contemporary outbursts of psychohistorical exuberance. A clinician for many decades, she knew how unsurprising, finally, so much psychopathology turns out to be. No wonder she was interested in what a person *does* with conflict, rather than a continual emphasis on its nature. For instance, on one occasion, a report on a rather disturbed child, a dramatically disturbed child, was presented to her. At the age of thirteen, the boy had set many fires, and spoke in apocalyptic imagery about the imminent end of life on this planet through a nuclear war. Miss Freud shrugged her shoulders and said that the "psychodynamics" were "all too familiar"—but then quickly added: "This boy is determined to let everyone know what is troubling him. He is announcing his problems as if they are accomplishments." An interesting perspective, I thought then, and still do, for a biographer to keep in mind.

In the mid-1970s I was all set to do a profile for *The New Yorker* on Miss Freud, having done one on Erik Erikson. Again she demurred. Instead I did a book review for that magazine—an essay, really, on some of her writing. After her death, and after I was well on my way to completion of the intellectual biographies of Simone Weil and Dorothy Day, I decided to do a similar study of Anna Freud, who in certain respects, as I shall try to demonstrate, belongs in their company. Like the earlier two portraits, this book is also intended as a memoir, an appreciation, a study of one woman's most substantial and varied professional labors.

Once again, I warmly thank Merloyd Lawrence for all her help as I have tried to do justice to three remarkable contemporary women of the West, each a pilgrim in her own way, each a moral visionary. Many times I heard Miss Freud remember her own youth, her "dreams of changing the world by changing people in it through psychoanalysis—and especially children." It is such a remark, and others like it, that inspired this book's subtitle—and prompted me to chronicle for others how those "dreams" turned out in one long, ever so energetic and significant life.

I also thank Jay Woodruff, who has worked with me and been of great help to me as I did the research and the writing of this book. He is a good friend, a real colleague, a fine, fine person. The same thanks go to Wayne Arnold, who also helped as I struggled with this book. Always, I make mention of my wife, Jane, our three sons, Bob, Danny, Mike—who have known, all along, in their bones, in their hearts, what some of us have to find out through the head's occasionally overwrought exertions.

Finally, I mention our beloved dog, Aran, named after the Aran islands, which Miss Freud had visited and loved, as did all of us, Jane and I and our sons. Everyone who knew Anna Freud at all well knew of her great love for dogs in general, and of course, most especially, for the dogs who figured in her life. Our dog shepherded us through many years with unstinting attention, affection, and I believe Anna Freud's face would break into one of her wonderfully charming smiles, were she here to read of my heartfelt nod to a great and beloved companion, Aran.

As the reader will see, I have tried to offer a view of Miss Freud's life—its biographical essentials first, and then its major themes. She had many interesting and productive sides to her, and I have tried to glimpse them, do them what justice I can. I draw on her books and articles; on her letters to me and others; on my conversations with her, which mostly took place during the early 1970s, some of which I taped; on my talks with others about her; and, not least, on some of her own "self-assessments," a phrase she occasionally used as we talked. My hope is that this book will further help others to know what I set out over twenty years ago to explore: the achievement of Anna Freud—an important one, indeed.

A LIFE WITH CHILDREN

Who could have known all that we know now?
Anna Freud

IN APRIL 1970, WHEN I broached the subject of her biography, Anna Freud, then sixty-four, made this comment: "I've spent most of my life trying to understand children. I have been lucky to be able to [do so]. But I don't think I'd be a good subject for a biography—not enough 'action'! You would say all there is to say in a few sentences—[such as] she spent her life with children!" I objected, of course—but she had made her point. Apart from her usual reluctance to take prolonged center stage, she spoke of her work with children in such a way that she and they were virtually indistinguishable. She went on to explain: "For most of my life I have treated children, or tried to learn from them. That is how the years have gone—and now I am entitled to be called 'old'!" At the time, she seemed to me genuinely perplexed at the thought of a biographical study of herself—although, of course, she knew that her life had not been without considerable intellectual and even personal drama, despite all the time she had given over to the long, difficult, demanding, relatively isolated and self-effacing work that characterizes psychoanalysis.

Her birth, on December 3, 1895, came at a rather momentous time in her father's life and work. Sigmund Freud was then thirty-nine years old, a Viennese psychiatrist who was readying himself for the writing of his masterpiece, *The Interpretation of Dreams*, which he would finish in 1899. He was then very much involved in an intense, intellectual friendship with another physician, Wilhelm Fliess. The two shared ideas relentlessly, and Freud, we now realize, turned this friend into an audience of one for his bold ideas about the unconscious, the significance of sexuality, the importance of dreams in our psychological life. As a matter of fact, had the baby Anna—the last of six children born to Sigmund and Martha (Bernays) Freud—been a boy, she would have been named Wilhelm, as her father made clear in a letter addressed to his friend: "If it had been a son I should have sent you the news by telegram, as he would have been named after you. But as it is a little girl of the name of Anna, you get the news later. She arrived today at 3:15 during my consulting hours, and seems to be a nice, complete little woman."

That nice baby was born into the nice life of the upper bourgeoisie in Vienna. Three years before Anna Freud was born, her family had taken up residence in a large, comfortable apartment at Berggasse 19, an address that would one day become famous. The Freud family stayed there until 1938, when Hitler's *anschluss* compelled their emigration to London. Since Anna Freud never married, never really took up residence on her own, away from her parents, that Berggasse 19 address was hers for forty-three years.

She was sent to good private schools, all of them near her home. At fifteen, she graduated from high school and did not seriously consider any further education. To be sure, women at that time were hardly welcome in Austria's universities (or in those of other European and American institutions of higher learning), but contemporaries of hers in psychoanalysis, such as Grete Bibring, Helene Deutsch, and Marianne Kris, had become physicians, and she surely might have done the same had she so wished.[1] Instead she chose to become a teacher, and (between the ages of nineteen and twenty-one) took training in an elementary school. Before that period, she had done much travel, and had begun the life of an only child—her older siblings now departed for independent lives. She had also begun to be her father's good friend and traveling companion, two of many roles with respect to him that she would eventually assume—along with secretary, nurse, confidante, colleague. Before becoming the last of these, however, she had been in analysis—with her father. She became a patient of her father at twenty-three.

I asked her once about her life as a schoolteacher. She was lively and forthcoming as she remembered fondly the years that preceded her psychoanalytic training: "I taught in an elementary school—all subjects. I often hear teachers talk about how exhausting their work can be, and I am sure they have good reason to feel as they do. But I must say—

perhaps it was because I was quite young then, and the school was a delightful, private school, with charming and appealing children—that I was happy with those children; they were good, solid students, and as I remember them, I realize how lucky I was to have them in my classroom. In those days, of course, we were all more formal with one another, but I recall the fun we had, much fun. I had yet to study dreams, but I loved listening to the children tell of their dreams—what they wanted to be when they grew up, and how they wanted to live: their daydreams. Later I'd think of them as 'fantasies'; [back] then we told stories to each other, and yes, we'd recite little poems, or we'd tell what was on our mind—maybe, better, it was what our hearts told us to say. In those days I read a lot of poetry, and I wished I could write poems that would have meaning for others, not only myself. (There is a difference, [between those two kinds of poetry], believe me, I gradually learned!) Some of the children were very talented. They would close their eyes, and see pictures, and then open their eyes, and give us beautiful descriptions of what they saw. I was fascinated! Later, when I began to work with children, and learn to do psychoanalysis [with them], I would often realize how hard it is for many children to be so imaginative, and so willing to share their thoughts with others!

"As you know, teaching children is not always so pleasurable—even under the best of circumstances. I learned to be firm and even strict at times—or else life gets hard for both the teacher and the students. But the children were mostly sure of themselves—from strong homes, [speaking] psychologically, and they took their teacher's discipline in stride! As I look back at my life, I realize how important those five years [of teaching] were to me.[2] They offered me a chance to get to know 'normal' children, before I started seeing children who were in trouble for one reason or another; and they gave me a chance to learn from children—and learn that children not only need to be taught, but need to have a chance themselves to teach! I can close my own eyes, now, and see those children, some of them, eagerly raising their hands, because they wanted to tell me the answer to a question I asked, yes, but also because they had something else on their minds, and they wanted all of us to know exactly what [that something else was]."

Anna Freud herself had something else on her mind during those years of her schoolteaching stint. She went on ward rounds with Heinz Hartmann and Paul Schilder at the Psychiatric Clinic of the Vienna General Hospital. Both of those young psychiatrists were brilliant clinicians, and Hartmann would later become one of the most distinguished psychoanalytic theorists in the world.[3] Without question, at that time she was their guest in her capacity as her father's daughter—but soon thereafter, Sigmund Freud was sharing his ideas with young Anna, discussing his writings with her, and by 1918, when she was still teaching, psychoanalyzing her.

Most of those who have written about Anna Freud take note of this rather special and unusual relationship—the first psychoanalyst and his last child. Such an arrangement—between a psychoanalyst parent and a child of whatever age—is now unthinkable. But the historical context is important, if we are to understand young Anna Freud's experience of psychoanalysis. In the early years of psycho-analysis—up to, say, 1925—there were no formal requirements for those who wanted to enter that fledgling profession. Men and women, physicians and those without medical degrees, began read-ing Freud's books on their own, wrote to him, came to know him, came to know others who knew him, became gradually part of a community, most of it spread across what is now Austria, Hungary, Germany. Freud and Jung informally shared and interpreted their dreams. Walks were taken, memories and experiences discussed. The emphasis was on intense, intellectual, and fairly brief exploration—a far cry from the years of complex, emotional interaction that now characterizes an analysis.

The enormous significance of "transference"—the manner in which we endlessly reenact with others, and especially our analysts, our childhood responses to various family members—was only beginning to be explored. Put differently, psychoanalysis was then a strongly felt intellectual and personal experience, but had yet to become the extended and profound exercise it now so often is—years of figuring out not only one's dreams and fantasies and every-day difficulties, but the ways one holds on forever, it seems, to one's parents and siblings by endowing various contemporaries (wives and husbands, teachers and colleagues and friends) with all the qualities of those important, remembered adults who figured in one's childhood. No formal psychoanalytic training had yet been developed. "We were trained by our personal analysts," Anna Freud once recalled, "[and] by extensive reading, by our own unsupervised efforts with our first patients, and by lively interchange of ideas and discussion of problems with our elders and contemporaries."[4] Some became psychoanalysts with no real experience of psychoanalysis— and it could be argued that none of those early analyses, and even many of those undertaken as recently as the 1930s, when training standards were being established, would today qualify as satisfactory for a psychoanalytic institute. The length of time was markedly shorter; the depth and breadth of interpretation, and the subject matter (what was examined, and with what degree of tenacity) were different. As recently as 1935, in a well-known letter to the Italian psychoanalyst Eduardo Weiss, Freud could write in this manner: "Concerning the analysis of your hopeful son, that is certainly a ticklish business. With a younger, promising brother it might be done more easily. With my own daughter I succeeded well. There are special difficulties and doubts with a son. Not that I would warn you against a danger; obviously everything depends upon the two people and their relationship to each other. You know the difficulties. It would not surprise me if you were successful in spite of them. It is difficult for an outsider to decide. I would not advise you to do it and have no right to forbid it."[5]

No question, that letter might also be subjected to its own analysis—even as, one suspects, Anna Freud's life might have been different had she worked with an analyst other than her father. Her particular challenge was how to use successfully the unique psychoanalytic experience she did receive as the particular analysand she happened to be. Moreover, to repeat, knowledge about psychoanalytic therapy (not to be equated with psychoanalytic knowledge about the mind's structure and function) has had its own history— decades of clinical experience that have enabled today's analysts to work with their patients far more knowingly than was possible in the 1920s. The complexities and subtleties of transference and countertransference, the ups and downs of human relatedness that take place as patient and doctor bring themselves, their childhood memories, their past yearnings and disappointments, to the couch or to a chair in an office, have by now been extensively documented. In 1920, when Sigmund and Anna Freud were working together as teacher and student, as analyst and analysand, such knowledge was obviously not available. As a matter of fact, the concept (never mind the reality) of a training analysis as a necessary precondition of future psychoanalytic practice had yet to become accepted as desirable by the relative handful of men and women who had associated themselves with Freud. Only in 1928 did the training analysis become institutionalized as a standard aspect of psychoanalytic education.

When I was studying with Erik Erikson—as mentioned in the preface, he was an analysand of Anna Freud—and working on his biography, I asked him about the nature of psychoanalytic experience back in the 1920s, and his account both brings to life a past moment in the history of a discipline and sheds light on what this father and daughter were trying to do: "You must realize, analyses were much shorter then. Visitors from abroad—later to become prominent analysts—would come [to Vienna] for the summer, and see Freud, or others, and that would be that! This was a moment of great hope—a utopian moment; and the emphasis was on the intellect—what the intellect could learn about the emotions. That [kind of inquiry] is different [from a kind that would emphasize] what we now call 'working through the transference,' something that can become—*has* become!—a matter of much time and energy; and yes, a whole subject matter: psychoanalysis as the development of, and the eventual resolution of, the transference neurosis, as opposed to psychoanalysis as a means of learning about the unconscious, learning about the way your mind works, learning about your [now forgotten] childhood."

This distinction is, of course, somewhat arbitrary. From the start, and to this day, psychoanalysis was meant to offer not only intellectual understanding (insight), but a reshaping of the patient's emotional life, a shift in feeling. Still, the emphasis has changed over the years. In the early years of this century, the tilt was toward insight as the essential liberator—as in Milton's insistence that truth makes for freedom.[6] It was a time of breakthrough scientific discoveries and high hopes—of faith in victorious rationality. I never had the nerve to ask Miss Freud directly about her analysis with her father, but I certainly did ask her about the intellectual climate that obtained in the 1920s, when she was learning to become a psychoanalyst (a subject she had, anyway, discussed in several of the lectures she gave in the 1970s at various psychoanalytic institutes), and she was anything but reticent: "Back then in Vienna we were all so excited—full of energy: it was as if a whole new continent was being explored, and we were the explorers, and we now had a chance to change things—to come back from that continent, you could say, with what we had learned, and offer it to the world, to people who hadn't been there. What could be the result? [I had asked her what she and others hoped might happen when their new psychoanalytic knowledge was made known to the Europe of the 1920s.] Well, we didn't know exactly, but we certainly hoped there would be some changes—some important changes. Even in the darkest years, the 1930s, some of that anticipation and hope could be found—amid the doubts and skepticism."

She then went into a fairly extended discussion of her father's last writing, especially his *New Introductory Lectures* and his long essay "Analysis Terminable and Interminable." He was always, of course, respectful of biology, she reminded me—the rock-bottom "drives," or constitutional forces, as he saw it, that set limits on any psychological intervention. But he dared dream of an altered world—a population of analyzed people, constantly growing in size, and ultimately of some import to, and impact upon, the civilized world. As always in a writer's life, or in the life of an intellectual movement, there is an evolution of tone and emphasis—the relatively younger Freud who taught and analyzed his daughter Anna was somewhat more optimistic than the older (and dying) Freud, who had ample evidence around him (the Nazi rise to power) of what the "death instinct" can come to mean.

"We were all trying to harvest a great crop," Miss Freud went on to say in the same interview, and she paused in the middle of that metaphor, then carried it through: "We weren't sure exactly how to do that [harvesting]; we weren't sure who should do what. We had no rules to fall back on. We had to make up our own rules! We weren't sure how our analytic work with patients would end—what would happen and when and how to say the job was done. Those were years of test and trial, and, sometimes, trial and error. By the middle of the 1930s, we were on somewhat more solid ground. It is hard, I notice, to create for today's [psychoanalytic] candidates the atmosphere of a half-century ago [the early 1920s]. That is always the case (isn't it?): we look back at past history with a vision that has been influenced a lot by the intervening history."

She had made an important point, and she stopped, to let it exert its authority over herself, never mind me. She sighed—a sign that such was the case. I remember thinking to myself that the endless speculations about her analysis with her father would benefit from noting that last comment. We are all too quick to make our evaluation of (and judgment upon) such a long-ago event in the light of what we now take for granted as a long-standing body of knowledge and experience.

This is not to say that we should avoid questioning the possible implications of that unorthodox analysis for her life. She never married, never really allowed herself to go out with men, and she most certainly was exceedingly attached to her father—especially after he became ill with cancer in 1923. His profession became hers; his interests, in large measure, hers. As her analyst, he became privy to her privacy, her dreams and thoughts, as other parents rarely are. He was, it can be said, irreplaceable for her—by any other man. Anna Freud did become strongly connected to certain women—to the writer and, later, analyst, Lou Andreas-Salomé, and above all to Dorothy Burlingham, who arrived in Vienna in 1925 as an American analysand of Freud and ultimately became a psychoanalyst herself and essentially a member of the Freud family. She and Anna Freud lived in the house where Freud died in September 1939, 20 Maresfield Gardens, until death claimed her in 1979—and her children were treated at various times by Miss Freud. To call their relationship complex is to underline the obvious; it is harder to spell out its psychoanalytic dimensions without having had the unlikely privilege of a specific discussion of the matter with Miss Freud and Mrs. Burlingham. I don't think, however, that it takes a psychiatric wizard to figure out that Anna Freud found it much easier and more appealing to get close emotionally to women than to men, and that her initially professional relationship with Mrs. Burlingham and her children became familial in nature—in a way that today would be certain to raise eyebrows among admission committees at psychoanalytic institutes. The two women were also colleagues and collaborators; they worked together, pursued research projects jointly, co-authored articles.

In 1965, as I was trying to place these questions in context, I had a long discussion with Grete Bibring, a Boston psychoanalyst who had been part of the Freud circle in the early years of this century—before the Nazis forced so many psychoanalysts to become émigrés. She was rather brusque: "What difference does it make—to know the details of her [Anna Freud's] personal life. What is important—is what she has done: decades of work, it is now, with children; important contributions [made] to psychoanalytic knowledge." I interrupted, to agree—but I also noted the irony: the essence of psychoanalysis is its interest in the exploration of motives, and so such an interest with respect to anyone, be it Anna Freud or the next patient that Dr. Bibring or I planned to see, would not seem to be merely indulgent or an exercise in sensationalism or prurience. "Yes," she agreed, but then added: "It all depends on what you are trying to do, I think. If Anna Freud came to see you or me, to be a patient, we would have plenty to do (wouldn't we?), as is always the case! But if you are looking at what she has done in life—that is a question of her activities, her research, her writing. If she does not come and talk about herself as our patients do, then we have no way of knowing various things about her—and you and I know that we can even say that after years of working with patients who try to tell us everything, and *still* there is plenty we don't understand about them!"

She said much more along these lines, and I agreed—emphasizing the long tradition of intellectual biography, as distinct from so-called "psychobiography."[7] Yet, neither of us was quite at ease, perhaps because we were both still worrying about the analysis of

Anna Freud by Sigmund Freud. Dr. Bibring finally took this blunt initiative: "Now—it would never happen. Then—well, I am not exaggerating: things were different; psychoanalysis was simply not what it has become today. But let's put the cards on the table: of Freud's children, she [Anna] became his treasured and loved companion and heir. His work became her life, and that's a lot to happen to someone! But I am back to pointing out what she *did* with that unique situation: she handed her father *The Ego and the Mechanisms of Defense* on his eightieth birthday—quite a 'sublimation,' there. Her life was full of such moments—this was no 'old maid' left to wither because she was victimized by a neurosis. She found love in her life. That she was unconventional, that she did not marry or become a mother— that is true; and I am sure her father, sometimes, felt sad about that. He was an ordinary family man, quite conventional—as well as being the genius he was. What are we to do with all this—maybe just accept it, appreciate it for what it was: an unusual 'moment' between two unusual people—and plenty of good came out of it."

The "good" that Dr. Bibring mentioned—perhaps a bit insistently—began to be apparent early in Miss Freud's professional career. She had become a psychoanalyst and started seeing patients. She also attended psychoanalytic meetings, participated in seminars, initiated her own discussion groups, trained future analysts (such as Erik Erikson), and presented her thoughts and ideas in written and oral form to her colleagues. In the 1920s, she was among a small group of men and women who took an interest in psychoanalysis not only as a body of knowledge that helps us to understand childhood, but as a means of working directly with children, or with those who, in turn, work with children, such as teachers and doctors, not to mention parents. She was certainly no stranger to the work of Dr. Maria Montessori, an Italian pediatrician who spent a lifetime trying to emphasize the child's resourcefulness and need for independence. She had herself tried, as a teacher, to give her pupils leeway, let them spread their wings, while giving them an overall sense of purpose—a sense that there must be a mix of freedom and control, both.

In several conversations with her about those early years of her psychoanalytic practice and research—when she was in her late twenties and thirties—I asked Miss Freud about the origins of child psychoanalysis, and heard her defer to others: Berta Bornstein, Alice Balint, August Aichhorn, Erik Erikson. She also deferred to her father, no rare occurrence—reminded me of "Little Hans," the five-year-old boy who developed an array of phobias, and who was "treated" by his parents, both members of the early Freud circle. (The father was Max Graf, a musicologist, and the mother had been a patient of Freud.) In a sense, the boy was the first child analytic patient—treated by proxy, as it were. Freud interpreted the boy's problems to his parents, who tried hard to be understanding and responsive to his worries, fears, anxieties. As psychoanalysis spread, some adult analysands were hoping that the psychological difficulties they had experienced as children would not be visited upon their children. Just as Freud did with the Grafs, their analysts offered interpretations of particular problems as they arose in the children, and even offered suggestions as to what might best be done for a child.

The analysands who were now coming to Austria from abroad established a nursery school for the children they had brought with them. Erik Erikson and Peter Blos were among those hired to teach those children: Erikson, history and art; Blos, biology. The two, not surprisingly, would eventually become child psychoanalysts. Here is the way Erik Erikson remembered those days, the late 1920s: "I was an artist then; I'd come to Vienna, and my [childhood] friend Peter Blos was there, and he told me I could get a job teaching children in a small private school. I took the job, and enjoyed [doing] the teaching. Later, I learned that Anna Freud had been observing us, and that she thought we'd done a good job—Peter and me. I met her, and she suggested I try to become a psychoanalyst who works with children. I wasn't sure what that meant—and I'll tell you, at that time I'm not sure she knew exactly what that meant. Those were days of great hope and promise and experimentation [for psychoanalysis], and it was a time when one man's ideas [Freud's] were being learned by a lot of people—and then applied. But it is foolish to go back to that time with today's thinking—you'd think we were all 'lost' or 'confused' or 'naive.' We were just beginning to learn how to *do* psychoanalysis. Freud had written about it—gave it to us, in his books. But he, too, was only gradually learning about the unconscious, and the way we struggle with it in our lives. His patients were teaching him—and he was going through failures [as a therapist] as well as successes, and he was changing his mind and revising his theories.

"Now Anna Freud, when I was in analysis with her, was seeing adults, and many of us would be called psychoanalytic 'candidates' today. She was also enormously interested in children, and she wanted to treat them. I'd change the way I just put that: she wanted to be connected to children—she liked them, and she was interested in them. No, she wasn't alone [in that regard]; but she was a very methodical and well-organized person, and she worked closely with her father, and she was certainly one of the most important people to take a direct interest, a systematic interest, psychoanalytically, in children—certainly in Vienna, while I was there. I remember hesitating about going into analysis—I was hoping to be an artist, and I liked teaching the children. Anna Freud several times told me I could combine those interests with psychoanalysis. I'm not sure, now, she knew how *exactly*—but I'm sure she was, *herself*, trying to connect psychoanalysis to her own earlier interests: children and how they learn. Of course, she had *her* 'artistic' side: she loved poetry, and I heard she wrote it; and she had memorized a number of poems. She loved to encourage the children to take music and art. There was that side [to her], and then there was, gradually, the side of the careful psychoanalyst, who had to be very watchful—and of course, an artist, a writer, can't be too watchful, of himself, I mean, without paying a price. If there is such a thing as a muse, it has to be given its freedom! So, you see, we were all struggling to find out how to use psychoanalysis effectively, and we were also struggling to extend it into new directions—and she was learning, then, how to do that with boys and girls: not the same, by any means, as working with adults."

This use of psychoanalysis marked a continuation of Anna Freud's life as a teacher. She had ostensibly stopped teaching school at the age of twenty-one, yet she never really forsook an active interest in the way children learn. The Vienna school, with Erikson and Blos as teachers (and Anna Freud as *their* teacher), would be one more victim of Nazi aggression, but once in London, she soon took an interest in education as well as psychoanalytic treatment—the instruction of children as well as attempts to learn about their problems and help solve them.

Well before Hitler's triumph in early 1933, all these psychoanalytic explorers were threatened by the ominous rise of Fascist politics. Austria had its own serious anti-Semitism, a long legacy of it. Immediately to the south, Mussolini had been in power throughout the 1920s, and the general economic and political and social instability that seized Europe in the latter years of that decade could not help but make precarious the future of a revolutionary intellectual discipline whose founder and practitioners were predominantly liberal-minded Jews. After 1933, of course, one psychoanalyst after another, in Vienna and elsewhere, began to leave for the safer territory of England and the United States—although not without regret, and in some instances a good deal of regret registered by the Freuds, father and daughter, and others who chose to stay. "I remember telling Anna Freud that we were leaving [for America, in 1933]," Erikson once remarked, "and she was not at all pleased! " He explained: "We were a community—all very close. We were beginning to know how to work with children. It was a lively time for all of us. It didn't take a political genius, though, to figure out what was going to happen in Austria, and the rest of Europe. But Freud had no intention of leaving Vienna. He was old and sick. He'd seen so much happen in his life—I guess he figured: Hitler, too, will pass. Anna—she was loyal to her father, of course; and if he wouldn't think of leaving, she wouldn't, either. She never discussed politics directly with me. I never thought of her as giving much thought to the subject. When I told her Joan and I were going to the States, she asked me why. I told her we didn't like what was happening in Germany and Italy—and in Austria, too: the Nazi thugs had plenty of sympathizers there. She shrugged her shoulders, and said she was sorry we were leaving. It was painful for us, and for her, but a lot more pain was to come as the Nazis grew stronger and stronger."

Even so, amid the rising tide of European militarism, and the likelihood that one day Hitler would claim his native Austria for the Third Reich, Anna Freud tried her energetic, levelheaded best to continue her psychoanalytic work. In those years of the early 1930s, she became much interested in the workings of the ego, an element of the psychoanalytic metapsychology that had hitherto been relatively unexplored. Freud knew, naturally, that we are not totally at the mercy of the unconscious "drives" that he had collectively called the id. He had formulated the superego as a powerful "agency," always on the alert as a conscience, a potentially punitive judge. He had also formulated the ego as that part of our mind which negotiates with the id and the superego—tries to connect us to the world around us, tries to make a kind of peace within us, as well: our consciences exhort, indict, condemn, and our yearnings and lusts and rages press upon us, and all the while the ego does its very best to keep things in some satisfactory order, so that from dawn to dusk, at least, a reasonably sane and civilized life is lived.

In 1935, then forty, Anna Freud gave the ego her full intellectual attention—and the result was one of the most important achievements of her life, *The Ego and the Mechanisms of Defense*, published in May 1936, on Freud's eightieth birthday. With that book she became much more than Freud's daughter, even than Freud's psychoanalyst-daughter. In this major survey of the ego's activity, and important investigation of how such activity works in adolescence, she broke important new theoretical and clinical ground. It is ironic—and maybe no accident—that she focused upon the ego and its functions at precisely the time that Europe seemed headed for political madness. Before the *anschluss* of March 1938, Nazis had begun to take posts in the Austrian government, and gangs of their followers roamed Vienna's streets, shouting anti-Semitic obscenities, a warning to anyone and everyone of what was ahead for that beautiful city. Freud was old and sick, and rarely left Berggasse 19. His daughter tried to maintain the semblance of a normal life. Indeed, as she wrote about the ego's struggles against "aggression," she bore witness to the rampant destructiveness of a mass movement whose leader mouthed unspeakable hate as a daily matter of course. Meanwhile, she and her friend Dorothy Burlingham had founded a nursery school for the poorest of the poor—a living out, it could be said, of the kind of altruism she described in *The Ego and the Mechanisms of Defense*.[8]

Their urgent effort to rescue psychologically the most vulnerable and hurt of children surely bore witness to what the ego can do under the most serious of duress.

In a most understated way, Miss Freud described to me those nursery-school days—spent under the shadow of a terror that became ever more threatening: "By 1936 it was clear that nothing would stop Hitler from seizing Austria—or, I should add, Austria from joining Germany. I am not remembering with the aid of hindsight—because I clearly remember several of us in the nursery [she had just established] wondering what would happen when (not *if*, but *when*) the Nazis took over. We had begun building important ties to those children, and we knew that at some point, not too far off, we might see all we'd accomplished torn down. What to do, though—well, we kept at our work. We were not denying what was likely, but we were not surrendering to fear and apprehension. Why did you not leave Austria *then*, people asked us politely, later—when we were in England. The answer was quite simple: my father was quite sick; he was in pain a lot of the time; he was nearing the end of his life—over eighty, with cancer; and he could not imagine any 'new life' elsewhere. What he knew was that there were only a few grains of sand left in the clock—and that would be that.

"There is something else I should say. It is always easy in retrospect to know what was right, to know what should have been done, and when it should have been done. It is always easy in retrospect to judge a decision—call it a smart one, or call it a big mistake. We see this in our work with children, too—how we look back at a child's life, and we say: oh, *that* was when things turned sour; and *that* was when we should have intervened, and a pity we didn't. The hardest thing in the world is to put yourself back in a family's life at a certain point in time, *and* put yourself back there [in time] with them; and similarly with adults, when you are trying to understand why they chose one course, or another course. Do you see what I am trying to say? It's not just that you must understand their choice, but you have to try to put yourself in their shoes at the time that choice was made. . . . I'm repeating myself [with that remark], because 'understanding' involves just that (at least *psychological* understanding does): a temporary surrender of yourself and your present point of view, so that you can see someone else's life as it was unfolding at a moment in time that's all gone.

"I am being a bit of a preacher here! I am trying to remember how we regarded the Nazis and their growing strength in 1937, just before the *anschluss*. Without a doubt, we could have left Austria then, quickly and with no difficulty. Now, as we talk, knowing what happened in Europe from 1938 to 1945, we look like fools for having stayed as long as we did—ostriches with not only our heads in the sand, [but] our whole bodies! But who could have known all that we know now? That is an old refrain, I realize. Some knew immediately—left Germany in 1933. But we were living in an independent nation, and we had yet to see what the whole world began to see . . . that Hitler was going to march with his troops and his murder into one country after another. The death camps, the conquests—they came later. Yes, the Nazi anti-Semitism was the worst ever [I had mentioned that accelerating phenomenon of the 1936–1938 period]; but even there, you have to realize that we had lived our entire lives under the shadow of a really shrill anti-Semitism in Austria. Today, here [in England, in America] you would be horrified if you heard even 5 percent of what we had grown accustomed to hearing. You'd get alarmed. We were alarmed, yes [I had asked], but we were also survivors of decades of such attitudes. I'm glad, though, that it's hard for me to convey the kind of world we'd learned to take for granted back then—because that means we are living in a much better world now."

When she had finished that last statement, she looked away, toward a window. This was uncharacteristic, for usually she looked with consistent concentration directly at the person she was addressing, and attended closely to what he or she was saying. When her eyes returned to the part of the room where we sat, I didn't know what to say. She understood my silence, I soon realized, better than I did: "I myself have trouble going back to that time! When I do so, I am going back through all the years I've lived [in her thoughts]. I wonder, sometimes, how we managed to live with such pleasure and enthusiasm those days in Vienna well *before* the Nazis came [given the endemic anti-Semitism and economic instability of the time]. There was so much trouble in Europe after the First World War—all you need do is read a history book, and you wonder how anyone wasn't in a constant state of anxiety: terrible inflation, unemployment, governments that collapsed, one after the other, hatred of many kinds. But most people don't think of their lives as if they were historians, writing a book about what's important that is happening! We went from day to day, and week to week; we were busy; we were trying hard to do our work. Time goes fast—and then, suddenly, something big happened, and we all had to stop."

Time stopped then, she remembered well. I knew she had been detained by the Nazis on March 22, 1938, nine days after German troops—unopposed, indeed, welcomed with wild enthusiasm—crossed the Austrian borders and in no time took possession of the country. I knew she was kept all that day, and well into the night, by the Gestapo, interrogated by them. I knew she had taken with her a drug that would have killed her lest she be tortured. I had read the words of Max Schur, Freud's physician—a description that indicates all too exactly the psychological climate of those fateful days: "It was not until quite recently that Anna Freud told me the following story and authorized me to publish it. When things were at their worst and escape seemed hopeless, Anna asked Freud: 'Wouldn't it be better if we all killed ourselves?' To which Freud replied with his characteristic mixture of irony and indignation: 'Why? Because they would like us to?' "[9] When I asked her about that moment in her life, she was much terser than usual: "It was terrible for us, but briefly; it was so much worse for thousands and thousands of others, who had no chance of ever getting out of Austria or Germany. I thought of those people while we were on the train, headed for Paris. There are times when you realize how lucky you are!"

As she rode on that train, she was saying goodbye to almost exactly half of her life. At forty-three, she was returning to England twenty-four years after her first holiday stay there. She knew the language, and liked the people. England would be her home, thenceforth—until her death. England would also be where her father died, on September 23, 1939, three weeks after the Second World War had started—in W. H. Auden's memorable line, "an important Jew who died in exile."[10]

In no time the war would push England to the brink of defeat—with thousands of bombs showered on its civilian population. It was then that Anna Freud and her friend Dorothy Burlingham began their own kind of heroic work: the establishment, starting in 1940, of nurseries for the care of children who had been sent away from their parents for safety's sake. For dozens of young boys and girls those nurseries would turn out to be psychological lifesavers—a place where affection and attentive understanding more than mitigated the strain and pain that accompanied the loss of the mother, especially, and the father. Several times when I talked with her about that work, Miss Freud downplayed it: "Yes, we did try to be of some use to those children back then." In fact, she and just a handful of colleagues worked long days with children undergoing enormous emotional stresses: the death of relatives, including parents; separation from families; the rain of bombs visited on England—the frightful noises of alarms, explosions, the shrill sound of ambulances and fire trucks and police cars. In the evenings, when the children were tucked in bed, she wrote long, carefully and lucidly stated descriptions of individual boys and girls; she analyzed the psychiatric symptoms she had witnessed; she tried to explain what worked and didn't work for the caretakers (herself included) as they attempted to calm and reassure and encourage and protect those children, and often, for a while, become their parents. This exemplary work, organized by a woman in her late forties who had only recently come to England, was surely one of the high points of a long life—the horror of the blitz became an occasion for several years of tireless devotion and generous, unstinting love on the part of Miss Freud and her co-workers, much to the advantage of those entrusted to them. "I do not remember the war fondly," she once said, "but I was so fortunate to be able to work in those nurseries." She was too modest to say that she had, actually, founded those nurseries, spent much energy getting them funded, and put in a grueling day and night schedule working in them.

When the Second World War was over, Anna Freud, now fifty, did not overlook other children who had suffered as a consequence of

Nazism. In Vienna, before the war, she had worked with young orphan children, taking them into a nursery she had established. In 1949, six children whose parents had been killed in Nazi concentration camps, and who themselves had survived the Theresienstadt camp—cared for by camp inmates under the hellish conditions that prevailed there—arrived in England and became the special concern of Sophie and Gertrud Dann. Those two sisters had worked with Miss Freud in her Hampstead Nurseries, and would now, along with her, be devoted guardians and teachers to boys and girls whose suffering was unimaginable. The effort with those children involved a huge commitment, years of dedicated work. In 1951, Miss Freud described what she and the Dann sisters had observed in an essay entitled "An Experiment in Group Upbringing"—a careful, scientific report that only by implication addresses the larger, moral issue of what this world ought do with respect to the Nazi war crimes: how to commemorate such tragedies; how to think about their occurrence in a "heart of darkness" located in one of the best-educated countries of the world, supposedly a centerpiece of Western civilization.

Miss Freud's writing in the essay is not a polemic, however, but that of a restrained psychoanalytic researcher and therapist. In her report, those six children would not be an excuse for political or cultural pronouncements. Nevertheless, she was in this instance teaching by example—showing that psychoanalysts could both extend the domain of their work and modify the manner of that work: nurture and teach children, and learn so very much from them, as well as analyze them for an hour or so four or five days a week. For her, the practice of child analysis was not only an end in itself (for those boys and girls in need of it) but a way for certain adults to be with children. For her, child analysts were watchful students, anxious to explore and be taught, to extend themselves with interest and concern and unflinching attention, and in so doing, to be, directly or indirectly, the one who helps mend, repair, nourish, restore.

Anna Freud could be a lively, compelling, even lyrical writer at certain times, even an intensely personal one—not, though, in the observations offered on those six children. Here, in retrospect, is how she explains the tone of this writing: "We tried very hard to be

respectful of those children. They did not need pity from us, or want
pity from us. They did not need us crying for their awful experiences.
They needed us to take the measure of their lives, so far, and then to
try to earn from them some trust—and that was a big, big thing to earn
from them. When I sat down to write about those children, I felt waves
of sadness come over me; but I also realized how tough they were—
and I don't mean by that 'callous' or 'hard-hearted.' All children—all
grown people!—can be 'tough' at certain moments, with certain people. Those children were not sweet and kindly—victims we could
regard as angels! They had developed certain strengths, and they also
had significant 'deficits' in their 'personalities.' We thought that we
owed our readers what the children indicated to us they wanted from
us—full and fair treatment. What do I mean by that? Well, I'll put it
this way [I had asked for amplification]: These children would have
been undone, I am convinced, if we had allowed ourselves to spoil
them or respond too eagerly or uncritically to their habits and requests
and demands. They had learned to survive against the worst odds in
the world, and now they had to learn to survive with us—and so we
had to stop and think not only what was 'wrong' with them, but what
we thought was the 'right' way to behave with them. If we ended up
trying to spoil them, because of the injustices they had experienced—
then that would only compound their problems. . . .

"When I wrote up our work, I decided to describe the children as
we first knew them, and describe them later. I didn't think the readers
of our piece would need me to state my abhorrence of the Nazi death
camps; and I didn't feel we ought shed tears in public for these young
ones. They themselves didn't know who to cry for—they had lost
their parents at such an early age. They weren't crying with us for the
past! They were united with one another against the future—the dangers they feared [to be] around the corner. We decided to let our
research speak for itself. Presumably our readers realized that we had
given much time and attention to these children, and would continue
to be a part of their lives. We decided to leave it to others to express
the shock we all felt at what took place under the Nazis in Europe."

I felt, as she spoke years later (1972) about those children, by
then adults, a certain tension—someone trying to constrain emotion-

ality in the interests of both wisdom and good judgment; as if, had she been less tactful, I might have heard that outrage and sentimental effusiveness and even tears are not all that difficult to summon, but *in whose interest*? She, who had always insisted upon "the best interests of the child," a phrase she used over and over in the course of her long writing and teaching life, was now trying to let me know that those children deserved a particular mix of analytic objectivity and compassionate subjectivity that did *not* include their elevation to some position of psychological privilege—an immunity from the earnest and sometimes skeptical observation she and her colleagues have extended to countless other children. Such a privilege would become, ultimately, no privilege at all—rather, she firmly believed, a form of indulgence on her part, at the expense of those boys and girls.

In any case, she never did know how to "make up for" all the horrors those six youngsters had witnessed, experienced. They ached for some kind of reliable, stable life; and she and the Dann sisters tried mightily to provide it. "We had never before worked with children who had lost so much, so cruelly—and who had already, when we met them, come together as a band of brothers and sisters (in spirit). We tried to learn from them. Right away we realized they did not wish for our tears! I recall saying to myself—and later, I repeated to Sophie and Gertrud Dann: 'Let us be taught by these little people, who have already lived longer lives—you could say—than any of us has lived or wants to live!' So, we tried to do just that. I won't say we didn't bend toward generosity—but we did [so] with the Hampstead wartime nurseries as well! We gave those six the best food in the world, and good lodgings; and we gave them our time and our affection. But when people on the outside [not working with the children] learned of their 'history,' and when they got upset and agitated, and when they shook their heads in deep sadness and shook their fists in rage at what had happened, and when they offered to give us 'anything,' or give us 'everything, everything'—then I tried to change the subject! I knew we owed it to the children to leave a lot of our ideas and emotions at the doorstep [of *their* lives] and walk into this experience [with them] not only open-hearted, but open-minded!"

Such clarity of vision was clearly part of what she believed psychoanalysis required of her—and numerous audiences received full measure of that quality of mind in the last three decades of her life. Those were exciting and productive years for her. She was invited to speak in psychoanalytic institute after institute, in universities all over the world. She received numerous awards, prizes, honorary degrees. In 1947, she developed a training center in Hampstead, outside of London, for those who wanted to be child analysts; and there she helped educate dozens and dozens of men and women, both physicians and laypeople, to understand and treat children. In contrast to more orthodox child analysts, she was inclined to stress the differences between adult and child analyses, and skeptical, indeed, about the capacity of young children to handle some of the interpretations that these analytic colleagues were tempted to offer. Throughout her career she was interested in the normal as well as the abnormal—an interest that today may seem quite appropriate and unsurprising, but which a half a century ago was itself an achievement: to connect analytic insights to the ordinary, the everyday lives of reasonably sound and solid children as well as to the lives of those who have gone emotionally astray for one reason or another. Such matters of theory, of course, influenced her life as a practicing analyst—her way with patients. She saw a substantial number of patients, both adults and children. She also attended all sorts of international psychoanalytic congresses and, in so doing, traveled back and forth across continents and oceans. She inspired and worked on a number of research projects, attended and led seminars associated with those projects, and wrote papers on what she had learned. She kept writing other papers, too—devoted to theory or to a kind of historical reflection. She looked back at what had been happening to her discipline over the decades of the twentieth century, whose span coincided exactly with that of the discipline, since Freud emerged from obscurity in 1900 with the publication of *The Interpretation of Dreams*.

Although she was much honored, and eagerly sought at all sorts of academic and medical meetings, and although she was obviously her father's namesake and, in important respects, his heir, as psychoanalysis reached a peak of acclaim in the Western bourgeois world, she took great care to keep her life rather quiet and orderly and under various constraints: "Remember, I am an analyst!" She paused at this point, with a wry smile. "That means I have to stay in daily touch with my patients. The nature of my work, the requirements of my patients—for those reasons alone I can't be wandering too far or too long from home, nor can my mind wander, either. I have to attend those adults and children carefully and conscientiously. And I help train future analysts here—a big job. We have seminars, lectures, conferences. We have to choose candidates and evaluate them as they are being trained, and we have to decide when (or whether) they are fit to graduate. We don't look at grades or test scores. We share our personal and professional knowledge of a [candidate's] character and temperament and way with patients (and with himself, or herself). Hours, many hours, go into such deliberation even as hundreds of hours go into psychoanalysis. . . . You ask about how I spend my time [I had, indeed!], and I would say: with patients, with colleagues at [the] Hampstead Clinic, and then, with my other duties—to give talks, to write, to keep track of our financial affairs [at the clinic]."

In that last regard, she was exceptionally able and scrupulous, as I well knew, because, as mentioned, I was on the board of the Field Foundation, which supported her work for many years. She wrote us the most comprehensive reports I've ever seen—full and thoroughly detailed accounts of how the clinic's money had been spent (down to the last penny) and to what effect. Nor was she afraid to acknowledge doubt, uncertainty, misgivings or regrets, even failures. She came and spoke to us several times, and I well remember her frank statement, at one point: "We had hoped to learn more than we have! Perhaps we were too hopeful; perhaps we have, so far, simply been unable to figure out what is happening [psychologically] to these children." The boys and girls she was discussing with us were from poor backgrounds, many Pakistani or Jamaican, and she was the last one to try to come up with an appealing theory about or explanation of a phenomenon she believed, deep down, she did not fully understand—in this case, the nature of the school problems experienced by children whose parents were poor and of minority background. She asked for more time, told us that more research needed to be done—but was frank to tell us, also, that she had not yet been successful in "figuring out" what was "going on" with respect to the "school lives" of those young people, or with respect to their "home lives, either." I remember writing down those phrases I have put in quotes in the sentence above—and thinking to myself that this was one "expert" sure enough of herself and honest enough to speak to us candidly and unpretentiously, and with no fear of saying "I don't know" (a statement she made three times in one afternoon spent with us) or "maybe we'll find out, if we're lucky," a statement she made twice that same afternoon.

The end came for her (through a stroke) on the morning of October 8, 1982. She was eighty-six years old, and had been in failing health for several years—although her mind was clear to the last. By then she was very much a British lady—a person whose command of English was superb, who knew the pleasures of a London life, an Irish summer vacation life; and a person who knew "all sorts and conditions" of her country's people the way a psychoanalyst does: those long hours in which stories of family after family are relayed, unfold, and eventually get put in perspective, a joint achievement of the two who share those consulting rooms, one in a chair, one on a couch, or sitting on the floor or at a table and playing with toys, or drawing pictures, or chatting about what happened yesterday or long ago.

Many of the obituaries stressed Anna Freud's family origins—a not insignificant part of her life, for sure. Other death notices emphasized, correctly, her important role in the development of child psychoanalysis. She herself anticipated such attempts to summarize her life at one of the foundation board meetings she attended in New York City during the early 1970s, when she was less than a decade from her own death. A person had asked her what she intended to do in the coming years. She did not answer immediately. Another board member, anxious to abbreviate what seemed like an embarrassing moment, tried to change the subject politely. But "Miss Freud," as we all addressed her, would have no part of that strategy. She suddenly gave us her answer: "I don't know anything else to do, but to be with children—and with those [adults] who also choose to be with children. So, I fear that is how it will go—until I am no more." She predicted accurately the remaining years of her life—the same, steadfast, even tenacious interest in young people, and in those who worked with them. Her answer told us something else: like her father, she was at heart, and philosophically, a materialist, although with a soulful side to her personality, and she was also rather self-effacing, despite the attention and high regard showered upon her for so long.

TEACHER

*Clinical experience—practical contact with
human beings as it was called at that time—
which was demanded from every analyst, was
supplied for me by teaching school, a five-
year contact with young children.*
The Writings of Anna Freud,
vol. V, p. 512

ONE AFTERNOON, AS Anna Freud was telling me about her early life, she made a comment that reminded me of her father's loyalty to the classical tradition: "I once heard someone called an 'educator,' and I immediately thought of the Latin derivation of the word—a person who *leads out* students from their ignorance to knowledge: a teacher! I closed my eyes for a second, and I saw my young students [back in Vienna], and I was 'leading' them: we were walking, and I was up front. Behind us were shadows, and ahead was a countryside scene, with the sun shining brightly on it. I was an 'educator'! The truth is that a teacher doesn't only 'lead out' students by making sure they know how to read and write and count." She stopped abruptly with that declaration, apparently reluctant to pursue her thoughts. I wanted to press her, but felt intimidated. Although she could come across as a lively raconteur when she wished to be, could be generous with comments, even effusive, and certainly edifying, she would sometimes stop short halfway through a line of reasoning.

A phone call rescued us from a silence, although I had already seen her eyes wander to a pot of coffee and some cakes—a way out of our potentially embarrassing impasse. When she hung up the phone—politely suggesting to the caller that she try another time—I heard her speak as if she were talking to herself, not to someone else: "I don't know whether I should pursue this subject. So many teachers judge themselves by what they get children to learn. If the children do well on tests—that is a great reward [for those teachers]. I agree. Who would disagree? But teaching is not only the presentation of facts to students, it is persuading them to be interested in the world, to want to learn about it—a state of mind. If you are to 'lead out' children, you have to persuade them to walk with you. The best teachers, actually, persuade their children to take the initiative in 'leading out' themselves! That is not easy to do. I worked very hard as a teacher—and back then, I was much stronger. I'd be exhausted at the end of the day, and I often wondered what I accomplished. I suppose, in a way, things haven't changed [for me]. I'm still trying to help people see more—gain knowledge. I'm still trying to help them to be leaders [in that regard]—to be almost one step ahead of me: to figure themselves out just a bit before any interpretation I might come up with. 'It is a good sign in an analysis,' my father said, 'when the patient has been prepared by the analysis to make the decisive interpretations himself.'"

She was struggling, then, with the question of insight—how to offer it most effectively to others, how to relay it in such a way that it informs a life rather than merely registers fleetingly in an individual's consciousness, one more grain in an accumulation of facts. Early in her adult life, she had sought something similar for schoolchildren, of course, and for those who worked with them, the schoolteachers of Vienna. She was inspired not only by her father's ideas but also by those of another writing physician, Maria Montessori, also in the Western tradition of respectful attention toward the individual child, already in important respects a person in his or her own right.

In 1928, she offered a group of Viennese schoolteachers four lectures on psychoanalysis, published later as *Psychoanalysis for Teachers and Parents*. And her choice of audience in itself was a statement. She and August Aichhorn, a lay analyst whose pioneering work with delinquent or "wayward" youth is still seminal, were then reaching out to teachers, to those who attended, in one way or another, troubled young people. The two of them were no strangers to poor and vulnerable children, and to their families and neighborhoods, a tradition in psychoanalysis not always pursued later, in America, as it became almost exclusively the property of the upper bourgeoisie. These teachers taught in a kind of after-school program: "The Hort is a kind of kindergarten, but particularly for children from six to fourteen years of age. The kindergarten itself only takes children up to six years or until school age. The children who come to the Hort are the children of parents who go out to work. They come daily and return to their parents in the evening. Here, in the Hort, they prepare their school homework, occupy themselves in light work or communal games, and are taken for outings by the Hort workers."

Many years later she would remark upon the obvious value of such an enterprise—a way of reducing the number of latchkey children. Back then, she was also full of admiration for what was a vigorous effort to work educationally with just those children who were most in need of adult companionship and pedagogical support. Indeed, the tone of her presentation, from the very start to the end, was instructively deferential—a former teacher making clear that she was, in important ways, still very much a teacher, was not determined to intimidate them, lord it over them with jargon or highfalutin formulations, or through a patronizing emphasis on what they need to know, but clearly don't know. She immediately remarks that "in one particular direction" she most certainly has "nothing new" to extend to her listeners. They are experienced with children, she observes, and are being tested constantly, strenuously. She spells out some of the challenges by describing the range of boys and girls who stay at the Hort centers: "from the physically and mentally retarded, the obstinate, cowed, lying and ill-treated children, to the brutal, aggressive and delinquent ones." Wryly and winningly, she then acknowledges to her audience that even such an impressive description is inadequate: "It is better not to attempt to give you a complete list, for you might well point out to me a large number of omissions."

It is, perhaps, rather too easy for the reader to regard such remarks as the inevitable rhetorical passages that precede a speaker's real message. But this speaker, no matter her psychoanalytic erudition, was clearly quite sincere in her long preamble. She goes on to emphasize the constant pressure the members of her audience face, the need "ceaselessly to *act*." She is quite mindful of their interest in the practical, the insights that somehow can help teachers work directly with children in a more satisfactory way. She points out an important distinction—the teacher as one very much in the middle of things, as against "a passive observer," someone who comes to classrooms to watch, take notes, and later write articles or books about what supposedly happens under certain sets of circumstances.

This distinction was not made by her as a mere throwaway compliment to overworked, underpaid teachers—although she knew how
hard it can be for teachers to keep up with the constant demands their
work makes on them. She was, rather, reminding herself of something, as she made clear, decades later, in a talk we had: "Someone
who comes to a classroom from outside [as a visitor, a social scientist]
is not always going to see the same class that a teacher who works
with the children sees. Teachers must keep in mind *the moment*—each
child's response, or failure to respond, when a subject is being discussed. Observers bring their special interests—and, of course, they
bring themselves. They sit and sift through the experiences they are
watching others have. It is a different relationship to the children . . .
[there is now] the presence of a new person, the observer. Many
teachers are made uncomfortable by visitors, and many children are,
too. It would be foolish to analyze that [discomfort] exclusively in
terms of psychopathology, I agree. I had in analysis a teacher who
knew she did a good job every day with children, but who fell
down—compared to her usual high standards of performance—when
a parent sat in on her class, or another teacher, or a professor doing
research. I thought for a while that she feared criticism, felt herself in
some way being 'exposed.' She did feel self-conscious, and there was
an element of 'inhibition' at work—as if this gifted performer was
now going to be reprimanded for displaying herself so readily! But
the better I got to know her, the better I saw her situation [under
those circumstances of being observed by her superiors or others]:
she felt 'inhibited' because the children *were* inhibited, and she now
had to work against that, and so, this was an entirely different classroom for her. If you go before teachers, and expect them to 'take to
you,' or hope they will, you owe them respect—but you owe them,
even more, some indication that you understand what it is that happens to them when people like you visit them, at work!"

She remembered, too, as we talked, how impressed she had been
with the Hort teachers; and, indeed, she pointed that out to them in
the course of her remarks—again, not with a facile compliment, but
with a respectful and detailed enumeration of the considerable difficulties they then faced as frontline protagonists, often working with

exceedingly troubled boys and girls. She said, right off, that she knew the Hort teachers were "obliged to receive all children exposed to various dangers in and out of their parents' homes in the intervals when they are not at school." She also was alert to the special role those teachers had carved out for themselves—not occupants of conventional classrooms, and not parents or relatives or even neighbors, and therefore free to try to be a new and special kind of person for young people troubled, already, by the adult world and its dealings with them.

, These children brought their own lives, of course, to any new situation in which they found themselves. In her lectures to her fellow teachers, Miss Freud was at pains to discuss the classroom (or the nursery, the playground) from the child's point of view, and she was especially interested in a narrative and chronological view of childhood—each boy or girl with a particular story, one with themes, characters, events, cumulative developments. Today we might take for granted such a point of view—the gradual emergence of certain attitudes in children, based upon their home life, especially. A half-century ago, however, such a way of looking at children was by no means common—and even today, in classroom after classroom, teachers shove aside such knowledge either because of the desperate urgency they feel, or out of their own lack of interest in what they often, with some disparagement, refer to as a "psychological approach."

A teacher in an elementary school north of Boston (Lawrence) once used that phrase in the course of a conversation with me in 1989, over sixty years after Anna Freud tried to connect the insights of psychoanalysis to the events that take place in schools the world over. Here is what she had to tell me—a reminder that a book such as *Psychoanalysis for Teachers and Parents* is not yet outdated, even if the message it presents is now to some extent (at least in certain neighborhoods) common knowledge: "I have over thirty kids to teach [third grade]. I want them to do the work I assign, and I let them know that flat out on day one, and I keep repeating the message! No fooling around in this class! Sometimes, yes, I have some problem kids. [I had asked.] But I don't bend any rules for them. This is a classroom, not a [psychiatric] clinic! I don't ask these kids about their home life—you start with that, and you don't have time for anything else! I think of them as kids who have to learn, and I'm there to teach them. If a kid starts hassling me—or another kid—I let him know quickly that we're not going to have any trouble in this room, *period*. Sometimes I have to say that a few times, but after a while the kid will get it—the message. This year I had a boy who started on day one with his speaking out of turn, and bullying others, and even challenging me. I called him up, and told him he could leave the school, for all I cared, and I wasn't going to let him give the rest of us a hard time, and that's that. Sometimes I can see that a kid is looking for a fight with me, but I haven't the time to find out more. You have to lay it on the line for these kids—tell them what you want from them, and go full steam ahead with the lessons!"

I had enormous sympathy for her, and admiration, too—her class was made up of boys and girls from the poorest and most vulnerable of families. She worked hard and long to teach those children how to read better, spell better, figure better with numbers. But some children, by her own admission, were "beyond" her, and for them her solid, no-nonsense, even stern manner did not work at all. Indeed, with several children she did have to shift gears a bit, have "talks" with them, try to learn what it is that made them so difficult, so obstinate, so hard to reach, "from day one," as she put it. She was not about to change her own "personality," she told me once, "to suit them," but she did wonder, at times, what it was that prompted such children to be as they are: "They'll come to the very first class, and there's something in the look they give me that spells 'trouble ahead,' that's what comes to my mind! With one boy, I knew five minutes into the first day we met that he and I were going to lock horns! I tried to ignore that [her premonition], and just get him to learn, but there was always something stirring in him, that's how I saw it, and whatever that 'something' was, it ruined things for me as his teacher. When he wasn't sulking, he was staring into space, and I thought he might have epilepsy, to tell the truth. I sent him to the [school] doctor, and they did these tests, and they didn't come up with anything, so they said it was all in his mind. We don't have a [school] psychologist here, but they said he should go somewhere, and they'd tell his parents. They never did, though—and I was left there, to fight it out with him all last year. He was the only kid in the room who didn't know how to clean off his desk at the end of the day—or at least he pretended he didn't. I never could figure out his reasons. I finally gave up on reprimanding him—and then one day, he fell in line. I almost didn't notice—until I did: that he'd left a desk without any junk on it! I was going to say something—tell him he was going to get an A+ from me for what he'd done, but something in me told me not to say a word, because if I did, then he'd start fighting me again. So, I didn't—and he kept his desk neat for the rest of the year, and he never left anything on it at the end of the day. I guess I became a psychologist myself, with him."

In her own way—a rather good way, too!—she was inching toward an understanding of what it is that a child may feel toward a teacher right off: an unearned, seemingly gratuitous emotional disposition that can be a powerful determinant in a child's educational life. For many of us, today, the word *transference* comes to mind when we hear about an encounter like this one in a Lawrence classroom. This teacher had a sense of what it is that patients in psychoanalysis continually find themselves learning: their manner of seeing and responding to the analyst they visit has to do with how they got on with one or the other of their parents. When Anna Freud addressed her fellow teachers in Vienna, she stressed the matter of transference with both clarity and tact. She noted that children often "bring with them a preconceived attitude of mind, and may approach the teacher with the suspicion, defiance, or feeling of having to be on guard which they have acquired through their personal experience of other adults." She pointed out that a teacher's "real individuality," including the way he or she functions in the classroom ("the actual behavior toward them," namely, the schoolchildren), can be as nothing, rather often, because the boy or girl in question is making the teacher over, to a certain extent, and quite unwittingly.

The exact and full significance of the so-called transference phenomenon—one of the major discoveries of Freud and his early coworkers—and its occurrence in our daily lives and the subtleties of it both there, and of course, in psychoanalysis, have been appreciated only over time and through years of careful study and reflection. Similarly with "countertransference"—the manner in which we doctors or teachers respond to an earlier life's mandates, yearnings, fears, worries, while working with someone with whom we are substantially engaged psychologically, as teachers most assuredly are (or ought to be!) with their schoolchildren. It is perhaps not surprising that the psychoanalytic literature on transference is greater by far than that on countertransference. Doctors find it natural to keep close tabs on others, while forgetting to be quite so zealous with ourselves—a contemporary version of the kind of behavior that prompted the old Christian caveat (Matthew 7:31) about the mote in one's brother's eye as against the beam in one's own.

In any event, for Anna Freud the teacher, and the teacher of teachers, the psychological reality of transference was one to keep uppermost in mind. She spent a lot of her time thinking of transference and countertransference as they took place not only in her consulting room, but in the nurseries she ran, the institutes where she taught or lectured, the seminars she gave at various universities. Thanks to her abiding common sense, she knew when to deal directly with such matters and when to be silent or only briefly referential in her comments: "If we can help teachers realize how it [transference] works, then we are able to bring to them a real service, I think. On the other hand, if the result [of such instruction] is a heightening of consciousness that turns into self-consciousness—then, I fear, we are not getting somewhere desirable!"

She smiled faintly, frowned, and then went on: "Teaching is not only the presentation of facts and directions about what to do, but an *art*, the art of exposition and persuasion—whether you can elicit from a student (or a whole classroom) what an analysand of mine once called 'glad assent.' He was a lawyer, and he had an interest in politics, and he used that phrase a lot, and I took to it—an English way of saying things. (I suspect Americans don't talk that way.) Once, I stopped him and asked him to explain the phrase. I don't have all he said on the tip of my tongue, but I remember quite well what he was trying to get across to me—the thoughtfulness and sensitivity required when one person tries to earn the cooperation of another. He was, I knew, speaking to me, as his analyst, though he wasn't quite aware of that [fact] as he spoke: he was being quite philosophical and conceptual, rather than personal. I realized, as I stopped him and asked him for a clarification of those two words, that I had my reasons as his analyst to explore with him the question of how one receives the 'glad assent' of another—because a psychoanalyst is also in a teaching relationship: the patient teaches the doctor, the analysand teaches the analyst, and vice versa. We tend to emphasize the handing over of knowledge (or interpretations) by the teacher, or the analyst, and we can sometimes forget that teachers and analysts learn a lot from their students, their analysands!

"It is true, a teacher has a body of *facts* that she has to impart to her students. [I had mentioned that aspect of teaching—a part of the teacher's job that has to do with what the teacher has learned not from her students, but from her own life as a student.] But [it is a matter of] *how* the teacher does that: the students can teach her how to reach them, how their 'glad assent' can be obtained. That is what someone like you or me can do when we work with teachers— remind them [and thereby, ourselves] how a careful [psychological] evaluation of students can enable a teacher to understand them in such a way that she can teach them—her knowledge *about* children helping the transmission of knowledge *to* children."

We both paused—her eloquence and lucid, direct phrasing had me in its grips. I then told her that as she was just speaking I remembered the important fourth lecture in *Psychoanalysis for Teachers and Parents*, which she entitled "The Relation Between Psychoanalysis and Pedagogy"—a subject that, in a way, she spent her entire professional life exploring.[1] In that lecture, too, she indicates her awareness of the everyday needs teachers have: "Probably you seek practical advice which will be a guidance to you rather than an extension of your theoretical knowledge." As always, she wants to be of help, but has no interest in the status of a seer or, in contemporary American terms, elevation to the position of an "expert" on something called "child development." Rather, she tells her audience that she can see matters both ways—that she worries about schools (and of course,

homes) in which children are being unduly punished and reprimanded for even the slightest assertion of their own psychological
particularity. Such an approach can be "crippling," she insists—but
then she makes sure her listeners, and later, her readers, understand
that she has no desire for "one-sidedness." At a time (the early 1930s)
when the cultural stage of Europe and, especially, the United States
was being set for a widespread permissiveness with respect to child
rearing among the middle class in the name of child psychoanalysis,
Anna Freud, one of its founding and guiding spirits, was eager to
point out that "the lack of all restraint" on children as they grow up
can be as harmful as "the injurious effect of too great repression."

She asks for "a *via media*," points out that "instinct-restriction
has to balance instinct-gratification." Such an insistence on proportion may have been welcome to the audience of Viennese teachers
she was addressing; but others, elsewhere, would not be so attentive—as she reminded me years later: "I was hoping to be of some
use to people I regarded as friends and colleagues [in late 1920s
Vienna]. It may be hard for you to imagine the nature of the relationship between those Hort teachers and me. I wasn't an 'authority' who
came to tell them what to do! They were working with some very
difficult children, and they had already taught me and August
Aichhorn [whom she mentioned with much respect in these Hort
lectures] a great deal. I was—to their minds, then—doing what we
would call 'experimental work,' or 'research.' They were open-
minded (to a certain extent), and interested—but they were not
eager and hungry. They certainly weren't gullible, ready to swallow
whatever was offered at an instant, [as was] sometimes the case later
on, elsewhere, when psychoanalysis arrived in other countries to the
west [of Austria]."

In our discussion, she made no mention of her own independence of mind and practicality, a match for that of her fellow teachers. She herself was never tempted to grant the instincts the kind of
unqualified leeway others did in their view of the mind, of the task of
psychoanalysis, and in their application of this new discipline to the
thinking of other disciplines. Freud had told the world of the power
instincts exert on us, and of the symptoms that those instincts can

cause as they relentlessly, if deviously, try to assert themselves. Analysts were soon at work "uncovering," as it were, those instincts, laying bare their presence, detailing their workings in the mind's life. Before long, analysts were worrying not only about the repressions their particular patients exerted on those instincts but also the repressive traditions of various social institutions and their consequences. But an analyst who a few years later (1936) would be exploring and explaining the considerable significance of the ego and the superego and the ego-ideal in our mental life—the importance of constraint over those instincts as well as "expression" of them—was not inclined to see such "agencies" of the mind disregarded in the name of either clinical work or pedagogy. "I think it fair to say," she once commented, "that I wanted children to be able to 'express themselves' (who, now, would be against that), but with reservations. Aichhorn and I saw what happened to children who had not developed internal controls—children the courts would end up calling 'delinquent' or 'antisocial.' " She elaborated on this: "Those children have no trouble 'expressing' themselves! They are at the mercy of their instincts in a different way [from] the inhibited or classically 'neurotic' child. The symptom formation may be different, but there is still a problem—and for the schoolteacher, it is often a more serious problem."

In the lectures to teachers, Miss Freud did not leave out clinical examples—conveyed, though, with an accessible narrative presentation that would become a hallmark of her writing. For instance, she offered the story of "an excellent woman teacher" who, at the age of eighteen, left an unhappy home life and became a governess with three boys under her care. The middle child had a "serious educational problem." He did poorly in school. He was shy and fearful. His older and younger brothers, in contrast, were outgoing and successful students. The teacher gave her all to the obviously reclusive and distressed child, and the result was what appeared to be a miraculous cure—a transformation in the child's personality and his academic life, both. But with that success, much appreciated by the child's family, came an abrupt, unexpected, and dramatic shift in the teacher's attitude: now she pulled away from a boy she had hitherto wanted to shower with affection and concern. Indeed, she resigned her position and left a family that had come very much to like and admire her. She pursued her teaching career elsewhere, but had continuing personal difficulties as a teacher—and so, fifteen years after the above-described episode, went into analysis.

Having told members of her audience about this teacher, and aroused their interest, their curiosity, Miss Freud explained what she learned. The teacher herself had felt herself to be an unloved child, even as the middle boy to whom she gave so much of herself had been slighted, relatively speaking, by his parents. "All the love and care which she had lavished on him," Miss Freud explains, "meant that she was really saying to herself: 'That is the way I ought have been treated to make something out of me.'" With success, however, came the end of that personal bond. The boy was now a stronger, more able person, and his teacher began to harbor anger toward him, a consequence of envy: "She could not help grudging him . . . the success which she herself had never attained."

A story bound to appeal to a roomful of teachers; a story that may well have had resonance for some of them; a story told with disarming simplicity, and with no show of pretentiousness. This story was given an appealing voice, the teacher's—her words given to her by an author well aware that such a voice would make all the difference to members of that particular audience, bring them closer to the teacher whose life story is being told, and thereby earn from them not only an intellectual response, but an emotional or personal one (the task every psychoanalyst has in mind as he or she works with patients).

Miss Freud as a teacher lecturing to other teachers had other strategies of the novelist or short-story writer up her sleeve. Once she has introduced her teacher's story in a gripping way, she risks a bold kind of irony: "You will say, perhaps, it was a good thing that this teacher, when she dealt with her pupil, had not yet been analyzed; otherwise we should have lost a fine educational success." Such a comment, potentially undermining to her own purposes, is meant to anticipate and put up for discussion (rather than smugly brush aside) a major complaint any number of critics or skeptics of psychoanalysis have stated explicitly or indirectly—that the so-called "neurotic" nature many of us have is commonly the source not only of our problems, but of our personalities, our interests and abilities: our passions as they become our achievements. It was such a way of thinking that prompted the poet Rilke (whose work Anna Freud dearly loved) to avoid psychoanalysis. He feared a "cure" that would leave him devoid of the desire—maybe even the ability—to write his haunting (and so often tormented) poems.

Anna Freud committed his poems, one after the other, to memory—and her long friendship with his close friend Lou Andreas-Salomé drew her even closer to him, even though her father was no fan of Rilke's, indeed, reportedly disliked him. She was willing to take up the matter of psychoanalysis and creativity in a direct and compelling manner—without loading the deck in her own favor. Yes, the teacher had left her pupil—but only after she'd done a lot for him; so this is not the case of an exceedingly disturbed and disturbing person who is doing harm to others and herself, no matter her capabilities, and whom, therefore, we are likely to judge an obvious candidate for analysis. However, Miss Freud offers this moderate opinion: "I feel that these educational successes are too dearly bought." She explains: "They are paid for by the failures with those children who are not fortunate enough to reveal symptoms of suffering which remind the teacher of her own childhood and so make sympathy with them possible for her."

Her use of the word *fortunate* in connection with children obviously in considerable psychological trouble is characteristic. Although she leaves that irony unattended, she raises our concern for those children whom that teacher won't be interested in teaching. By implication, we are asked to contemplate the teacher's own sadness and loneliness: she had to walk away from a real accomplishment—her evident victories hostage to her own prior defeats as a child.

Many years later, as I sat with Miss Freud, holding a well-marked paperback copy of her book, with an appealing picture of her in young middle age on the jacket, and tried to bring us both back to that spirited and important and instructive fourth lecture of hers, she stopped us short at a certain point: "I could have expanded on the point, yes—discussed with admiration what that teacher *had* done with the boy. But I made a judgment—that her success was apparent and one of the major points of the case I was presenting. The boy profited from another's problem—one very much like his own. There can be no doubt that there are many other such cases—how often it is that someone undergoing pain can understand another person's pain, and help that [other] person, whereas someone who hasn't known such pain won't be motivated to do so! I would never want to deny that [such chains of human circumstance are to be found in abundance]. Life is full of paradoxes! I think I wanted to acknowledge that—but I also wanted to ask those teachers [the Hort teachers] to consider when the cost of success is too high. . . . Remember, the key thing here is that the teacher chose, on her own, to go into analysis. I don't suggest we should go after people and tell them: you should go see an analyst! There *has* been some of that [approach to people], I know. [I had suggested as much.] I would expect to be greeted by teachers with a great deal of disapproval if I went before them and told them they must go to the doctor soon—many of them. I was trying to be a teacher myself when I spoke to them. I was trying to say this: there are times when a person falls down on the job, and the person doesn't know why—and if that keeps happening, then there is something you can do; you can investigate. But it is a step further—many steps, maybe: to urge everyone to do that [to 'investigate,' to go into analysis]."

She was, yet again, being both tactful and modest. In fact, she had shown extraordinary restraint in her presentation, with respect to the question of psychoanalysis as a recommended pursuit for most teachers. Any number of analysts, at the time, were having visionary ideas about this new and powerfully probing discipline—hopes that through its application the world would be different, because people would be different, once analyzed. To some extent, Miss Freud's remarks to the teachers in her fourth lecture were a response to that utopian enthusiasm—a measured effort on her part to affirm by example what psychoanalysis can offer, while at the same time stopping well short of investing it with a messianic glow that, even back in the late 1920s, she knew would ultimately both fade and disappoint. "I was, perhaps, cautious when I gave those lectures," she later observed, the word *cautious* itself a cautious way of putting the matter. She smiled when I pointed this out, then said firmly: "The Hort workers would accept nothing less [than caution] from me! They were very hardworking; they weren't rich, to say the least; they had very demanding jobs—and like many teachers, they weren't getting the social approval they deserved. There they were, doing the most important work imaginable. . . . They did not need me to come before them and tell them they were all in trouble psychologically, and the sooner they saw an analyst, the better—*and then* all would be well. I wanted to explain to them what we had been learning. I remember August Aichhorn's advice to me: the teachers have been learning from children all along, just as we try to do—and if you remember that, they will receive you warmly. It was an 'attitude' he was recommending to me, and I did try to remember."

Here she was getting at the heart of the matter with respect to teaching. A specific teaching experience had challenged her not only intellectually, but personally, even morally. Her references, in old age, to the social and economic vulnerability of the Hort teachers she had met as a young woman are an instructive example of an "attitude" that had lasted a lifetime—a capacity to stand back and take a careful look not only at others but at oneself and one's immediate world. Teachers (she knew back then and realized all through her life) are an all-too-easy target for both moralists and psychoanalysts—and so the double jeopardy of a presentation to humble, ordinary schoolteachers who work with ordinary children.

Miss Freud for many years had her own ways of combating such occupational hazards. A shyness, a bemused capacity for irony, a plainness of manner, a delight in humor, in the telling of stories—all were of help. Her comments on her friend August Aichhorn—in an obituary published in *The International Journal of Psychoanalysis*—tell a lot about her as well as about him, and reveal her as someone open to what others offered, no matter their formal education or training. She praises Aichhorn's "modesty." She declares that "he had as much to offer to psychoanalysis as he could hope to gain from the study of the new science." She goes further: "He did not need analytic insight to learn how to handle delinquents; he was a master at handling them, individually and in groups, before he had ever heard of psychoanalysis." She follows with a quite astonishing remark for a psychoanalyst: "He did not even need analytic psychology to understand delinquency. His understanding of dissocial manifestations was intuitive, based on an automatic, effortless identification with the delinquent or criminal individual with whom he had to deal."

This tribute to an old friend was a tribute, also, to an old teacher, a statement of continuing gratitude. An acknowledgment, too—that teachers often appear before other teachers in the unlikely incarnation of one of their students: Aichhorn as the psychoanalytic candidate, ready to be educated—yet, already an educator in his own right, a graduate of the rigorous program known as "life," or "hard knocks," psychological division.

Even in her seventies and eighties, Anna Freud seemed to remember, word for word, her friend August Aichhorn's way with troubled young people. She also made clear his spoken influence on her as she became a teacher of teachers with her lectures to the Hort workers and involved herself in other informal contacts with Vienna's social workers and school officials: "He wasn't only able to reach children otherwise unreachable; he influenced a lot of us who weren't 'wayward youth' or 'neglected youth.' We had a lot of enthusiasm, and we had ideas—[whereas] he had a secret in him that he was ready to share, if we were willing to become his students: how to put others at ease, so they will be able and willing to learn. I have used the word *intuitive* to describe him; and that is a word we shouldn't try to break down. . . . But some people are 'natural teachers,' and Aichhorn was an *especially* natural one! He knew how to pace himself—build up his presentation first, with a description of the problem under discussion, then give some examples, and then lead a discussion. He invited people to be as open-minded as he could be. So often, teachers are in a hurry to get their students to *know* something, to *have* the right answers: a possession. Aichhorn knew how to scratch his head and say: Well, we can look at this [delinquent] boy in this way, but we can also look at him in that way, and there may be other ways, too. He was challenging us: can *you* do the same—focus and refocus, shift your angle of vision, adjust your point of view? It is true, one *has* 'intuition,' or one doesn't—but an intuitive teacher will want, also, to share his gift with his students; so, they will, over time, become 'intuitive'! I think a teacher does *that* intuitively—doesn't hoard such a gift, and thereby give students the idea that all is hopeless, because one is either born with this wondrous, amazing gift, or one isn't.

"I knew teachers [whom she met when she taught school] who were very much like him [Aichhorn]. They weren't necessarily the brightest graduates of universities—where so many people learn in the name of ambition to have 'higher' aspirations [than that of being a schoolteacher]! They were extremely bright in their own way, though. . . . Sometimes, when I hear a child being described as 'bright,' I will ask the parents, or the social worker, or the doctor, or the teacher: what do you mean by that? I am not trying to be 'difficult'; I am wondering whether they are telling me that the child does well academically, or whether they are speaking of other qualities—a child's quickness with people, an ability to understand them and communicate thoughtfully with them. That is a kind of 'brightness' I found in those teachers [she had just mentioned]—and I believe *we* can always learn from them, as well as the children they teach."

Such a willingness to take instruction from the widest possible sources—and indeed to define knowledge ("brightness") rather flexibly—informs her lectures to teachers, and too, strongly informs the ending of those lectures. She offers her audience the words a child used to express his feelings about "the wrong things grown-up people do." The child's opening sentence is a clarion call: "Here, you grown-up people, listen to me, if you want to know something!" The boy both pleads and remonstrates. He wants people of his age (he wants himself) to be heard, respected, rather than be constantly given orders, denied their rights to go in their own direction. He even insists that some of his age-mates "can do many things" even better than those who are their elders. He is, finally, upset and angered by the seemingly ceaseless volubility of parents and teachers and others who, he clearly feels, patronize children far too often. He exhorts them (us) in this fashion: "Don't always talk so much; let the children sometimes get a word in."

Miss Freud then shows how a child's assertions can fit into the values of one or another social and cultural world. Some teachers, she observes, would obviously be outraged by this boy's behavior. (He also made "blasphemous remarks about God.") Someone whom she describes as "a conservative teacher of the old school" would surely want to exert the most serious kind of discipline upon the lad—let him know, for his own sake, that enough is enough. On the other hand, someone whom she calls "a modern educator" might well turn to the boy with high hopes—might even, she says, "expect to see in him a future leader and liberator of the masses." At this point in her presentation a certain dramatic tension has arisen. After all, in this latter category are to be found a number of her own colleagues, not to mention all those who saw the experience of psychoanalysis itself as an important step in the liberation of individuals—and who were, even then, hoping to apply psychoanalytic knowledge to all sorts of social and political problems. Perhaps many of the Hort teachers themselves regarded their young lecturer and her work with children as potentially liberating in its impact on them and their future professional activities.

Yet Miss Freud rejects not only the "old school" but the "modern educator." In a compelling narrative voice, she brings her audience what she regards as the rock-bottom psychological truth about this boy. He is, she says, "a harmless little coward," a description hardly in keeping with the psychiatric and psychoanalytic jargon one sees in journals the world over. The boy "is in terror when a dog barks at him" and "is also frightened to go along the dark passage in the evening, and certainly would not be capable of injuring a fly." We then learn about the origins of the child's rebellious braggadocio, as written in his aborted dream of a novel. This youngster had been rather sternly educated at home and in school, and had gone through his fair share of intimidating encounters with doctors. He became afraid, as boys do, that he'd be sexually mutilated, denied his assertive masculinity—"the fear which psychoanalysis names *castration-fear*." Such a fear, she explains, turned the boy against all authority: the one with power is the one with the power to punish, to maim, to castrate. Deeply troubled by such fears, the boy did his best to appear (to himself as well as others) unworried, imperturbable. The more he was tempted sexually to "play with himself," the more he feared punishment for such temptations, or indeed for any independent initiatives he may have had, which in his mind might have been linked to his struggle to balance his sexual interests with the strong anxieties those interests got going in him. Miss Freud refers to "his quite harmless attacks on those in authority" as a psychological ploy by a child who is trying to whistle in the dark (in this case, shout in broad daylight), lest he break down in apprehension, even panic. She then turns from the clinical analysis she has made to a controlled, terse plea to her listeners on behalf of the boy: "What he needs is, indeed, neither admiration of his efforts nor harshness and restrictions."

In other words, he ought to be regarded neither as a victim of an outmoded educational system, nor as a promising reformer whose childhood avowals and confrontations augur well for some future political moment, when a new breed of activists will confront stale pieties and policies. Nor did Miss Freud conclude—as many would today—that the boy needed "therapy." She calls for "an abatement of his fear," but doesn't directly and specifically suggest that he go to a psychiatric clinic or be referred for psychoanalytic treatment. She urges that "by some means or other" that "abatement" take place. In the following paragraph, she mentions "the psychoanalytic method of treatment" as one means by which this might be realized. She is not there, she notes, to describe that "method"—not then, at least, under the sponsorship of the Hort teachers. Indeed, it is interesting how restrained and unpretentious she is when she contemplates the transformative possibilities for this child: "By some means or other." Was this a mere rhetorical device—a desire not to be haughty and too sure of herself? Did she consider various other ways in which this boy might be assisted—of which child analysis was but one?

When I asked her these questions, she first replied with characteristic firmness—"No," she wasn't using a "rhetorical device." She then decided to take on my second question: "I was hoping to say something of use to those teachers. That was my intent. I did not regard myself as an 'authority.' The boy I told them about had his objections to 'authority,' but I didn't feel I was the representation of the authority he was resisting and denouncing, out of fear. After all, many people in Vienna and elsewhere—many important people— felt that psychoanalysis was also meant to undermine 'authority.' So, when I came to give those lectures, and then told of that boy—it was a double dose!"

She paused, smiling, and then resumed: "I did not feel that it was fair to tell teachers about a boy who had gotten into trouble and then tell them that I knew how to get him out of trouble, and that was that: nothing else but an analysis would work! Here was a boy who kept a vivid diary, and was dramatically anxious to take his case to others. Perhaps a teacher might have gained his trust—just as an ana- lyst would try to [do]. Maybe the teacher would help the boy to feel less threatened—just as an analyst would try to [do]. I don't think most teachers—then, at least—would have figured out what was troubling that boy; at least, the way we [child analysts] do. But chil- dren have a way of dealing with their problems on their own; and if they have an understanding teacher, they are the better for it— stronger, so they can tackle these matters.

"I guess I was trying to suggest the value of psychoanalysis to those teachers; and I was trying to show them what we could make of certain kinds of behavior that otherwise seem quite confusing or hard to figure out. But I would not have been a very credible speaker if I'd told them that boys such as that one, and all the other children they knew who were having their troubles, have only one hope, and that is to come see us. There weren't enough of 'us' then, and there still aren't, and there never will be; and besides, the question then becomes: what about 'us'—what *is* our role with these children, and with their teachers? That's an important question!"

She wanted time to think about that "question"—one she'd pondered many times before. She had always encouraged teachers to work closely with people like her, when a child's difficulties required collaborative efforts. But she did not want professional distinctions to become so blurred that both child psychoanalysts and teachers were in one another's way. There was the danger that the two kinds of professional people would begin to lose track of their own responsibilities and capacities, as they became caught up in their collegial involvements.

"It is possible for analysts to overlook the normal changes that take place in children—their ability to 'grow out' of a problem. It is possible for teachers to overlook the irrational side of life, and keep going after a child who is in trouble in such a way that he gets worse, not better. Both sides have to be considered: the analyst who lacks a 'commonsense' perspective, or as some would put it, a 'longitudinal perspective'—the changes that naturally occur in children, including children who seem very troubled one season, but can get much better the next; and the teacher who gets upset with a child, or by a child, and tells the child to stop doing something, only to find that the child has no intention of going along. Certainly discipline is important [I had mentioned it as one of the 'means' she might have had in mind when she mentioned 'abating' the child's fear by 'one means or other'].

"I know that some teachers have equated psychoanalysis with 'permissiveness,' or hedonism. We heard that in Vienna, and we've heard it in London; and you must have heard it in America. There *is* a basis for what has been charged: some of us may have forgotten the needs children have for order and control and predictability—and what I think you mean by 'discipline.' But some children can't respond to 'discipline' in the way teachers intend. Some children become wilder, the more we bear down on them. Some children lose their rationality, as we try to make them more acquiescent with our 'discipline.' If a child lacks 'discipline' from within, and lacks the willingness or capacity to pay attention to someone's request that he be more 'disciplined'—then what ought a teacher do? At what point will a teacher stop and say: I have tried, but to no avail!

"We have met with teachers over the years, and heard their problems; and sometimes, we have little to offer but the recognition of how troublesome some children can be. But most children are not [troublesome]; and it is these children who give their teachers the confidence to deal with the few who *are* troublesome. A teacher once said to me: 'I have one child who drives me crazy; but I have twenty other children who make me feel I know what I'm doing, and I'm doing it well—so it is those children who are helping their one class-mate by helping me to be patient with her, and not take the things she says to me personally.' I thought that was a nice way of putting it. By the way, when we learned of that girl [who was driving her crazy]—what she did and said in school—we did *not* recommend psychoanal-ysis, or psychotherapy. We felt it best to work with the teacher; she seemed to have a strong handle on what was going on, and besides, we suspected that this girl was not 'locked into' her predicament—and was cooperative enough and sensible enough to profit a lot from the 'special time' she had gotten for herself with her teacher. So, you see, I meant what I said when I used that phrase 'by some means or other.' A teacher, a parent, a relative, a neighbor, can sometimes begin to figure importantly in a troubled child's life, and how that happens depends on the child—what the boy or girl is doing and saying, and also on the way a certain adult 'rallies around.' I like that expression; we hear it often in England!''

My questions about her final "charge" to the Hort teachers in that fourth lecture led us to long discussions—to a prolonged effort on the part of both of us to figure out how children in psychological trouble can be helped, short of treatment. After a while I began to realize how strongly committed she felt to the teachers she had come to know over the years, in Austria and in England, how respectful she was of their ability to work with children emotionally as well as intel-lectually. Not only did she regard herself as a teacher who had become a child psychoanalyst, but she never, of course, stopped teaching. She also never stopped consulting with particular teachers of children—all those who worked in the nurseries she ran during the Second World War and afterward, or came to the Hampstead Clinic, which she also helped run, for advice, or in connection with a child who was in treatment. Some teachers followed her lead and, under her aegis, took psychoanalytic training, became analysts who there-after taught children in a different way.

On another occasion, as we were looking at some children's drawings and paintings I had brought her, the subject of "art classes" came up—their value and purpose. She asked me if I spent much time asking the children what they had in mind when they drew or painted.[2] I said I did, a bit too quickly, perhaps. She surprised me with her response: "It is always a balance we have to aim for—isn't it?"

"Yes," I said—but I wondered what she meant. She explained: "A child is trying to tell both himself and you or me something, with the drawing. On the other hand, who wants to feel someone breathing down your neck! I've been told that—'Miss Freud: don't push me so hard!' I remember that girl very well. She must have regarded me, too many times, as acting like her schoolteacher, and not her analyst! There are times for us to listen and be relatively quiet—even with children, who want a more active person [working with them] than the analyst who works with adults. There are other times for us to surprise both ourselves and the children—with a remark we make. That same girl—who could, rather quickly, get 'fresh' with me— once told me, after I'd pointed something out to her, that I was an 'all right teacher.' She was a little begrudging, always—but those two words, for her, were meant to be an enormous gift to me, and I was more pleased than she may have realized, though I did smile with appreciation, and she saw by my look that she'd got to me!"

The little girl had, I suspect, not only "got" to her, but "got" at what was central to her, always. She made it clear many times that, for her, teaching is learning twice: first, one learns as one prepares for one's students, and then one learns from them, as one works with them. She constantly insisted upon the capacity children have to teach us—I remember, for instance, what she said one day, as I picked up and put back in a big black leather carrying case a sheaf of drawings and paintings, which we'd both looked at especially hard and long: "Well, the children did well with us today!" I was a little nonplussed. To be sure, I'd heard her comment on those times when children become our instructors, when they inform, enlighten, even guide us. But this remark, in its relaxed tone of pleasure and satisfaction, caught me a bit by surprise, as did her next comment: "They showed us the ropes—with those crayons and paints!" No question, they had taken us by the hand psychologically, as she was surely suggesting, but at that moment I thought I heard and felt something else at work—an elderly teacher who had looked at what schoolchildren of eight and nine and ten had chosen to represent, had found herself challenged, put to the test (what meaning to find?), had eventually found herself edified (found that meaning), but had also found herself taken in hand by those boys and girls, "brought forward" a bit as a human being the way someone's words or pictures can occasionally manage to do for us. Yet again, a teacher brought face to face with herself by students who thereby did, indeed, "do well" by her, and by themselves as artists and fast-growing tutors.

THEORIST

It is not the analytical work that is so difficult, for one can accomplish this with some human reason, it is the everlasting dealing with human fates.
Anna Freud to Lou Andreas-Salomé,
August 19, 1926

I N HER TOUCHING TRIBUTE to her friend and colleague and teacher August Aichhorn, mentioned earlier, Anna Freud pointed out that "instead of looking for ready-made theoretical answers to his problems, Aichhorn began practical work in the analytic field as soon as his period of training was completed." She then describes Aichhorn's many sustained efforts as a therapist with exceedingly troubled and often quite refractory delinquents, and as a psychological guide for social workers, police officials, and others who struggled so vigorously (and often unavailingly) with those "wayward youth." Her comment on Aichhorn's relationship to theory implies that here was someone who had all sorts of interesting thoughts and ideas but didn't become exclusively preoccupied with them, didn't try to turn them into a raison d'être. Nor did he lean upon the concepts of others in such a way that he allowed himself, even by proxy, to derive his major view of what obtains in life from conceptual statements, from formulations and generalizations. In contrast, he "began practical work," a series of everyday endeavors and commitments she is at great pains to spell out.

Twenty years after she wrote that obituary, I asked her whether she had any particular reason to point out this contrast—the conceptualist as compared to the person engaged in the everyday psychiatric and psychoanalytic treatment of patients, or in consultation with those in other professions. She did not answer right away, and I had the distinct feeling that she was either puzzled or irritated by my inquiry. "I don't remember my reasons. [I had brought with me a copy of the obituary she wrote and read to her the pertinent section from it.] But I'm sure the major one was to try to do some adequate justice to Aichhorn's life."

I took the unusual silence that followed to be a reprimand—her way of telling me that she saw clearly through my question, aware that I had a personal ax to grind. But I was wrong. She then told me that Aichhorn's work had always impressed her—especially his uncanny ability to engage with youngsters whom others off-handedly or self-servingly dismissed as "unsuitable" for treatment, for psychoanalysis. She described his virtues at length: his obvious flexibility and resourcefulness as an analyst, his capacity as well as willingness to take risks, to bend the rules, even make up some of his own rules, in order to get things going with young people inclined to be wary of the adult world, including its doctors, lawyers, social workers. Then she got back to the matter of theory: "Aichhorn had his own way of being 'theoretical'; he carefully observed the young people he worked with, and he tried to figure out how to work with them, not an easy thing to do. He told me many times that working with delinquents, in the first stage of treatment, was like working with much younger children: you had to show them that you are well disposed to them, and even are ready to be of use to them. Later, sometimes much later, comes the kind of serious discussions that take place in psychoanalysis—about one's parents, and one's dreams and associations. 'If I tried to push some of those young people into a regular analysis,' he once told me—and then he laughed—'they'd tell me to go have myself analyzed some more!'

"That was a moment I still remember—and you can see why: it tells a lot about him and how he was able to do what he did. He had a sense of humor; he knew how to approach people to earn their trust; he could be self-critical; and he wasn't afraid to see in himself some-thing of what he was treating in others, though he didn't forget the difference between himself and those he was treating, or trying to treat. 'Each of them [his wayward youth] is different,' he once told me—and he truly believed that. Perhaps a person has to think along those lines, if he is to work successfully with very disturbed (and disturbing) delinquents. [He's] not the person to build up a big the-ory; he's the one who feels his way down a path, hoping for the best, but worrying about trouble ahead—and not with a grand view of it all."

Of course, she knew well that Aichhorn had, in fact, managed "a grand view of it all"—had built an understanding of the nature of "wayward" or delinquent young people. During my residency in child psychiatry, I worked rather intensively with delinquent youths, and especially with delinquent young women (aged twelve to seventeen) who were confined to a so-called industrial school (the toughest of the youths, the most truculent and agitated). Scarcely a week went by when I didn't consult Aichhorn's writings, on my own or when I was told by a supervisor to do so. Often those supervisors would cite Aichhorn, chapter and page—his views, his experiences, his clinical narratives, his portrayals of certain kinds of young people. But this writing of Aichhorn's did not strike me as theoretical writing—rather, as a great clinician's essay-writing.

Miss Freud knew what I meant when I said as much to her—but she also wanted to discuss the matter, even take issue: "Aichhorn is not Fenichel¹—if that is what you mean! But theory need not be without its pleasures. Some writers are more interested in winning over their readers than others. Some writers of theoretical essays will never give clinical examples; others will give many. I suppose the fair thing to do is state one's preference—that is everyone's right. It need not be *either/or*; we can make general statements, and back them up with clinical vignettes—to illustrate, or even advance a theoretical position or argument. That happens all the time. . . . We have all been in those seminars—when the language gets quite 'thick,' and tempers can sometimes follow suit! I think the reason that [the emotional turbulence she had just mentioned] happens is the same [reason] that people become so agitated or 'defensive' in courtrooms: a law is being handed down, and many of us remember the pleasure we had when we were young—defying rules. When an analyst describes a patient, the listener is being told someone's personal story; when an analyst hands down a theory, the listener is often being asked, by indirection: agree or disagree? That is a temptation—to shake one's head and say no! It can be another kind of temptation, I agree, to say yes. [I had begun to suggest as much.] A theorist, let us say, is someone who tries to understand, and communicate [that understanding] in terms of general principles."

After stopping for coffee, she asked me what I thought of what she had just said. I told her I could hardly disagree, but the language of some theorists seems to me impenetrable, and I find it hard not to be irritated. She smiled, and probed further. Was I responding with aesthetic disapproval, or was there a "personal" or "emotional" reason for my reaction? I laughed, and said, "Both." She smiled. We seemed at the end of this particular road. But she pulled back, now, from that line of questioning—and became, herself, more "personal," and yes, a bit "emotional." She noted the ease with which her father moved back and forth—from illustrative examples, drawn from his practice, even from his own life (his dreams), to general remarks: the discursive essays that flowed so continuously from his pen throughout his working, writing life. She also made some interesting (and for me, unexpected) comments about psychoanalytic training, as it has evolved, and the impact of that development on "theory making."

To draw on a few moments of what was a bit of a lecture: "My impression is that *dense* theory—the kind you don't seem to like, [the kind that is] unconnected to clinical information—has become more and more available to us. I don't know why, exactly. Perhaps some of us equate it with 'science.' Perhaps our choice of candidates has something to do with this—we are after those who enjoy propounding and dissecting the law. We aren't attracting the poets or novelists. I used to think that doctors would be the ones who want more case histories; but many doctors are not at all put off by dense theory! In my experience, Aichhorn has his followers today [1971] in some of our social workers and nurses and pediatricians, who aren't interested in using their intelligence in the way theorists ask us to. . . . They are quite attached to their patients, and their memories of patients they once worked with, and they want to do more [for them], or more for others, who will be following them [as patients], and that is why they want psychoanalytic training—not to sit and exchange (and develop!) ideas! Of course, many psychologists are well versed at that [the communication of, the nurturance of ideas] and many psychiatrists, also—they have only 'put up with' medical school, and are glad to be away from that kind of clinical life, and maybe, when they go into psychiatric training, they forget how valuable their clinical way of looking can be: each case is different. If you remember that motto, you'll be quite careful about how you make your 'general' remarks, I suspect.

"If I keep talking, I'll be found to have rambled on beyond reason! It would be ironic if I make a theory, today, about theory making or theory makers—who they are, and why they do what they do. I think most of us [in psychoanalysis] move back and forth in our minds when we are seeing patients, [or] attending seminars that are *meant* to stress the discussion of theory. We pay the closest attention to what our patient says, or does, and then we pull back, now and then, and say to ourselves: what does all this add up to, and how does this person compare with others, others we've seen, and others described in the journals or textbooks? We may not all go the same distance—some may stop there, and others may think of all kinds of theoretical constructs, even as their patients keep talking, or [if they are children] doing what they are doing with toys or with paints or crayons. If it is true, as the saying goes, that 'each person is different,' it is probably true that each person uses 'theory' differently, and has a distinctive attitude toward it."

I found myself, as she concluded, remembering silently the introductory sentence to the third chapter of her landmark book *The Ego and the Mechanisms of Defense*. She had just reminded her readers that the ego is "the seat of observation," and she had just described, with breathtaking clarity, "the application of analytic technique to the study of the psychic institutions" (a summary, really, of the purposes of analysis, and the obstacles in its way), and she was all set to discuss the ego's "defensive operations considered as an object of analysis," when she made a break with a highly abstract mode of presentation, and wrote: "The tedious and detailed theoretical discussions contained in the last chapter may for practical purposes be summed up in a few simple sentences." As I sat with her, I remembered coming upon that sentence for the first time: her book had been assigned by a psychoanalytic "preceptor," as he was quaintly known in the late 1950s. Even then I wondered about the use of the word *tedious*—surely no accident for any psychoanalyst engaged in what seems to be straightforward theoretical exposition and explanation, and especially noteworthy, I thought back then, and still think, in the case of someone so conscious of words, so sensitive to language and its shades of meaning.

We got going some more on "theory"—on the balance in her father's writing between the personal voice of the doctor who has had dreams, or his patient who has suffered nightmares, on the one hand, and the master of incisive, rational analysis of human affairs who wants to make general statements, and do so in a way that a broadly literate audience will readily comprehend. Still pondering her remark about "tedious theoretical discussions," yet reluctant to ask her about it, I found myself commenting on the "tension" in some of Freud's writing—the clear-eyed writer, anxious to clarify for his readers, as against the theorist who adds up ideas and tries to endow them with both symmetry and the weight of significance. She nodded, but a quizzical smile told me that she had taken note of the word *tension*. I tried to move us toward the general, tried to be a bit theoretical myself—remarked upon that "tension" as part of the emotional experience felt by many social or psychological observers: their desire to do justice to human particularity and complexity, while at the same time integrating what they have seen and heard into constructs and ideas.

She responded warmly to this not very original observation. I had worried that she might be critical of my skepticism with respect to some kinds of theory making, and want to drop the subject. Instead she launched into a heartfelt and moving statement with respect to her own life as a theorist: "Some minds work better with theory than others. Some love to develop it; others find no pleasure in doing that—or in contemplating it. I know analysts who are comfortable discussing theory, but who would never take it upon themselves to write it. Of course, there are always those who write it— and are comfortable only in discussing what they have written, and not what others have written! A patient of mine, a writer of fiction, once told me of the 'vanity' he saw in his fellow novelists, as they talked about their work. He had been talking, during that hour, about his own 'vanity'—his struggle with narcissism, a consequence, we were both beginning to realize, of a childhood in which he had been alone far too much: his parents had been divorced; his father left England for the south of France, and then South America, and his mother had her own life very much on her mind—she had a successful career, and it was important to her that men gathered around her.

"I recall my patient contrasting the 'vanity' of writers with the kinds of emotions he believed to predominate among psychoanalysts. Needless to mention, I asked him what he believed those 'emotions' were—and he had nothing in particular to say about us. After he told me how 'good' we are, he once more told me how 'bad' his writer friends are, himself included. I asked him a second time around to spell out what all that 'badness' was about. He came back to the 'vanity' theme, and I began to notice a certain boastfulness in his talking—writers as gifted, but vain, vain, vain! More so than anyone else, a kind of accomplishment! I remember chuckling . . . we have our fair share of 'vanity,' too. He asked me to say more. I didn't want to say too much; I wanted to hear *him* speak some more on the subject. But I did mention that we do some writing, too. He quickly observed that our writing is 'different.' Of course, I asked him to tell me the 'difference,' and he did: I got a lecture on how much of himself a writer of fiction puts into his stories or his novels—whereas 'you people,' meaning all of us who write 'scientific papers' (he called them), report 'the truth,' our 'discoveries.'

"I had to chuckle again. I told him I thought the distinction he made was very generous to people like me—too generous. I went no further, then—though we came back to the matter months later, and by then we were able to have a quite different conversation. By then he was not surprised when I declared that 'vanity' can be found among psychoanalytic writers, too—who are human beings, after all. He constructs novels, putting himself into what he does, his talents and his warts; we construct theories, some of us, and the same 'investment' of ourselves [into the theory] takes place. When I finished drawing that comparison, I felt I'd perhaps said more than I intended! I think at times when I have been a bit skeptical of theory, I am holding myself to strict account, the way my patient did. Like him, I am worrying about 'vanity,' the ambitiousness and high self-regard of a theorist—especially when little effort is made to 'check out' the theory with the actual lives of people: see if there is supporting clinical evidence.''

I certainly was not about to argue. I heard then what I had heard before, and would hear again: a side of Anna Freud that did, indeed, I feel sure, prompt that comment in *The Ego and the Mechanisms of Defense* about "tedious and detailed theoretical discussions." Her own two chapters that she criticized so sternly are not all that detailed, and are not tedious either. They are brief (less than thirty pages in all) and crisply, lucidly written—a vigorous, well-paced presentation of the fundamentals of psychoanalytic work. At a time (1936) when not all that many psychoanalytic writers had made the effort to explain just what it is that takes place in analysis, she outlined the "resistances" met by the analyst; the strategies employed by the analysand in an effort to avoid anxieties; the development of the so-called "transference neurosis," with the patient connecting the analyst to emotions and attitudes directed earlier at parents, and the analyst getting immersed in the tug of those emotions himself or herself, responding in ways that have their origins not in the patient's childhood but in that of the person sitting behind the couch. Although not completely comfortable in her role as a major theorist—hence her apologetic, if not self-critical, aside—she was not deterred from completing a book that has become a major theoretical statement: the ego explored with care, thoroughness, precision—its importance newly, convincingly emphasized for a profession hitherto heavily preoccupied with the unconscious instinctive life collectively known as the id.

"Somehow or other," Miss Freud writes, "many analysts had conceived the idea that, in analysis, the value of the scientific and therapeutic work was in direct proportion to the depth of the psychic strata upon which attention was focused." With those three words "somehow or other"—delightfully vague and innocent, a phrase she used often—she is choosing to avoid a long discussion of the hold that ideas and theories can have on certain people under certain circumstances—the "somehow or other" that had to do with her father's emergence as a major twentieth-century intellectual figure. She could not help but have in mind the range of her father's writings, including his last major theoretical effort, *The Ego and the Id*, published in 1923, thirteen years before her own book appeared. In that book, Sigmund Freud the clinician and theorist is mightily impressed by the power and authority of the id, and conversely, the vulnerability of the ego, which at one point he calls "a poor creature," constantly at the mercy of "three masters and consequently menaced by three dangers: from the external world, from the libido of the id, and from the severity of the superego." Still, he was also anxious to indicate what the ego could do: "The ego develops from perceiving instincts to controlling them, from obeying instincts to inhibiting them." He goes into the matter of sublimation at some length—that major, yet everyday victory won by millions of egos as they struggle with millions of ids. Freud's own hard-won psychoanalysis (including all the books he wrote) stands in witness to what one of those egos was able to achieve over one of those ids. The military imagery that Freud often favored is mobilized on behalf of all those who would be the beneficiaries of Freud's self-analysis, through the intervention of his various followers: "Psychoanalysis is an instrument to enable the Ego to achieve a progressive conquest of the Id."[2]

The greater the power accorded the id, the greater the admiration, I suppose, felt by the rest of us for those who struggle with that id: our psychoanalysts, and we who as patients follow in their steps. But the growing renown and success of psychoanalysis throughout the Western bourgeois world eventually cast doubt on the id as an omnipresent, powerfull protagonist, before which all else seems a weakened, feeble opposition, always on the verge of being toppled. In fact, many of Freud's patients were ironic witnesses to quite the opposite—the excessive power of the ego and the superego over their instinctual lives. True, Freud's Eros and Thanatos had pressed hard on those men and women—but by no means had either of the two putative drives taken control. The price may have been neurosis, that universal condition, Freud told us—but the result was an id all too successfully checked, hemmed in, held at bay, all too thoroughly "civilized," to the point that the sexual lives of these patients were often nonexistent and their aggressive energies often thoroughly routed, or transformed into such unheroic qualities as shyness, humility, fearfulness, anxiety.

By the late 1920s and early 1930s, Freud himself began to turn his attention to Thanatos, which seemed newly influential not only in his thinking, but in the world of Hitler, Mussolini, Stalin. Meanwhile, a growing number of analysts kept taking up arms against the id, and, especially, the drive Eros, which could always be counted as a worthy and formidable antagonist. By the 1930s, such a struggle earned any analyst who pursued it reflection in Freud's growing glory—and the distinction of being considered a brave clinician, a (self-designated) follower of a clearheaded man increasingly regarded as a twentieth-century seer, if not an icon. To find himself the object of intense veneration might not have surprised Freud, even in the early and mid-1930s. Long before, he had given his earliest colleagues rings, as though sealing their association with mystical bonds—lonely seekers after elusive truths in an alien, unfriendly world. As might be expected, disagreements followed, and given the intense, quasi-religious nature of this association—initially, of middle-aged, middle-class, preponderantly Jewish men—those arguments turned into defections, which soon became consolidated into rival "movements." Just the same, the original circle continues to predominate in many intellectual and cultural worlds, and in the medical world, especially that of the English speaking nations, with the United States foremost. While Freud himself was putting his own ideas through careful and at times quite substantial revision, others were fastening their hold, embracing him and his books with that zeal often seen among the agnostic intelligentsia, for whom the anathema of explicit religion is replaced by other fervent enthusiasms.

Grete Bibring, a psychoanalyst of Freud's 1920s Vienna circle, once described to me what she and her analyst-husband experienced upon their arrival in England, then America: "We were exiled from our homeland, remember; and before that happened we were hardly popular there. Suddenly we come to a foreign land, and people treat us with respect, even admiration. It is a completely different reaction to us. We were invited to do this and that, and meet one person and another—I had to pinch myself and say: is this the same world where I've been living all these years? Well, it wasn't, that was what we began to realize—from night to day, as they say! From the darkest part of the night to a day with bright sunshine. Once, my husband [Edward Bibring] said to me: 'This attention, it is a bit too much, don't you think?' I said yes, but we could tolerate it for a while, after all we'd gone through. But we began to realize that there are times when such favorable attention can be a mixed blessing. When people listen to your every word, when they *hang* on your every word—then you have to watch your every word! In Vienna, we met and talked and agreed and disagreed and changed our minds—and no one cared, except us, among ourselves. Now, I'd make a remark, and the next thing I knew, people were quoting it as if I'd stepped out of the Bible. I began to feel I should be serious all day long, and I should never tell a joke, especially on myself."

What Dr. Bibring experienced only in exile, Anna Freud surely by 1936 had known for years. As her father's secretary, she was privy to the escalating adulation he had been getting from people far and wide, no matter the parochial hostility, and deteriorating political situation, that obtained in Vienna. Freud had entered history, and the result was a legion of adherents, admirers, would-be followers, if not disciples. His every word became a matter of great import, even though he himself changed his mind on certain points, shifted his emphasis, and in general let his writing reflect the fallible human being he most assuredly was. But ardent recruits to an intellectual "movement," especially one that also has a therapeutic side to it, rarely exhibit a shred of worldly skepticism, even though under other circumstances the same people can be highly skeptical, even cynical. "Every day," Grete Bibring went on, "I heard: 'Freud said this, Freud said that, Freud wrote this, Freud wrote that; I heard myself intro- duced, all the time, as 'one of Dr. Sigmund Freud's colleagues'; and I even began to hear that 'Dr. Freud and Dr. Bibring say'—it was, I'd say to myself, 'just too much!' "

Against this historical background, the following sentence, the third one in *The Ego and the Mechanisms of Defense*, takes on particular importance: "Whenever interest was shifted from the deeper to the more superficial psychic strata—whenever, that is to say, research was deflected from the Id to the Ego—it was felt that here was a beginning of apostasy from psychoanalysis as a whole." An "apostasy" is the abandonment of one's moral or religious or political or spiritual convictions, a heretical alteration of one's values or beliefs or principles. To use that word in connection with a group of scientists—to suggest that they leveled such an indictment on their co-workers, their fellow researchers and scientists, is to suggest that psychoanalysis had become a kind of creed even then, while its founder was alive, intellectually alert, and himself still making new formulations, new judgments with respect to causes and effects. Put differently, Anna Freud the theorist was declaring her own values and principles—especially that of open inquiry in the tradition of scientific research.

Decades later she would try to carry herself back to the time when she used the word *apostasy*, a still young psychoanalyst full of ideas and ideals: "I had no one specific in mind to rebuke, no. [I had asked.] I was not so much being a scold as [being] ironic. I knew how much devotion my father inspired in many people by that time [the early 1930s, when she was at work on her book]. I knew his ideas mattered enormously to them—and they wanted to do and say and think as he did. I felt they weren't following him carefully enough—that was part of my reason [for writing as she did in that early sentence of her book]. I also felt that things were getting a little out of hand—that psychoanalysis was being, I guess, 'shortchanged,' because my father always had in mind that we shouldn't confine ourselves to the [analysis of the] drives. We are not only *driven!* To be obvious, we who have our psychoanalytic profession are people who analyze drives—meaning we have egos that are fairly strong, I hope. We have learned how to explore the minds of others, and our own minds, too; we are not doing that without rather sturdy egos, I hope. If we are to understand how we ourselves function, and how our patients function—and they tend to be, many of them, rather able and accomplished people, even if they do have their 'problems'—then we had best cast a fairly wide net. If we don't do that, then we'd better explore the reason: an 'inhibition,' perhaps?"

She stopped to smile, as I savored her remark. But she quickly brought us back: "It's not easy to go backwards in time, and see things the way others did. When I was working on *The Ego and the*

Mechanisms of Defense, I was nearing forty, I recall. [She was forty-one when it was published.] The original group of analysts were of another generation. Some had already died; others were in their seventies and eighties. I was suggesting that the time had come for new explorations; but they remembered how difficult it was to make their own discoveries, and how deaf the world was for so long—and when it did pay attention, the reception was angry. When you have been misunderstood and insulted, and your own motives called into question for trying to learn how the mind works—then you will hesitate when someone comes along and says the time has come for a new approach!"

Such an effort to understand others with whom one disagrees does not come easy, she was frank to say later in our talk. Moreover, she reminded herself (as much as me, I thought) that too much of such "understanding" will stifle the expression of one's heartfelt convictions. "I went ahead and said what I believed ought be said," she recalled—and then added: "Perhaps I could have made some of the points I just made—provided a context for the remarks I made." But, she added: "At the time, I was not looking for 'contexts'—I mean, for those older analysts. I was trying to supply one for my own generation of analysts."

She was trying to map the ego's terrain as carefully as possible—show how it works (its "mechanisms") and illustrate these theoretical assertions with clinical examples. She was especially interested in claiming part of the unconscious for the ego—lest the notion prevail that the unconscious is, in sum, the instinctual life (the "seething cauldron," Freud in one of his more vivid moments called the id). We are certainly "driven" by the lusts and rages Freud lumped together, metapsychologically, as the id—the urges and cravings that usually don't surface directly, or if they do, cause us discomfort and apprehension. But there is another side to our unconscious life—the learned maneuvers we as human beings acquire from early childhood as our means of coming to terms with those urges and cravings. Some of us learn to attribute them to others rather than face their presence in ourselves. Some of us learn to guard ourselves exceedingly well—even restrict the range of our interests and involvements—lest those "drives" assert themselves. Some of us work hard to turn things all the way around—assert praise when we feel the desire to blame, assert affection when we feel resentment or envy. Many of us learn to take the energy connected to those drives and find expression for it in the "higher" realm of hobbies, professional activities, interests such as art, literature, science. None of this aspect of our humanity seems all that surprising to us today—for half a century psychoanalysts have edified themselves and us about such mental tactics: the "projections" we find convenient to construct for ourselves; the restrictions of the ego we find useful to assert; the "reaction formations" that have us behaving like Uriah Heep, when "deep down" we'd like to slap and punch and scream at someone; the "sublimations" that let us use our passions in intense, continuing commitments to the arts and sciences or in a lifelong devotion to a job.

Yet, in the early 1930s, those dimensions of our unconscious had not been given the prominence they deserved—by virtue of the psychological authority they have in our everyday lives. In a sense, psychoanalysis had begun as an investigation of the night—the dreams that reveal our otherwise hidden yearnings. The night stretches into the day, Freud told us—the daydreams we have, those slips of the tongue we hear coming from our mouths, the misreadings we make, our jokes. Such telltale shadows kept the early psychoanalysts, guided by their mentor of mentors, Freud, busy trying to comprehend. But we don't only stumble significantly in our speech, or reveal ourselves in our attempts at humor, or spend time letting our thoughts and feelings carry us all over the place with people we invent or merely glimpse in the street or in advertisements, only to include in our most intimate fantasies. We also—huge chunks of time—live in the light of day as able, active men and women, committed to particular people, loyal to particular obligations.

It is that knowledge which Miss Freud keeps in mind as she spells out her theory—a consciousness, on her part, of the ego as tough and resilient as well as overworked, even battered on many occasions, vulnerable to the powerful demands of biology and society and culture, of neurophysiological reality and historical reality as they get translated into each person's daily experience at home and at work, in a family, a neighborhood, and beyond. She gives us the "nine mechanisms of defense," which a measure of humility permits her to say "have been exhaustively described in the theoretical writings of psychoanalysis." Her own book, however, was surely as comprehensive and searching an effort in that direction as had ever been attempted. To these nine mechanisms such as projection and introjection, repression and reaction formation, she adds a "tenth, which pertains rather to the study of the normal than to that of neurosis: sublimation, or displacement of instinctual aims."

The fact that she is aiming for more than a theory of defense mechanisms becomes apparent with the emphasis she gives to sublimation—reminding us that "the normal" should also be stressed by the psychoanalytic theorist. She is constantly calling on the lives of patients to illustrate the points she makes, and no doubt it was these stories—or, more exactly, her wide-eyed, open-minded response to them—that kept her theoretical inclinations in firm check. For instance, she was tempted at one point to attempt a "chronological classification" of the defense mechanisms—that is, which ones appear when in the life of the child. But she desists because she acknowledges "differences of opinion." She points out apparent inconsistencies, contradictions—admits to "all the doubt and uncertainty which even today attach to chronological pronouncements in analysis." Her use of the word *pronouncement* is, of course, no accident—a subdued thrust at the inclination among psychiatrists to find order, structure, certainty, and chronology at all costs, eager as we are to impose those characteristics on what William James described, unashamedly, as the mind's "booming, buzzing confusion." "It will probably be best," Anna Freud concluded, "to abandon the attempts to classify them [to make a chronological enumeration of the defense mechanisms] and, instead, to study in detail the situations which call for the defensive reactions."

That remark, seemingly a resigned afterthought by a theorist who has by then (a third into the book) shown herself to be a master of the subject she is discussing, is a kind of "antipronouncement," the implications of which are enormous. Her examination of the mind's struggles, its interiority, takes on a different character when she suggests a careful investigation of the various "situations" that elicit particular psychological responses from particular patients or from subjects of research. In essence, Miss Freud was urging what she would later continually call "direct observation," of a kind that stresses family life, social pressures, forces at work in schools—the situations that encourage or discourage one or another kind of defense mechanism to take place. She is, in this regard, becoming very much an environmentalist, psychologically—contrary to what is said about her and most psychoanalysts, by those who understandably have chafed at the almost unqualified importance laid upon "drives" and "instincts" (libido) in traditional psychoanalytic theory, that is, in Freud's own writings and those who followed his direction. Erik Erikson later led psychoanalytic theory, heavily weighted toward the influence of "nature" in our lives, towards recognition of "nurture." But it was his analyst and teacher Anna Freud who helped set the stage for his work, published some fifteen years later, when she pointedly asked for a situational look at children—at the particular world that engages the child's ego as well as libido.

During several long talks with Miss Freud in the 1970s, we kept coming back to this passage in her book. At one point, I told her how I had taken it to heart when I lived in New Orleans in the 1960s and did work with black children initiating school desegregation, often against great odds. At the time, I was also, as mentioned earlier, in analysis, and taking seminars at the New Orleans Psychoanalytic Institute. I had remembered her words while trying to figure out what was happening to small black children (first graders) who had to make their way past mobs in order to attend schools boycotted by white parents and their children. When I told Miss Freud about those children, and others I met across the South, I spoke a lot about the "defense mechanisms" the boys and girls summoned. She listened carefully to me, and to the tapes of the interviews I did with four black New Orleans girls, and eventually with white children, as they returned to school. (At times I was taping my conversations with Miss Freud, as she listened to tapes of interviews done with those children—two layers of "oral history.") She pointed out to me psychological events I hadn't picked up: the manner in which, for instance, the crowd's denunciation of those children subtly informed their attitude toward themselves, making them feel inexplicably "low" at certain moments, despite their brave efforts to hold their heads high; and the manner in which those same children dealt with their own worries and fears by the interesting (and morally challenging) strategy of extending pity to (and expressing an earnest religious worry about) the people in the mob who harassed them.

Miss Freud's response (here I have pulled together comments scattered amid the flow of one morning's exchanges): "You are right: those children were stoic and, it turned out, stronger than you believed possible. I agree with you—it serves no good to look for trouble if there isn't any that is getting in anyone's way! But perhaps we could look at the children a bit closer—not to look for trouble, but to try to find the truth of their experience.

"When the little girl tells you she feels sorry for the people in the mob [heckling her, threatening her], I'm sure she does. When she prays to God that He should forgive those people, I'm sure she means it. [The girl, Ruby Bridges, had invoked Jesus in her prayers— 'Please god, try to forgive those folks—because they don't know what they're doing!'3] I think sometimes when we try to understand a girl like this, we worry that we're in some way doing an injustice to her—adding our swear words to those of the mob! I don't doubt you have heard some people in psychiatry or psychoanalysis use a language that does not sound very favorable to this girl, or others like her. [I had said as much, shown my irritation.] But the misuse of a technical language is no rare thing. Without question, some of us are only comfortable talking about pathology—and we see everything through that lens. But more and more we have tried [in child psychoanalysis] to look at the normal development of children; and if we analyze that development it is not in order to demean it. If some of us do so [analyze reductively], then that is the way it goes—the well-known rotten apples in the barrel! Maybe there are more than a few—I agree. But even a lot of them should not get us so distracted that we are concentrating our attention on them, not the issues that ought to concern us.

"If I may say so, you are letting that point of view [the reductionist kind] get to you a bit! It is as if you are saying: I'll have no part of their analysis rubbing off on my children! Why can't we understand the defensive maneuvers of these children as a tribute to them—evidence of their capacity to survive? This child's prayers are not tarnished or spoiled if you and I take note of their usefulness to her—apart from their moral or spiritual content.

"When the girl feels sorry for others [the mob], she surely had in mind [obtaining] a bit of sympathy for herself. Had you asked her, she might have smiled and said yes, she would like the Lord to help her out!" I then protested that, on the other hand, Ruby might *not* have been so pleased with such a line of conversation—might have felt it to be distinctly unlike the kind of devotional Christian talk she had grown up hearing: 'pray, pray hard for those white folks, pray that the Lord gives them His hand, because they surely need it'—the words Ruby heard her Baptist minister use repeatedly.

"Well, all right, perhaps I don't understand the religious life of Ruby's family! But I have heard many Christians marvel at 'the mysterious ways of God,' and perhaps they—some of them—would find our defense mechanisms to be part of his 'mysterious ways.' No matter what happens, if you are a believer, God figures in it—or so many believers have told me. Perhaps Ruby and her family would think of us as friends if we told them that the mind is part of God's world, and we are trying to understand his world through our studies—and [to do] that is our way of understanding him.

"If we were, by some miracle, given a chance to talk to those [New Orleans] children, as they faced those mobs, we might try to see how they pick and choose their way through the 'defenses' available to them. When they get sad, perhaps the accusations of the mobs became their own [accusations]. When they asked for mercy [from God] for the mob, perhaps they were asking for mercy for themselves. When they told you they paid absolutely no attention to the screams of the mob, and never even heard them, some days, then perhaps they had learned how to block out a lot—to 'deny,' to restrict their ego function in some way. When they boasted of the pity they felt for the mob, perhaps they managed with such claims to persuade themselves that they lacked the anger and bitterness and resentment that may have been pushing hard for expression in them, only to be kept 'below the surface,' as we put it. Of course, I must say that in 1960 I myself might have been as silent as you were with the families—for the same reason you were, I suspect: here were people going through a terrible time—so much stress!—and one certainly doesn't want to 'tip the cart over' with questions that can be as upsetting in their own way as a street mob can be! Analytic work requires tact as well as perseverance—and not all of us learn that, I'm afraid.

"Perhaps intuitively, you were standing back a bit from these children, and letting their lives unfold—without feeling the need to take their pulses every day, or week, or even month. I suppose, when we monitor defenses we are doing that, taking the pulse. If you'd heard these children say something that worried you, I'm sure you'd have become their day-to-day doctor! As it was, you tried to be an observer. Would you mind the phrase 'longitudinal observation' as a description of your work? At Hampstead, we gradually learned to take a longer view of things. We held back our statements about psychopathology—as you did. We tried to ask ourselves not only what something means with respect to id-ego-superego, but with respect to the child's gradual emergence as a certain kind of person. I am not being as clear as I'd like to be: we have learned to hold our breaths rather often, and let the children show us how they are going to 'put it all together'—I like that phrase. For you, perhaps, what mattered was not Ruby as a child who resorted to projection, introjection, restriction of her ego, reaction formation (her defenses), and, of course, sublimation, but Ruby as a child who was gradually moving along with respect to her independence, her ability to get along with people, her loyalty to certain adults and to those of her own age, her ability to be conscientious, thoughtful, and a reliable child—all of that has to do with the ego, and all of that tells about the 'lines of development' in a child, and that's the phrase we've been using, a part of our *own* 'line of development.'"

That phrase became an important part of her thinking in the last two decades of her life, and figured prominently in her last major theoretical statement, *Normality and Pathology in Childhood* (1965). She had no reason to forsake the psychoanalytic truths that her father's generation had come by—the progression children go through as they deal with the intake of food, the control of bodily secretions and waste, a rising sensuality and sexuality. But she had never allowed those terms *oral, anal, phallic,* to dominate her thinking in the way they did for so many others for so long. Back in the 1930s, she had looked at the ego's progression—its slow mastery not only of the id but of the respective worlds (schools, playgrounds, camps) children learn to inhabit. By the early 1960s, she was prepared to be bolder. "So far, in our psychoanalytic theory," she declares, "the developmental sequences are laid down only with regard to particular, circumscribed parts of the child's personality." She mentions, in that regard, the "development of the sexual drive," and that of "the aggressive drive." Here, in one fell swoop, with no great flourish and even disarming offhandedness, she has categorized those two drives as "particular, circumscribed parts of the child's personality," a sweeping reappraisal of their significance, and a challenge of enormous proportions to traditional psychoanalytic theory.

She is determined, she makes clear, to look at the "assessment" of any child's life in a much broader manner than usual among psychoanalysts or cognitive psychologists. She includes among her "assessments" that of a shift "from the young child's egocentric view of the world and his fellow human beings to empathy, mutuality, and companionship with his contemporaries," an assertion quite in keeping with what her onetime student Erik Erikson had formulated fifteen years earlier in *Childhood and Society.* Such a remark, like much of Erikson's writing, certainly helped me understand what the children I met in the 1960s were accomplishing (apart from the desegregation of a city's schools!): They were beginning to have a sense of what had been denied their people, and what they as young citizens had to offer—the long march from legally enforced, racially connected egocentricity to a knowledge of "others," a daily experience with those "others" that had all sorts of personal meaning and consequences for them. In a poignant and compelling remark (the antitheorist yet again at work), Miss Freud insists that "far from being theoretical abstractions in the sense here used, developmental lines are historical realities which, when assembled, convey a convincing picture of an individual child's personal development."

That is what, finally, she had spent her lifetime trying to envision (the root meaning of "theory" has to do with a view of things): her way of paying the fullest regard possible to the lives of children—so that their sexual development, their moral struggles, their social competence, their growing intellectual competence, are each and severally acknowledged and (in discussions) rendered convincingly. She dares to use, for instance, phrases such as "emotional self-reliance" and "responsibility" in bodily management, and she has a marvelous section not only on Winnicott's well-known notion of the "transitional object" (the child's move from attachment to the mother to attachment to "objects" such as blankets or play-animals that receive emotions hitherto connected directly to her), but on the importance of play for children, and the way it foreshadows a person's work life: what we learn to do in games (compete and cooperate both) we soon must learn to do at work. Yet again, she was walking down a road Erikson would explore—a road that enabled her to look clinically at children without yanking them out of their social and cultural and historical and ethnic and racial and familial context and slapped with various ominous words that announce irrevocable "pathology," in the name of psychoanalytic theory.

For Anna Freud, psychoanalytic theory was no mere intellectual fancy, or temptation. She was never a university student, never learned to show off for a professor, or as one. While growing up, she loved poetry and novels and short stories, and tried writing both poems and fiction on her own for a while. While her father was a brilliant theorist, revealing himself in his writing to be not only a psychoanalyst but a penetratingly analytic thinker, he was also a shrewdly pragmatic physician. He was anxious to make things work for his patients, and for himself as the one trying to heal them. He was also a brilliant essayist, with an engaging gift for narrative presentation. His daughter followed suit—called upon theory without embarrassment or difficulty, although sometimes with barely concealed reluctance that hinted at her preference for allusion and image rather than the dense formulations of social science, for the concreteness of human experience rather than the wordiness of abstraction heaped upon abstraction.

Anna Freud was a theorist, as a poet can be; she sought through metaphor, simile, a semblance of control over life's astonishing, limitless variation. She used theory as a quiet resting place rather than a final destination—and she tried hard not to lose her sense of proportion or irony as she elaborated that theory, or discussed it with others. "I hope our ideas (or speculations) can be of help to both of you [Jane and me] as you try to understand those children, but perhaps they will be the ones to give you food for thought." My wife and I loved hearing her put matters that way—her unassuming tone, her tentative attachment to her own ideas, her willingness to let others learn in their own manner, from children as well as colleagues. No doubt she had other sides to her relationship to theory; no doubt she could be a tough fighter for positions she wanted to uphold at all costs, and a mordant critic of the positions and conjectures and suppositions others held dear—but the slope of her thinking was ever down from lofty orthodoxy to the broad clinical plains, where live all those children, each with a germ of human particularity and complexity, each with a "line of development," a singular story line.

HEALER

*All analysts are curious, very curious, but
not all analysts are healers.*
Anna Freud

O N SEVERAL OCCASIONS, as my wife, Jane, and I talked with Anna Freud about our work with black children and youth during the eventful years of the civil rights movement, and later, in the ghettos of northern cities, we both remarked upon the enormous courage some of those children had shown us—their determination against great odds to prevail morally as well as psychologically. Miss Freud listened attentively—she had spent years in Vienna reaching out to poor children, and similarly in London. Whenever I wondered about the defense mechanisms used by these children, Miss Freud would oblige unfailingly: in a few sentences she could clarify what this or that boy or girl meant by a particular remark or intended to show through a drawing or painting (we took many of those works of art to New Haven for her inspection). One day, however, Jane said this to her: "It's been a great privilege to know those children. They've not only taught us a lot—they've *given* us a lot: they are healers; with all *their* troubles, they try to be so kind to us on our visits. It's very moving!"[1]

I thought we'd soon be "back to business," discussing more of those defense mechanisms, and was, in fact, about to produce another child's vivid painting of a racial confrontation in the south Georgia city of Albany, when Anna Freud chose to respond earnestly and with some animation to my wife's observation. During the next half-hour, they had an extraordinary discussion of the healing that children can offer one another, their needy parents or teachers, and some of us who observe them, treat them. At one point, Miss Freud remarked: "This is a matter [healing] that we often don't directly take up [in psychoanalytic writing]. We mention the 'problems' and the 'variables,' but we are made uncomfortable by words like 'healing.' Some [of her colleagues] would be tempted [upon hearing that word] to think of 'the transference,' and they could be quite correct—many children have learned to become their parents' healers and so, naturally, would want to get into a similar relationship with their analysts. But even so, we should be interested in how it is that a child becomes a healer. (Then, we'd have some idea of how certain adults become healers.)

"Many doctors, and many analysts, are not primarily healers. They want to know, they want to figure out, they take pleasure in fixing something—but they aren't [doing] what I think you are describing when you talk of the healing those children offer. Words like *empathy* come to mind—but what are the roots of it? Why do some children show compassion or empathy even when quite young—as you've seen—and others are far too preoccupied with themselves? I don't think we'll get the answer by speaking of 'narcissistic' children as against those who are far less so. [I had suggested as much, to my wife's dismay.] It is true—by definition—a highly narcissistic child isn't going to be inclined to put himself or herself in someone else's shoes, but plenty of children who aren't excessively self-preoccupied still don't let the predicament of others worry them. These children you describe seem to have been an inspiration. Isn't that what you mean. Isn't that what was so 'moving' to you—so 'healing'?"

We went round and round—and she was quite persistent, quite eager, it seemed, not only to understand what had been "healing" to Jane or to me—but what it is that enables certain people to accomplish such a feat. Words such as *identification* and *conscience* came up. She also spoke of "reaction formation" and the challenge that a segregationist world must have put to the parents of the children we had been mentioning: "I have never been in the South, but I would imagine that many black children there had to learn to 'reverse' themselves—be 'nice' when they really had other feelings at work. I'm not only talking about a conscious 'niceness'; I mean a more profound shift from annoyance and anger to constant ingratiation; and of course, under such circumstances, victims can go one step further, and begin to feel that they deserve what their bosses (or tormentors) give them in the way of punishment or disdain. Now, it is interesting to think of all this in connection with 'healing'—a person making such a strong effort to understand others, to make sense of their behavior, that he (or she) speaks like them and reacts like them and upholds their opinions or views, no matter how unfriendly they are to that person, and his race, his people. That [psychological maneuver] is not 'healing'—but it shows that through fear and anxiety we can make quite a leap toward another person, or other people."

She stopped and for a couple of seconds seemed quite lost in thought. I frankly felt we weren't going anywhere that we hadn't already visited rather often. Jane was of another mind, however, and she pushed hard on the distinction between fearful "identification with the aggressor" or anxiously sycophantic appeasement of an oppressor, on the one hand, and the kind of experience she had felt as she taught certain black children, came to know them, during the height of the civil rights struggle, on the other. It was then that Anna Freud spoke in this interesting manner—surprising to us, and ever so helpful: "I think we are talking about something else, here. I think I should go back to the word *inspiration*. You used it first, and then I used it, but we didn't get serious about it. These children you met were already quite 'civilized,' and that is no small achievement— especially when the society is trying to keep them more than a little 'outside the pale,' and so not 'civilized': they are compared with 'animals' by many of their enemies, we all have read. It is their moral achievement that you admire so much—not just their politeness, as you said, but their 'goodness, through and through' [Jane's phrase]. When a child shows us that [achievement], we take notice, we are impressed—it *is* inspiring! Maybe that is a bigger part of 'healing' than some of us [in psychoanalysis] realize—the strength our own conscience gets when it is in contact with someone else's that is unusually worth respect and admiration. There are so many forces and demands pulling at us—but there those children are, with all that is bearing down so hard on them, and yet they stand up for the good values their parents have taught them, and we are impressed. They help us follow in their footsteps—as happens sometimes."

Shortly afterward, we went back to those drawings and paintings—but Miss Freud's words have remained with me. Here was a child analyst in her seventies, reaching the end of a long life of work with children, service to them, looking beyond insight, beyond the resolution of neurotic problems, at something altogether different: the inspiration some can offer others, and with it, a kind of healing.

Not that those children were little saints; they had their rambunctious moments, their irritating, provocative qualities—even as any grown-up healer has flaws of one kind or another. Still, as she talked I thought of her own struggles in wartime London, her extended efforts with children who survived concentration camps, her interest (with Dorothy Burlingham) in blind children, her intense curiosity with regard to those brave children who put their own lives at risk in order to rescue others, her efforts in the 1970s with London's poor, and her collaborative work at Yale Law School with Joseph Goldstein and Jay Katz and Albert Solnit—in the hope that "the best interests of the child" would be heard in courts of law, in divorces, foster-care placements, adoptions. She would be the first to emphasize the "scientific" side of all that activity; yet, she was also trying hard, it seems, to make an implicit moral statement. While helping others in obvious distress, she was also, like the children my wife described, both witnessing in others and finding for herself a certain healing, a purpose and meaning in life.

In her "discussion remarks," at the end of a paper on "Problems of Psychoanalytic Training" (Writings, Vol. VII), she reminded her colleagues that in the early years of psychoanalysis there were no elaborate application procedures for would-be analysts to pursue: "In the past this [procedure] was very much a self-selection—we selected ourselves for the profession of becoming analysts, very much on the basis of one particular factor, namely, a burning curiosity about how human beings function, what makes them function normally or what makes them suffer abnormally, and lastly what makes them develop from children into adults." But the teacher in her knew that "curiosity" has to be satisfied in such a way that the one who was initially curious and, later, had become enlightened is thereby changed or transformed psychologically, morally. As she spells out the various "problems" that come with modern analytic training—the dangers of hierarchical, authoritarian education, among them, with the training analysis itself a hostage to the candidate's careerism and the analyst's mixed role as an educator, judge, and healer—she abruptly moves away from an emphasis on difficulties and "problems" (the essence of the discussion the panelists had been having) into quite another direction: "We have heard very little about the positive side [of the psychoanalytic candidate's training analysis], and my feeling is that in this discussion, we—or you—have undervalued the process of learning. I do not believe that any process of learning proceeds without a personal attachment to the teacher, an identification with the teacher, and something that makes this a lasting identification. And this is not only so in analysis, it is so from early childhood onward, and remains throughout life so long as we are learning. I would therefore advocate that, besides identification, and transference, and indoctrination, there is also another attribute of the training analysis which I would call inspiration." She goes on, typically, to give examples, and then tersely but powerfully describes what a successful training analysis achieves: "a lasting identification with something good, an inspiration that is allowed to remain"—all of which she distinguishes from more conventional descriptions of what takes place (and ought take place) in analysis. She concludes with an interesting rhetorical question: "Should they [those analytic candidates inspired by their analysts] really have resolved, outgrown, all that, together with their transference?"

Here she throws a gauntlet—a question about the very nature of psychoanalytic treatment, its objectives and hoped-for outcome. In this statement before her colleagues—assembled in Surrey, England, from various countries—Anna Freud goes beyond the matter of technique and perhaps beyond the usual limits of discussion with respect to the efficacy of psychoanalytic treatment. For her, the ultimate therapeutic issue may not be the degree of "insight" a patient has obtained, or even the degree of harmony that exists among the three "agencies" (id, ego, superego), but rather the overall character of the person who emerges from analysis.

"Knowledge and reason only play a limited part in a child's life," she observed in *War and Children*—a reminder of the limited patience youngsters have with the "reality principle." But sometimes,

in the topsy-turvy world of the emotions, a child's apparent indifference to the world's all too pressing (and dangerous) realities can have
its own impressive worth and dignity. In an elaboration of the remark
just quoted (about the part played by "knowledge and reason" in the
life of the young), Miss Freud points out that a child's "interest
quickly turns away from the real things in the outer world, especially
when they are unpleasant, and reverts back to its own childish interests, to its toys, its games and to its phantasies." Soon after making
this point, she offers a marvelous story. "There is the observation
made by one of our colleagues during a day-light air raid in a surface
shelter into which a mother had shepherded her little son of school
age. For a while they both listened to the dropping of the bombs; then
the boy lost interest and became engrossed in a story book which he
had brought with him. The mother tried to interrupt his reading several times with anxious exclamations. He always returned to his book
after a second, until she at last said in an angry and scolding tone:
'Drop your book and attend to the air raid.' "

This engaging little parable makes one wonder whether all the
clever awareness some of us prize so highly is quite what it's touted
to be. The boy had his own way of sorting things out and didn't
manage too badly. What might we learn from him? Perhaps he turns
out to be, in certain respects, at least, wiser than his all-too-alert
mother, having found his own "cure" for the predicament in which
he found himself. In a way, Miss Freud invites the boy to show how
wary we ought be of received wisdom. Full of his "denial," limited
by his "developmental inadequacies," he proves far more solidly able
to deal with the very "reality" his mother anxiously hectors him to
attend.

The connection of the above Blitz story with the critique of
psychoanalytic training is not hard to find. In both instances, Miss
Freud, the open-minded clinician, aware of doctrine and theory, is
able at a critical moment to set them aside, find her own human truth,
full of clues for us who work with children or with young psychiatrists in psychoanalytic training. While we want, surely, to impart
"knowledge and reason," and help both patients and trainees negoti-
ate successfully the turbulences of the transference, we also want

something else for them—for ourselves, too. What, though? The transcendence of a child reading a book while loony adults bomb other adults, and anxious adults pay exacting attention to such a reality? The transcendence of an analysand who can't stop being inspired by his or her analyst, transference or no transference?

Toward the end of her life, I heard Grete Bibring give a disquisition on analysts—how they vary as therapists. She distinguished between "engineers" and "healers"—between "those with great technical skills" and those with "heart and soul." She emphasized that "it is not a matter of either/or," but rather of "a distribution curve. . . . Most of us have the ability to do a reasonably successful analysis with certain kinds of patients. But that brings us back to the big question: What do you mean by a 'reasonably successful analysis'? We are now up against all the variations in the analysts as well as the patients. I have seen candidates [at the Boston Psychoanalytic Institute] who are ready to graduate, because their analysts have said 'Okay, the analysis is over,' and they have taken their courses and done their control analyses—and yet some of us have to stifle a scream or a long sigh! Of course, as you know, sometimes we're ready to scream or sigh when we look around at one another [the training analysts], never mind the candidates. I still think there are two broad classifications [of analysts]: those who are out to work within the traditional confines of analysis, and hope that over time the patient's neurosis gives way to insight—the 'resolutions' we talk about. Then there are those whose patients experience 'resolutions'—but something else, too. I don't know how to say exactly what—the spirit of the analyst becomes part of the spirit of the patient. Perhaps we have to admit that some of us don't have much spirit, so what I just described doesn't happen between them and their patients.

"There is another division among us, [and] we haven't given enough thought to it. I have spent countless hours on panels in recent years—so much talk about the qualities that we should look for in our future psychoanalysts. Candidates should have *this* character structure, and *that* character structure! I look back at all of us—and wonder sometimes if any of us would have been admitted to some of our institutes today! But in all those discussions we have about 'admissions,' or 'the ideal candidate,' I don't hear much thought given to the difference between those who have worked with children, and those who haven't—and those who want to be child analysts and those who don't have an interest in that [field]. You get a range of 'character types' in any applicant group, I know; but after a few decades in this 'business' I think I should pay special attention to someone who has worked with children and wants to work with them: it's a longer road, those extra years, and we have fewer people willing to do it, *interested* in doing it. Those who *are*, though, I find many of them gentle and good-natured—more so, in general, than others [who apply]. I suppose it's obvious—they are more childlike; I mean it as a compliment. Anna Freud once said to me: 'All analysts are curious, very curious, but not all analysts are healers.' I think of that a lot when I interview candidates. No, it's not necessarily a question of giving preference. [I had asked.] Some people who are intensely curious have serious character flaws; they would not make good analysts; and others, who are highly motivated to heal—they have serious character flaws, and would be risky candidates. We have to look at the whole picture. (You've heard that before!) What really happens, if you try to be honest with yourself, when you sift through all those applications—you are saying something to yourself, and to your colleagues: this is what I believe is important about psychoanalysis; this is what I think we should try to be—this kind of doctor, this kind of person sitting in that office, listening to the patients.

"We make mistakes! I'm not sure the most rigorous evaluations would prevent that. Actually, the most rigorous evaluations might encourage us to make one kind of mistake—[whereas] a 'looser' evaluation leads to another kind. Anna wanted to train child analysts separately; she worried that people who would be very talented child analysts would not be accepted by many institutes. She was right, too. She trained teachers, nurses, social workers, gifted human beings who brought no degrees, just themselves. Yes, [such people are] like her. [I had suggested the comparison.] We train doctors. There is a difference. The one book of Freud's we don't take so seriously is *The Question of Lay Analysis.*[2]

"Who can be stuffy for too long with children? Those who want to work with children have to be able to 'take' children, be on the receiving end from them, or they will fall flat on their faces—or they'll give up working with children. Children know how to laugh at us, and mock us—and do it much better than the occasional [adult] analytic patient who gathers up enough courage (and hostility) to tell us off! I have wondered why we don't think of separate 'tracks' for adult and child analysts—though some would want to be both, and go through the progression as it is now: [adult] psychiatry, child psychiatry, psychoanalysis, child psychoanalysis. Have you ever heard Anna Freud's joke about that [the length of time involved]? [She said] that we in America are training grandparents to do child analysis. She was working with children as an analyst when she was in her late twenties and early thirties. These days, *medical* students are that age.

"She was always a serious person; but she had a sense of humor—a quiet sense of humor. She loved repeating stories the children had told her. She saw how 'wise' children can be, and she looked for that side of her patients. We do that, you know—we 'bring out' sides of our patients that 'connect' (I don't know the right word here) with our own personalities or character. I knew that if I were treating some of her patients, I'd notice different things, or maybe they'd reveal different things to me. She always took a strong interest in her patients, as we do, most or all of us, but she went further: she was dedicated to them. Most of them were children, and she knitted for them and, of course, taught them how to do things, fix things, play games. She became an important person in their lives, as we do with our patients, no matter their age, but as I said, she had to go further: with children you don't just sit back and pay attention, and let the patient tell you whatever comes to mind, and see the transference [neurosis] develop; you have to play with them, and *earn* your relationship with them. You have to be inventive, versatile, pragmatic, lively, or as Anna once said, 'full of the devil,' with the children, so that then you can learn the nature of the devil that's bothering them. Not very many of us would talk like that—and she doesn't in public. She can be very funny with the kids—and about them. She seems to remember *everything* they said and did, and she shows great pleasure in talking about them. They are 'her children' in a way—of course!—but she never gets too possessive about them, a real credit to her therapeutic skill: knowing when to distance oneself with children, that is a special challenge.

"She is an analyst who heals; some figure things out as carefully as possible, and their patients leave having done the same, figured themselves out down to the last dotted i and crossed t, but it's different when the analyst wants to stand out as someone: not only stand *for* someone [transference], but *as* someone. Today, she stands for her father—that's how many people see her—but with her patients she is a warm, energetic, sensitive person; she is not only Freud's daughter, she is *herself*, and anyway, with the kids, it is no big thing to be a professor's daughter. What they would like was her way of taking them *very* seriously, and showing them that she was ready to go a long way to make them comfortable with her, and to be worth their time. Children are very jealous of their time, and they won't just hand it over to someone, unless they've learned to think it's a good idea. She can both be herself—and she is *very much* herself!—and shed herself, and be for those kids what they wanted and needed. It is a rare gift—and she is generous: she gives of herself to as many kids as she possibly can take on, with all the other responsibilities she has."

Such a description confirms what even a casual meeting with Anna Freud, or attendance at one of her clinical conferences, certainly suggests—a degree of passion brought to her profession, to one child, then another, to discussions of those children, and to conversations with others who are also involved with them (their teachers, doctors, nurses, social workers). I remember a pointed and lengthy talk I had with her about the special problems of children born to unmarried teenaged mothers.[3] She was very troubled, naturally, by the news (in the 1970s) that this phenomenon was on the rise in American cities; and of course, were she alive now, she would be even more troubled by the statistics. Yet she quickly moved from surprise and alarm to the contemplation of *action*—what to do, how to go about doing it, and only then, almost as an afterthought, with figuring a psychoanalytic rationale. I had expected quite the reverse: a lengthy resort to theory—the "primitive" mental structure of many of these young women, the "acting out" to which they are so prone, a form of behavior unlikely to stop with a first pregnancy and delivery, and so the poor prognosis for them psychologically, socially, economically. Instead she showed no evident interest (at first) in such a traditional kind of contemplation. "Let us wonder out loud what might be done," she exhorted—whereupon, I felt like saying: I have, and without success. In no time she was doing that, "wondering," leading me to doing some more "wondering" myself. Although I had not considered her all that savvy about the racial and social problems of American ghetto families, her energetic and resourceful comments and suggestions, pulled together and extracted from several talks, ran along these lines: "There is no point trying to talk about their 'pathology.' The longer we do that, the more hopeless the whole situation will seem to be. We have to go to these young women and ask them what we can do to be of help. I can imagine they will be hard for us to talk with [I had suggested as much], but they have their needs—and we have ours. We could start by telling ours. We could say that we work with children and their parents, and we want to be of assistance, and sometimes we know pretty much what we can do to be of help, but other times we don't know, and it is then that we turn to the people we're trying to work with, and ask them."

She stopped, and I decided to present some of the situations I'd encountered: the utter silence, no matter my various comments, questions, tactics, ploys; the *sullen* silence—which made me look at my watch and think about how to leave politely but quickly; the outright skepticism, even hostility and, sometimes, rudeness, such as television turned up, phone calls made. I suppose I was looking for pity, for praise, or perhaps testing her as I myself had often felt tested (only to flunk miserably). Perhaps I was trying to arraign not only her but the entire field of child psychiatry, child psychoanalysis: what in the world *can* we do, really, given the seemingly infinite barriers that separate "us" in those fields, no matter our intentions, from "them," whose lives, whose assumptions and aspirations and expectations, are so different from, even at odds with, ours.

She did not hurry to respond. She looked at her hands. She looked at a nearby table, with some books on it, some writing paper.

She looked back at me, and saw that I already felt a bit uncomfortable with the unqualified bleakness of my portrayal of ghetto life, and of the reception professionals can expect if they attempt their various "interventions." Only after serving me some more coffee and cake did she speak. "I don't know what I'd do. I'd want to turn around and leave, I'm sure. But I doubt I could do so. I think I'd try to get away from the feeling of helplessness and immobility by looking around, and then getting up and trying to do something. Do the floors need a sweeping? Is there some cooking to do? How about shopping—has that been done? I'd bring my knitting with me. I'd try to show that I have an interest in the people, and am ready to work."

At that point, I interrupted at some length, mentioning what I saw as an overeagerness on the part of some of us, white, middle-class, professional men and women. I asked what it means to people when we arrive full of energy and ideas and promises. It seems a statement about them (their lack of those qualities), or else a temptation or invitation to further acquiescence and passivity and apparent helplessness. Our initiatives ostensibly on their behalf (but more likely on ours) are yet another variation of noblesse oblige, with all the attendant risks on both sides—white arrogance and smugness, black ingratiation that can quickly turn into resentment, bitterness, even rage.

She listened and nodded, more vigorously than at other times. When she resumed her side of the exchange, she was a little more measured and slower in her delivery as she tried to take into account what she had heard, but no less resolute in asserting her point of view: "There is always the risk that our purposes will be misunderstood—with our patients who are rich as well as poor, and with white people as well as black people. We are all prepared, at times, to have second thoughts about others, even the people we're closest to— maybe especially them! . . . Remember, when we go to someone's home, or when they come to our [clinical] home, we are almost instantly quite close to them—because we are talking about personal matters, their children, their income or means of survival, their difficulties at home, or with the social welfare system, or the courts, or their children's schools, the probation officer, the guidance counselor: you know, the list [of such officials] is long, and often most of them or all of them are of another race, another class, another neighborhood. When a rich, white, well-educated, grown-up person comes to see me, even then there are many possibilities for our misunderstanding—the usual projections and distortions of perception. When we are in need, or in pain, we are vulnerable. We feel weak, and we feel ashamed. We search for ways to be rid of those feelings; we find scapegoats, dump them [those feelings] on someone, or a whole group of people. We convert our frustrations into anger, or we turn a would-be friend into an out-and-out enemy, because we are prepared to think the worst of ourselves, and so find others to do that for us—a very sad outcome, both for the one who gets such an emotional chain reaction going, and for the person who becomes, thereby, wrongly regarded, and so a victim, at least for a while, and sometimes, for the longest time."

She stopped abruptly. I was following her line of thought, was impressed by it, although its fundamental assumptions are widely known: the psychology of fear, self-loathing, hate, and prejudice. She took a deeper breath than usual, then switched direction a bit: "Whenever a child comes to see us, and we try to forge an alliance, we are taking the same gamble—that every attempt to earn trust and to ease apprehensions, and to attempt to establish some basis for communication, and even to make evident our usefulness, will be met with a heightening rather than a reduction of anxiety and fearfulness in the patient. And before you know it, [this happens] in the analyst, too, because these things have a way of going back and forth: you try to be warm and open to another, and are rebuffed, and your guard gets up, and then *that* becomes part of the equation, because it is noticed, and so you try harder, and *that* is noticed, perhaps with a heightening suspicion (why is the doctor trying *so hard*?), and after a while you are in what the mother of one child I treated called an impasse. She was a journalist, and had a sense of the dramatic, and she would come to see us and say: 'Well, both of us tried having a frank talk, and before long we were at an impasse.' When I would ask her to tell me about the 'talk,' and the 'impasse,' she'd do so with a rapid-fire delivery, and invariably the sequence would go like this: child is despondent and withdrawn;

mother makes friendly overtures; child rejects them—a repetition of earlier times, when he'd been left, had become quite sad, and the mother tried to make amends on her return, only to be held at bay by the child; and then mother tries harder; child decides she is putting on a real production, and so is not sincere, and so pulls back even more; and then mother flies off the handle and is virtually at the boy's throat—which she politely calls an 'impasse'!

"I had no great solution for her, but I did tell her that the less she talked when she tried to get closer to her child, the better, and I thought things would work out. I encouraged her to try to find a way to be affectionate or thoughtful *without* being too obvious about it—hard for her to do, because she had a bit of the actress in her: even a simple talk with me turned into a 'production' sometimes. She got herself 'worked up,' she'd realize, eventually, and say so, though not until she'd already said much more than she ought have. But we had some success with her as well as the boy—I mean, we tried to help the boy see how his earlier experiences [of presumed abandonment] were constantly tugging at him, and putting a chip on his shoulder; and we tried to help the mother realize what the boy had felt, and still felt, and even was *made* to feel, once more, each time she showered him with attention.

"That word *showered*, as a matter of fact, turned out to be a crucial one in the conversations we had with her. She told me one day that she realized she showered too much attention on the boy sometimes, and that she had to learn to be less assertively maternal; and then I told her that she had told me on an earlier visit that she remembered showering her son [when younger] with presents upon her return from an assignment, and often he showed no interest in them, or he grabbed them, tore off the wrappings, made a bad face, or quickly played with the thing, and managed to break it! I wondered out loud whether her son, now, couldn't make a clear connection between the past 'showering' of presents and the present 'showering' of attention or concern. She wasn't immediately convinced—but after a while she let herself be the one to teach her [self] the connection. She observed the way her son reacted to her at certain times, and she recalled in her mind some of his earlier reactions to her, and she said 'yes' to my observation one day: 'Miss Freud, I think you have a bit of a point there.' From her, a tough, skeptical reporter, that was a big compliment!"

Anna Freud then returned to the ghetto world whose heavy burdens we had been discussing, pointing out that many ghetto parents feel as weak and defenseless and vulnerable as children, and are regarded as such by those who have no use for them, or even by many who go see them as welfare workers, social workers, truant officers. This analogy between psychoanalytic work with children and the efforts of social and political activists and professional caregivers to improve the lives of ghetto families was one that she knew could be regarded as patronizing or condescending, yet one she felt to be grounded in certain psychological truths: "Whenever I see a patient, I try to remind myself to think of what has brought him to me (or her), and to remember how sensitive people are about themselves—worried that others will take advantage of them. It is a real challenge in our field: we see people who need to see us, most of the time—and yet it is precisely those people who are the most afraid that they will be exploited or looked down upon by people, and that fear gets directed at us, naturally. We have to press ahead, take our chances, in the full realization that during treatment it is two steps forward and one step backward (not the other way, I hope!), and that is the way it goes: no matter how smart we are, and how carefully we've figured out the 'psychodynamics,' and how gentle and considerate we are, there will still be doubts and second thoughts and misgivings (and worse) directed toward us. The *reality* is, so often, that the people who need help—need psychotherapy or psychoanalysis, need social and political help—are upset and dependent and depressed or forlorn: all the things that bring people to city agencies if they are poor and don't have jobs, or to analysts, if they are in personal trouble. On the other hand those same people don't want to feel that others are living off them—I mean by that that [those] others are feeling good themselves by looking down at the 'neurotics' they see, or 'the poor' they work with. We don't want to give the impression we are 'living off' these people we want to assist when, really, it isn't true [that we are doing so], and yet we can easily be *felt* to be in the wrong—a phrase here, a comment there, an offer, a suggestion, and *that does it!* [Emphasis hers.] So, every word can count, and even so, we can stumble—if someone is looking for us to stumble, or if we on our own relax our vigilance and say or do something that can too easily be subject to misinterpretation."

There was more, much more. I remember being impressed by the extent and intensity of her self-scrutiny—the willingness of an elderly and distinguished analyst to take direct aim not only at the problems of others that make for distortions in human communication and relatedness, but at her own (our own) potential blind spots and temptations. She was clearly trying to examine and reexamine the complex ups and downs of our involvement with one another— the way class and race as well as the unconscious persuade us to feel one way or another. Moreover, she was doing this kind of personal introspection with a purpose in mind, a hope—that something would be *done* with whatever self-knowledge is acquired: improved treatment, or more sensitive social and political intervention, or indeed a combination of the two.

Years later, I thought of that conversation with her (the depth of feeling she brought to the talk we had, the power of communication, too, the range of her intellect as it surveyed a most complex and knotty problem, above all her clear desire to be of help) as I read a book by one of her youthful analysands of the late 1920s. *A Child Analysis with Anna Freud* is an extraordinary document about one of her first child analyses—with nine-year-old Peter Heller, who was then a resident of Vienna and now teaches literature in the United States. Miss Freud's extensive reports on her work with the boy are included, along with his poems, drawings, short stories, and psychological self-descriptions. "My memory tells me," Anna Freud wrote, "that these notes [with respect to the progress of the boy] are so much more extensive than any I made about any of my other cases of child analysis because I gave a very long lecture on this case at the Psychoanalytic Association at Budapest." Valuable, too, are the efforts of Peter Heller sixty years later to reconstruct that analysis— to remember Anna Freud, to figure out what was happening in his life that prompted the analysis, and what happened during it, as he recounted his dreams, said what came to his mind, poured his heart and soul into drawings, into fiction, into touching, compelling poems. Here is Peter Heller's description of the Anna Freud he remembers: "I see the radiant and illuminating eyes and hear the purifying voice and interpretations of Anna Freud whom I loved and revered as a child beyond all other humans." At another point, looking back at his childhood self as if he were a different person, he writes: "Anna Freud's ability to enter into the world of this boy as she did in analysis, to understand him, to enlighten him, to draw him out of himself, and to raise him above himself, seems to show her to me in the very best light, in *her* unique, lucid (at times all too lucid) intelligence, her humor, her capacity for a purifying, cathartic response which did not allow any collusion or complicity with weaknesses, yet did them justice. A moralistic element, a slight admixture of what Nietzsche called *Moralin*, may occasionally be detectable but it seems justified by her position as adult and educator."

As one reads Miss Freud's notes in response to Peter Heller's dreams and drawings and declarations made during his analytic hours, one realizes how earthy and wide-eyed and detached, yet caring and responsive, the young woman analyst was. She may have been a touch moralistic then—and would always be so—but she was far from prim or puritan: her notes abound with knowing and explicit interpretations of a boy's lusts, jealousies, rages. The body's various noises and functions are quite familiarly noted and discussed in her comments to herself and her young patient; and her way of talking about sexual matters, or the mean and spiteful side of life, shows a sophisticated, relaxed, even easygoing attitude with respect to human nature. Anna Freud had a rock-bottom worldliness and tolerance, the consequence of daily exposure to all the frankness and bluntness that boys and girls can muster with a sympathetic person like her. For my wife, Jane, and me, Miss Freud did have a certain austerity about her, and at times, a righteousness that became strenuous, hence verging toward self-righteousness—but Peter Heller as a child tested her with his wild sensuality and his outbursts of resentment, and she didn't become a prim scold, quite the contrary: his candor elicited from her a similar openness, and his suffering made her giving and sympathetic rather than aloof and judgmental. Would that those of us who are afflicted with *Moralin* had in our lives enough young Peter Hellers to dethrone us now and then.

Early on as a psychoanalyst Anna Freud chose to emphasize the importance for her of "working with the positive transference". This is by no means automatic with analysts; some, even those who work with children, choose to place less emphasis on a close relationship, or work quite comfortably with its opposite: they become substitutes for the feared, disliked, hated people of their patients' earlier lives— and eventually help those patients realize what has been going on. Healers come in many sizes, shapes, colors; and some who work the negative side of the transference may be the bravest and toughest of all. However, there are a fair number of psychiatrists and analysts who, one suspects, bring to their work an aptitude for eliciting the dislike of others: they are not especially warm or kindly or generous-hearted men or women, and so are not in the least likely to elicit affection from their patients, thereby muddying the waters of an analysis based upon the "working through of the negative transference."

Anna Freud, in her work with patients and in her various research projects, sought to be an ally of those she treated and studied, although an ally who reserved the right to say what had to be said, an ally who would not settle for sugarcoating when bitterness had to be acknowledged in the interest of truth. I think I saw an important part of her— the healer whose bemused reserve masked a maternal warmth—when we talked (as mentioned earlier) about some of the black children I knew in the American South who went through mobs to enter newly desegregated schools, and also when I presented her with the first interviews I did in the early 1970s with *favela* children in Rio de Janeiro.[4] Those latter boys and girls were living under as wretched circumstances as one could imagine. Some were essentially street children— huddled in makeshift shacks or in side alleys, trying to get through one night at a time, while spending their days begging, doing "tricks" or whiling away time with contests, fights, games, which often featured a mix of sensuality and betrayal. I could see that she was horrified by what those children said, did, and drew—although, as a veteran of many analyses with many children, she knew that "primary process" (the urges and fantasies that are kept under wraps by so-called "normal" or "mature" or "grown-up" people) is no less "shocking" in a child (or adult) of privilege than someone who lives under the most sordid circumstances. After almost two hours of a virtual monologue on my part, interrupted by her occasional questions, she slumped back in her chair, and began this fervent response: "We are so helpless in the face of all that you've mentioned—we join the company of those children. They can't do much to change their world; and we can't do much! People tell me there are some problems only governments can solve, but certainly the Brazilian government doesn't seem interested in solving the problems of those children—and we know how many children in England and the States are in trouble, and everyone throws up his hands, and says someone else should try to make things better!

"When we [she and her Vienna colleagues] were all young, and began working with children, we thought we'd be changing the world that way. We thought we would help some children to live better, to *be* better, and with their emotional state improved, they would help others, and soon you would see a difference: from neighborhood to neighborhood. I'm afraid we were naive! There are too many people for only a handful of analysts. Besides, in many countries we don't exist—or, if we do, we're only seeing children whose parents have a lot of money. We know that there's plenty of trouble among those [rich] children, and maybe that's the only kind of trouble we're able to handle. But when I think of those [*favelado*] children, I want to go do something! I don't know what—but something. That's part of us—a big part of us: to want to help, even if we don't know what we can do."

At that point I felt compelled to ask, "What would you do if you visited Rio, and were asked to give advice to people about the *favela* children?" She frowned, then replied: "I would feel as helpless as you must have felt! You're asking me to tell you what I'd do—but I have heard you say how helpless you felt, and I've felt like that, even in England, and so what would I have to offer there, in Brazil? Maybe we have no choice but to acknowledge what we *can't* do. But that is not something that is easy to do—not if you're the kind of person who tries to remember how the poor live, or even goes and sees for

himself. The trouble with 'seeing,' as you have done, is [that] it pro-
vokes conflict, but doesn't necessarily provide a means of resolving
the conflict. You want to change Rio de Janeiro, but you have no
power to do that! You know what those children need—a family,
food, shelter—but you have no power to offer them that. You only
have the power to write—and stir others to thought. But you are
probably aware, by now, that even if thousands read your words,
they [the readers] end up doing nothing—in the sense that they feel
as helpless as you feel you are."

Although these all-too-realistic words made me feel even more
helpless, I could not let the question go: "What would you try to do
if you found yourself living full-time in a city like Rio de Janeiro?" As
soon as I said this, I wanted to withdraw the question, apologize for
asking it. She had already let me know, after all, that she understood
my frustrations, indeed, shared them. She gave me a quick, direct
glance—her eyes meeting mine head-on for a couple of seconds. I felt
myself reprimanded: the stern moralist-teacher about to collar the
student and let him know that a certain territory had already been
covered, and enough is enough! But once again I was mistaken about
what she was thinking and feeling, because her voice when she next
spoke seemed full of anguish rather than impatience or annoyance,
and the lines of her face struck me as melancholy but not reproving:
"I was asking myself my version of your question earlier as we spoke.
I wasn't actually asking the question directly; I was letting my mind
wander—as if I had taken a flight to Brazil, and was now in Rio de
Janeiro, and was going to stay there for a while, and was wondering
what the next stop would be for me. I assumed I'd know someone to
call, and I pictured myself asking that person what an analyst like me
could do. I didn't get much further, though. I couldn't visualize the
person I'd be speaking with. That tells me something! The next
thought I had—I could visualize that, though: I'd be trying to set up a
nursery—just as Mrs. Burlingham and I did during the [Second
World] War. That is as far as I got. . . . Maybe if I actually went to
Brazil, that's as far as I'd get, and I'd be lucky to get that far: a nursery
for those slum children."

She read my face exactly, answered my unspoken demurrer:

"You are right: even if we had a hundred, or two hundred children, there would be hundreds of thousands who would not be with us in the nursery. I remember how hard it was in London [during the war] for us to say no to anybody—and yet, we had to." She stopped—as if remembering. I remembered, too—a narrative passage in *Infants Without Families* when she and Dorothy Burlingham talk about the press of applicants for an inevitably limited amount of space. Days later, I went back to read the exact words: "Most of these requests [for admission to the nurseries] were so urgent in nature that it was very difficult to refuse them. It seems all wrong to let one child live in comparative safety and comfort and to explain to the next mother that her child cannot be given the same advantages." She and her co-workers bent rules, made exceptions, fitted in children here and there, did the best they could to accommodate emergencies, knowing all the while that almost everyone's situation amounted to an emergency: children who had become homeless, or sick from living in shelters, or whose fathers were at war and mothers at work. Her comment in the reports on those Second World War nurseries showed the same moral anguish she obviously felt as she tried to imagine staking out a postage stamp of psychological sanctuary amid the vast disorder and sorrow of Brazil's *favelas*. (A letter that she wrote me in 1969, and that I offer in the appendix, shows that the plight of masses of deprived children, while beyond the reach of psychoanalysis, was not beyond the reach of her heartfelt concern.)

It was that anguish which, finally, told me as much as I'd ever learn about Anna Freud's relationship to the suffering of the many children she had allowed herself to come to know. She was not about to exhibit the tears her mind and heart might have shed at many moments in her life—or even make explicit reference to them. The fact that she got those nurseries going for children during the Blitz, and later, for the children who survived concentration camps, was in itself her personal statement, as was her Brazilian fantasy. Through her work as a child psychoanalyst, she wanted to do all the healing she could in any way she could: with individual analysands; in communal settings for children; in training programs to increase the number of psychologically sensitive men and women who work with children; in consultations with others (teachers, nurses, social workers) who have much to offer to children, but who run into quandaries and blind alleys, and so need a little healing themselves.

She did not, however, let this "nursery-fantasy" get out of hand. Earlier, I had once told her about some nuns who ran a school and an infirmary at the foot of a Rio de Janeiro *favela* I came to know especially well. At the time, she seemed not especially interested, but now, much later, she came back to those nuns: "Perhaps they are the clue: you could go and work with them, and learn from them their secret." I waited for her to continue, but she kept silent. The word *secret* carried a certain charge, so I replied: "Those nuns don't seem to have any secrets. They work day and night, and then tell anyone who will come and eat (and drink wine) with them that they feel themselves getting nowhere—but that's what they should be doing, even so!"

"Well, *that* is their secret," she responded. "If you have come to some peace with yourself about what you are doing, and why you are doing it, and what you can do, and what you cannot do—then you've got the answer to any doubt you have. You have learned to say to yourself: I've already admitted what I can't do, and I think I know what I can do in such a way that I'll be able to keep at it!" I wondered if she were convinced by what she had just said. Suddenly, she smiled and added: "I think if I were going to Brazil, I'd have *no plans* at first—except that I should go to see those nuns, and ask them if they would become my teachers for a while, so that I could someday find a way to work with children there." I thought then of something Dorothy Day once said, contemplating the limitations and opportunities that came with her work in the soup kitchens she set up on the Lower East Side: "The first step is to know what you can't do, and the next step is to find those who can help you learn what you can do—and then you can begin to stand up, and help others stand up."[5] An image of childhood, actually—children learning themselves to stand, and then helping others to stand: the healer as one who abandons prideful self-assurance, crawls back to childhood, learns yet again to stand up, side by side with others.

LEADER

Many of us were politically very active. . . .
For us psychoanalysis promised personal
"liberation" not for its own sake, but so that
we could work to "liberate" others. . . .
Political activity, social activism, they were a
big part of our lives . . . especially for those
[of us] interested in children and adolescents:
they were going to be analysts who helped the
world in so many ways. . . .
Grete Bibring

SIGMUND FREUD WAS NO solitary doctor or intellectual. He developed intense friendships among his colleagues both before and after his career as the "first psychoanalyst" began, in the late 1890s. His associations with Breuer and Fliess are, by now, the stuff of biographical legend—as are the relationships with Jung and Adler, Ferenczi and Abraham, with Sachs and Jones and Reik: a series of names that have entered history largely by association with Freud. Freud's involvement with so many men and women who chose to work with him, share his ideas, was not simply a matter of gregariousness, or even charisma. He had in mind, early on, the formation of a distinct movement—hence the regular meetings he encouraged with his colleagues, and the rings he gave the chosen, the handful who first gathered around him. In his forties, in the first decade of the twentieth century, he became a leader—unknown as yet to the world— eager not only to explore the mind, to write of what he had learned or surmised, but also, to have others join him in the search, and very important, as fellow practitioners of an original, demanding way of treating patients.

In 1969, as I was working on a biographical study of Erik Erikson, I went to see Heinz and Dora Hartmann, both psychoanalysts. Heinz Hartmann had been a supervisor of Erikson during his days as a candidate at the Vienna Psychoanalytic Institute, and it was important, for that reason, for me to talk with him about a person who had now become well known some four decades later. Hartmann was also an extremely important figure in the history of psychoanalysis—an analysand of Freud, an original and compelling theorist, a teacher of Anna Freud, a broadly literate and cultured person whose personal dignity and refinement earned him immense and near universal respect from others (in this profession with its history of cliques, schisms, warring schools, gossip, and psychologically reductionist name-calling).

Hartmann was nearing the end of his life: he talked openly with me about his cardiac problems, even as he and his wife, Dora, and I enjoyed some good sherry in their comfortable New York City apartment on Fifth Avenue. In no time, it seemed, we were carried back to an earlier decade of this century and a singular precinct of the European world: "Freud's [psychiatric] practice was his laboratory, his research library. He did his investigations in his office. His patients told him of their troubles, and he tried to figure out what was causing them to be in such trouble. When he thought he *had* figured out the trouble, he wrote his articles and books—and remember, he was a doctor, addressing other doctors: here is what I've discovered, and here is how I've discovered it, and if you're interested, you can try a similar plan with your patients. This was a big part of Freud. I'm not sure it's been discussed enough, in the biographies of him: how anxious he was to have others discuss things with him, and even more important, see patients as he was seeing them—so that there would be something to discuss. The clinical side of his life was extremely important, and he didn't want to be one clinician, working all by himself. He'd worked with Breuer—the tradition of a great man who shares his greatness with others. Some are happy to be 'great' all by themselves! Others need companions—and yes, I agree, an audience [I had suggested the latter]. But I'm not sure *audience* is quite the word—it applies, but there is more to it. A doctor doesn't only want to share his ideas with others; . . . a doctor wants to work with other doctors, and discuss with them what his patients said and did: how they are doing. Freud wanted to sit with other analysts and exchange *ideas*, absolutely—but also exchange *experiences*. It is true, he was a forceful person, and he inspired people—the word is *charisma*: he had it, even if he was a short man and he wasn't the kind who is a spellbinding speaker. But he was also someone who learned from others, and who liked to know that what he was doing, others were doing: we doctors are working that way!

"I agree, he urged 'lay analysis.' That is a separate subject—important, but beside the point. You have to go back in time, and you have to think of Freud in Vienna in the early years of this century. It's hard to do that now, if you're talking about him in the last third of this century, in America—so much has happened. Now, everyone knows him, and everyone takes his influence for granted. But this was not a man who wanted to write books and then wait for book reviews. This was not a man who wanted to get a good, tenured professorship someplace, and be looked up to that way. He *did* want critical acceptance, and he *did* want the kind of university acceptance others—less interesting people—easily got, I agree. But his big fight, early in his career, was for—what is the right word?"

He stopped there longer than was usually the case—he was a vigorous and stimulating speaker, and although his German accent was substantial, he spoke with a compelling, fluent clarity. I had to be fast and determined if I was to interrupt, or change the direction of our discussion. Now, though, he was searching through his English vocabulary—to no apparent avail. His wife, Dora, finally came to his assistance: "Others to talk with him—he felt he was all alone."

"That's true," he said, "but there was more going on. He knew how much—what is the word, flack?—he'd be taking. He was regarded as an outcast, a pornographer, that is not too strong [a way of putting the matter], by lots of 'respectable' people, in the universities, the [Catholic] church, the medical profession, which was conservative. This Jew with odd or crazy ideas about sex! I think he hoped that if there were a few people practicing psychiatry as he was—psychoanalysis hadn't become a profession then—things would work out better."

A rather noticeable pause, and when he resumed, it was as if someone had spoken, said something provocative, something to which Dr. Hartmann now wanted to address himself: "He was a fighter, no question; he wasn't ready to let it go—that he'd made a discovery, and wrote it up. That's what we [doctors] are used to doing; we do our research, and then we write a paper—maybe, a book. Freud had something else in mind."

Silence, again; and I wondered whether this urbane, sophisticated, utterly knowing, and quite thoughtful person was really at a loss for words because his ideas had gotten ahead of his linguistic capacity, in English; or whether, in fact, he wasn't quite sure what he actually wanted to say. Suddenly, Dora Hartmann again intervened: "His first circle—they were followers. He gave them rings, remember. They were a small army."

She was about to elaborate, or maybe qualify herself—when her husband did it for her, politely but with some insistence: "A *small* army! *Very* small! They were a handful—I'd think of them as a band, a band of outsiders. The military image—well, it does suit [the historical situation] somewhat. Freud definitely waged a war on behalf of what he believed, and he definitely did *not* do that alone. He wanted others to be with him—some [in Vienna] called us 'the Freud circle,' and others were not so nice! I remember a friend of mine, when I first took an interest in psychoanalysis, told me I was becoming 'a follower.' He was sarcastic: he meant to make me feel ashamed—I'd lost my independent thinking. I was about to get into an argument with him. I was about to defend myself. I stood there, and all I said was 'Yes.' He looked at me, and wondered what had happened. I think he wanted me to apologize for what he claimed had happened or to try to justify myself—or show him how wrong he was. But I said to myself: I'm lucky I've found this whole new world of knowledge, and I'll go my way, and if he wants to talk that way, let him. I think by then many of us weren't afraid to feel that Freud had changed our lives, with his ideas—and, very important, with what we were learning to do with them: to practice psychoanalysis. He *was* our leader!"

By the 1930s, when Anna Freud had become not only a psychoanalyst, a teacher of psychoanalysts, a writer of psychoanalytic articles and books, but also the psychoanalyst to whom Sigmund Freud was closest in so many personal ways—her father, her patient (because of his painful cancer, she nursed him constantly), her teacher, her analyst, her traveling companion—psychoanalysis was no longer an insurgent Viennese movement. While at first it had been seen as a group of mostly Jewish doctors who had strange flights of fancy, often tied, scandalously, to sex, to bodily functions or pleasures not discussed by physicians or professors, never mind ordinary members of the bourgeoisie, people had now begun coming to Vienna from all over Europe, and from America, during the 1920s, and

Freud had already become a living legend—although his ideas were still attacked vehemently, vociferously. Institutes had been opened in many cities, journals began to flourish—and controversy, too. The quarrels between Jung and Freud, or Adler and Freud, with a consequent total rupture of relations, gave way to relatively more muted disagreements and arguments or mere differences of opinion, choices of emphasis: tonal distinctions. In the remarks quoted earlier from *The Ego and the Mechanisms of Defense*, some of those variations in point of view are more than implied—the "conservatives" (as early as the 1930s) who wanted to pay major regard, always, to the instincts or drives and their struggle for expression, as against innovators such as Heinz Hartmann and Anna Freud (and, later, Erik Erikson), who wanted to do their own kind of exploration, each generation's right and opportunity. Of course, no institution is without generational tensions—although Freud the elder statesman, as it were, was far less hidebound and possessively rigid with respect to his ideas than some of his compatriots who had fought alongside him at the start, and were not about to give much ground to a succeeding generation of analysts, many of them dispersed across the continents by Hitler's actions. Even so, no matter the arguments, Freud's ultimate triumph over his early disputants (or rivals) earned him the unquestioned leadership of a worldwide movement, one with intellectual, medical, and nonmedical but therapeutic aims. Well before the rise to power of the Nazis (1933), he was the internationally "important Jew" whom Auden later memorialized. Yet he had, then, become not only sick and elderly, but an icon—and, inevitably, one whom others fiercely claimed as theirs.

William Carlos Williams, no psychoanalytic theorist but a shrewd observer of his fellow Americans, and fellow physicians, once described the "Manhattan psychoanalytic scene," as he called it, rather bluntly:[1] "I crossed the river a lot in those days [the late 1930s], and a lot of my writer friends were being psychoanalyzed. They'd talk about their doctors as if they were gods—and they'd talk about Freud as if he was the God of gods! They'd tell me they'd see pictures of him every day—in their analysts' offices: the man who founded the whole thing! I'd get a little ornery, sometimes; I'd say,

'Listen, I'm a doc, and we've had plenty of smart people come along, and tell us a lot, but we don't turn them into *religious* figures!' I'd be exaggerating, but I was touching a sensitive nerve, I knew—because some would react violently; they'd tell me about my prejudices and my 'resistance.' I'd shrug my shoulders and say, 'Okay, if you want to cut off all discussion that way—fine.' But it was a damn shame— people who were smart and savvy suddenly turned into *believers*. There's a difference between being a patient, I'd say to them—the ones I could keep discussing the subject with—and being a believer. They'd nod, and then rush to show me how rational they were, and how 'troubled' *I* was. 'You're afraid'—I kept hearing that. 'You need analysis; that's the only way to understand what we're talking about.' I'd hear that, too. 'Who analyzed Freud?' I asked that a few times, and they laughed—and told me he was the one big exception. That really got under my skin! It was such a way of dismissing everyone else, anyone's ideas—setting Freud up on a ridiculous pedestal, as if he was the only person in the whole history of the world who could be taken seriously, apart from his 'problems.' A 'king of kings'! I often wondered what in the world he made of all that, if he even knew that such shenanigans were going on in his name.''

Surely Freud did, indeed, realize what had happened to him at the hands of his various associates and followers. Early on, well before extraordinary success came to him, he interpreted his falling-out with Jung psychodynamically as well as substantively—more than a matter of intellectual disagreement: Jung's ''problems'' eventually undid their harmonious association. Such thinking, picked up by his followers, would only increase with the years—beclouding rational discourse (and disagreement) with the constant specter of neurotic, even psychotic ''acting-out'' as an explanation for any and all ''deviation.'' Anna Freud herself more than hinted at the existence (and nature) of such a development in the section from *The Ego and the Mechanisms of Defense* that I quoted in an earlier chapter. Under such circumstances, a tenacious orthodoxy can develop, not unlike the kind one encounters in religious institutions. Freud the inquiring and imaginative scientist, who constantly tried to give new shape to some of his ideas, becomes Freud the much respected ''founding father"—and in no time proper respect and admiration give way to a kind of veneration that smacks of the neurotic mental activity Freud himself kept describing in *The Future of an Illusion* as the mainstay of those who go to churches, mosques, synagogues.

Yet the pictures of Freud in psychoanalytic office after office—very much a part of the atmosphere of both analytic offices and institutes during the 1940s and 1950s—can be correctly regarded as the well-deserved respect a brilliant "conquistador" (one word Freud used to describe himself) had more than earned. Those institutes and offices, after all, would not have been there had it not been for his great intellectual and emotional breakthroughs, *and* his determination that his ideas be given a continuing institutional life—put into daily implementation by dozens, and soon hundreds, then thousands of others. These not only embraced his thinking, as many of us do when we read someone's books, but gave their working lives to such thinking, an altogether different order of commitment, and one that certainly raises the emotional stakes: one's entire sense of oneself is, in certain respects, put on the line socially and economically. Freud was not only an exceptional thinker, he was, in a sense, a political, an organizational, genius. He took on not only nineteenth-century bourgeois culture, but also the profession of medicine, the specialty of psychiatry—the world that decides what is respectable (or utterly outlandish and unprofessional) with respect to psychological therapeutics. That latter achievement was accomplished against great odds—a long, tough battle waged in country after country, city after city, a battle for the hearts and minds of each man and woman who would decide to enter psychoanalytic training, and for the larger social and cultural "climate of opinion" that would eventually make psychoanalysis a respected profession, with psychoanalytic institutes located in medical school settings or connected in various ways to universities.

In an address to the New York Psychoanalytic Institute, given in April 1968, Miss Freud herself took pains to remind her audience of successful analysts how far her particular profession had come, and against what opposition: she points out that Freud's early papers "are not reread often enough by the present generation of analysts to impress them vividly with all the advantages which they enjoy in contrast to their predecessors." She allows herself to chastize this audience of grown-up men and women who, as a matter of fact, had spent years reading just about every word Freud wrote. "A qualified analyst today, especially in the United States, will take it more or less for granted that respect is paid to his intensive training; that this will be an asset when he competes for professional appointments; that he will have no difficulty in building up a practice and earning a living; and that, if he sets out to write, he will encounter no difficulty in finding publishers or editors ready to accept his scientific contributions."

You who are here listening to me, she seems to be saying—on the occasion of the Freud Anniversary Lecture, no less—have it pretty good in many ways: money; the respect of others; established outlets for your ideas. Yet many of you have forgotten something, and it is my right (or duty or choice) to remind you that such expectations "have to be contrasted with the disbelief, the ridicule, the suspicions and the professional ostracism to which the first generation of analysts were exposed."

She now spells out, further, what happened to members of that "first generation," on whose behalf, presumably, she speaks: "They were, in fact, pioneers, not only because they ventured out into the unknown, where they had to break new ground, but also in the sense that their endeavors ran counter to and ignored the conventional restrictions of their time; that they risked their social and professional status, and, last but not least, in many instances gave up a secure and profitable career for financial uncertainties and hardships."

Of all ironies, the speaker is telling her listeners, who spend their days helping patients recover the past, remember what has been all too significantly forgotten, that they themselves have become victims of a substantial impairment of memory: what others went through has slipped their minds. Why so—what has happened, and with what consequences? One rejoinder might be that the past is the past, and there is no point dwelling on what once was—especially if the result is self-accusation or the development of unqualified awe toward those who lived in an earlier age. A more assertive rejoinder might insist that those in attendance at the lecture most certainly did know—and keep in mind—what had been presented to them but chose to act as if such was not (always, or ever) the case. An even more skeptical, if not truculent, response would take the apparently innocent form of the standard psychoanalytic inquiry: what is the real reason for such remarks—the hidden agenda of which they are a part?

Of course, Miss Freud was giving her lecture in 1968, at a time of great social and political upheaval in the country where she spoke. She was talking to comfortable, well-educated men and women who saw, by and large, quite well-to-do, if not wealthy, patients in the urban, cosmopolitan setting of Manhattan.[2] She is frank to say, in the same lecture, that the profession she knew when she was in her twenties and thirties is no longer the same, is in danger of losing its appeal to the young; "which was very pronounced at one time, especially after the First World War and in the early '20s of the century when Siegfried Bernfeld propounded the revelations of psychoanalysis to large audiences drawn from the Youth Movement." In those days, she said, psychoanalysis was seen by young people "as the embodiment of the spirit of change, the contempt for the conventions, freedom of thought about sex and, in the minds of many, the eagerly looked for prospect of release from sexual restrictions."

After evoking with evident nostalgia a time now gone—her own youth—she turns her attention to the here-and-now of the late 1960s when she is in her early seventies, with about fifteen years of life left. "For young people," she declares, "psychoanalysis is now in the hands of the parent generation and as such suspect . . . it has lost the aspect of being dangerous, a forbidden matter, accessible only to the courageous, a useful weapon with which to attack society; instead psychoanalysis is looked on and avoided as a procedure devised to deprive them of originality and revolutionary spirit and induce them to adopt and conform to existing conditions, which is the last aim they have in mind." She them attempts to get closer to the spirit of the late 1960s young by pointing out another dimension to their disillusionment with psychoanalysis: "After all, analysis never offered anything except enlightenment about the inner world, about man's struggle within himself, about his being his own worst enemy. This conflicts with the present battle cry of youth of 'man against society.' "

There are, needless to say, other ways of regarding the loss of interest in psychoanalysis that Miss Freud attributes to young people. Actually, the question, always, is *which* young people she (or someone taking issue with her) has in mind. Many young people in 1968 (and today, more than twenty years later) were and are quite interested in psychotherapy, if not psychoanalysis. They cannot afford the latter, but they surely seek out the former. Nor is the issue necessarily generational, as she would have it—parents trying to foist analysis or therapy on their children, and parents using psychology to discredit the social or political aspirations of their sons and daughters, although plenty of both could (and can) be documented.

She is, perhaps, too tactful to mention, as an explanation for the youthful disenchantment she has described, her own earlier remarks about the price paid by the century's first analysts (ostracism, lack of privileges and status, social and economic vulnerability) in contrast to the success that today's world gives to graduates of psychoanalytic institutes. Younger people who live relatively marginal professional or intellectual lives, those who take up a somewhat unpopular or much denounced cause, as the antiwar movement was in its early stages, will find within themselves a greater political and cultural bond with (and empathy toward) others who are in such a position. The issue therefore is not only the young, and their desire to strike at their elders, but the felt allegiances and commitments of the analysts themselves. After all, the enthusiasm the young of Vienna felt toward psychoanalysis, so poignantly described by Miss Freud, was surely a response to some of the attitudes many analysts had in common with those young men and women: "We were rebels, in our own ways," Grete Bibring once observed, and when she spelled out the nature of that rebelliousness, it was not too hard to see why a common cause was established, even if the analysts were from one generation, the members of the "Youth Movement" from another: "Many of us were politically very active. We were socialists, or 'liberals' who wanted to change the society. We stood with the poor, and wanted to fight for their interests. For us psychoanalysis promised personal 'liberation' not for its own sake, but so that we could work to 'liberate' others. Political activity, social activism, they were a big part of our lives— not for all of us, but for plenty of us, and especially for those interested in children and adolescents: they were going to be analysts who helped the world in so many ways—to work with 'delinquents,' to help children grow up in healthier, stronger families, to improve the schools so that children were treated with respect, and so that they learned better. I think young people sensed, right away, that we were on their side!"

Perhaps as Miss Freud looked at her audience that April evening in 1968—Martin Luther King killed only a few days earlier, Robert Kennedy soon to be killed, and, every day, American and Vietnamese people being killed in Asia—she may have noticed that the issue was not only generational, but what can happen to a profession with increasing influence, authority, power, and money, the variables she had already touched upon earlier in her address. Young people can take the measure of such a historical outcome—the rise of psychoanalysis to fame and fortune. But no political rebel, old or young, was going to be invited to say as much to the members of the New York Psychoanalytic Institute, and she surely must have known that to be true. She was there because she was one of their most respected leaders. For years before 1968, and for years after, a big part of her work had to do with the giving of such important lectures, receiving applause, congratulations, honors of various kinds. She moved from city to city, institute to institute, often becoming an honorary member of the institute she addressed. She was also, by then, receiving honorary degrees—an ever-more-sought-after presence in the intellectual life of the West. When I told my Harvard tutor Perry Miller that I had heard Anna Freud speak (in 1950, as described early in this book), his immediate reaction, his two words, said everything, said what thousands have said and thought: "Freud's daughter." Miller was hardly a social scientist, but he knew the relationship between individual talent and cultural values—knew how Emerson and Thoreau, for instance, fitted into nineteenth-century life in Concord, and into America's evolving social and intellectual history. "Someone has to receive the adulation Freud was beginning to get in the last years of his life—why not his daughter, who has carried on his work?" I don't think at the time I fully understood all that Perry Miller, with such a comment, was trying to get across, he who knew so much about cultural puritanism, and the instinctual life it is meant to keep under harness.[3]

In a sense, as Freud became an icon for the secular bourgeoisie, his radical glimpse of our urges and lusts became obscured, if not blotted out altogether. He could be celebrated—and his "ideas," now shorn of their powerful implications, could be recited endlessly in the safety that abstractions offer. The fierce opposition he and his colleagues sparked had about it an honesty, a candid responsiveness to rock-bottom psychological truths that contrasts tellingly with the ready acceptance psychoanalysis now has in so many quarters. Glib clichés, intellectualized palaver, have replaced the alarm and fear of those who knew in their bones that some raw nerves had been touched. By the same token, even as society as a whole has neutralized the psychological radicalism of psychoanalysis by its eager embrace— searching, unsettling clinical experiences and social observations turned into dreary, sophisticated chit-chat—the profession of psychoanalysis has itself gone through a similar transformation. At the start, there were men and women ready to stand up to the conventional, stand apart from the intellectual "principalities and powers," but psychoanalysis then became an accepted profession working by and large for the well-to-do who seek personal insight, for purposes of "adjustment," but rarely to share the social or political implications of the radical, visionary side of psychoanalysis.

In her lecture to the New York City psychoanalysts, Miss Freud was willing to spell out what had happened to a profession in a half-century or so, a profession her father founded, a profession she had by then practiced for some forty years. "When we scrutinize the personalities who, by self-selection, became the first generation of psychoanalysts," she starts out, "we are left in no doubt about their characteristics." Once men and women chose to seek a way of thinking, a way of being and working with others; now applicants come before committees, having filled out forms, are evaluated and evaluated, scrutinized to the point where one wonders whether any member of that early cohort of Freud's, himself included, would be deemed acceptable. Miss Freud makes the comparison in this way: "They [the early analysts] were the unconventional ones, the doubters, those who were dissatisfied with the limitations imposed on knowledge, also among them were the odd ones, the dreamers, and those who knew neurotic suffering, from their own experience." She then turns to our time: "This type of intake has altered decisively since psychoanalytic training has become institutionalized and appeals in this stricter form to a different type of personality." She never does amplify that last remark—a most intriguing one. But after all she was in an analytic institute, addressing those latter-day practitioners who possessed this "different type of personality." She did, however, return to the subject of "self-selection," a crucial one for any profession—since those who get admitted determine its future life: "Moreover, self-selection has given way to the careful scrutiny of applicants, resulting in the exclusion of the mentally endangered, eccentrics, the self-made, those with excessive flights of the imagination, and favoring the acceptance of the sober, well-prepared ones, who are hard-working enough to wish to better their professional efficiency."

She has damned with faint praise many in her audience—and made the trials and tribulations of her generation of analysts seem attractive by comparison. She herself doesn't quite sound as marginal as her portrait of those whom present-day scrutiny would exclude, although she surely knew (and knew that her audience knew) that no young candidate like her (or her analysand Erik Erikson) would ever today have a chance of admission to an American psychoanalytic institute. She had no college education, let alone medical school degree. She had learned to be a teacher by teaching—an apprenticeship not preceded by years of courses in "educational psychology." She had been analyzed by her father. She seemed not at all interested in a love life with men, and tended to seek out the company of older women, to whom she became quite attached. She was no stranger to "flights of imagination"; there was in her a shy, slightly melancholy side. She wrote poems, stories, spent much time daydreaming, and was utterly bound, it seemed, to her family, never having established an independent life for herself.

As for those who are accepted these days, what does it mean when someone such as Anna Freud comes before such people to describe them as "sober," "well-prepared," "hard-working," hence able to use psychoanalysis as a means of improving their "professional efficiency"? What does it mean when Erik Erikson addresses his colleagues with respect to their professional lives and mentions as aspects of such a life "identities based on talmudic argument, on messianic zeal, on punitive orthodoxy, on faddist sensationalism, on professional and social ambition"?[4] Are these older analysts being unfair to their younger colleagues? Is their intellectual leadership marred by nervous righteousness, self-righteousness? Or are both these elders (each of artistic sensibility, neither university-trained, neither physicians) worried that psychoanalysis has become the province of Eliot's the "cautious, politic, meticulous"—its creative surge long past, its life in the hands of bureaucratic custodians who endlessly mull and munch over trivia?

Erikson's indictment is more vigorous and explicit, but it was rendered in a book meant for the general public; Anna Freud's was worked into a speech and taken to the very heart of the psychoanalytic establishment. Her remarks are polite and seemingly meant to be historically descriptive, yet they might have been more appreciative of the day-to-day burdens (and opportunities) that go with, say, the psychoanalytic work that is done today in hospital and clinic settings, in consultative work with schools, in research done in communities, in teaching carried on with medical students, social workers, graduate students in psychology. Still, she had taken the measure of late-twentieth-century psychoanalysis in its heartland, the United States, and used her leader's prerogative—to criticize, even rebuke.

In Chicago, two years earlier, she had spoken in a similar vein. Her talk was entitled "The Ideal Psychoanalytic Institute: A Utopia," and in it she made clear that she objected to certain common practices that were powerfully determining the nature of the profession. Again she was concerned about admissions procedures—aware, as mentioned earlier, that those who get accepted for training determine in the long run what the word *psychoanalysis* will actually mean. She embraces an essay of Heinz Kohut, written in 1961, in which he spoke of the desirability of a "slow and careful consideration of the defenses" of the applicants—a process that he contrasted with various "efficient selection procedures where secrets were quickly wrested from the candidate through the use of psychological tests, group interviews, stress situations or deeply probing individual interviews." Once again, she is worried about "efficiency"—what it can come to mean both for those who practice it and for those who experience its (for her) dubious consequences.

She and Kohut were not simply urging an old-fashioned (and sometimes much needed) civility on their fellow analysts. Something more was at stake: the danger that what she calls "a truly analytic atmosphere" will be forsaken—one in which the complexities of anyone's personality are evaluated carefully, thoughtfully, with due respect for a particular person's idiosyncratic talents and handicaps, both of which ought to be fitted into the context of an ongoing life, its everyday achievements. She remains true to her long-standing conviction that an enormous amount may be learned from observing someone, talking with him or her, in a reasonably relaxed and cordial manner—without a need to launch a frontal assault on that person's personality through the kinds of maneuvers Dr. Kohut had mentioned. She even tells her audience that when she read Kohut's essay, she took it to heart: decided "to take his warning into account whenever I had to share the responsibility for selection procedures." She wants, with respect to those "procedures," not only courtesy and thoughtfulness, a more relaxed pace of evaluation, but a different notion of who might or might not be a valuable candidate. To be sure, she is prepared "to rule out the more severe psycho-pathologies and character disorders such as psychopathy, psychotic risks, depressive risks, perversions, and delinquent trends." But she wants to balance such a necessary skepticism toward applicants with this reminder: "Essential technical, clinical, and theoretical contributors to psychoanalysis have been made by individuals not only on the basis of different professional backgrounds, but in spite of, or prompted by, all sorts of personal characteristics, qualities, and idiosyncrasies." Then comes her punch line: "To imagine these historical figures in the role of present applicants for training may do much to dispel prejudices and to lessen some of the restrictive practices which govern selection at present."

She is asking for a leap of the psychological imagination. She is trying to leap across an entire historical process that, to her mind, has made psychoanalysis far less adventuresome and exciting and captivating than once was the case. Addressing a distinguished Chicago audience, she is not afraid to put her cards on the table. She acknowledges that "theoretical training" can become a "chore" rather than something keenly sought and appreciated. She insists that the so-called surface of the mind can be as important as its depth—each will express the truth of a person's psychological experience. She worries that various concepts will become mere "artifacts"—ideas unconnected to ongoing human life as it is directly observed. In that regard, she boldly urges her listeners to leave their conventional terrain, their consulting rooms and seminar rooms, for another kind of observational territory—"[to place themselves, for example] in maternal hospitals or in young families." She adds other locales, too—"the daily routine work of the infant welfare clinics," and, not least, "a nursery school." She is emphatically *not* suggesting such work as an "application" of psychoanalysis—a chance to show what a profession can offer others, with all the attendant problems of noblesse oblige. She was, rather, the ego psychologist once again suggesting that in the everyday life of schools and hospitals and courts psychoanalysts have everything to learn: "The candidates will go to maternity wards, welfare clinics, nursery schools, juvenile courts strictly as observers, by no means as advisers; their visits will have a learning, not a teaching, function."

Here she was not suggesting a stance of humility, pure or false. She was worrying about stale air in a profession, as well as asserting her particular way of seeing clinical psychoanalytic exploration—that one works inward from the ego and its defenses toward the harder-to-grasp psychological realities of the id and its drives. She was also speaking and writing as a genuinely public-spirited person—the Anna Freud who hastened at the outbreak of the Second World

War not only to set up nurseries for psychologically and physically endangered children in order to do research, but to render a service to the country that had given her and her family haven, whose tradition of middle-class decorum and politesse she obviously had found congenial.

Anna Freud's preference for respectful observation rather than intrusive assault in clinical exploration as well as selection of candidates is reflected in her well-known struggles with Melanie Klein. Here she got down in the trenches, in a hard-fought contest over the very nature of child analysis (and the training of candidates for that kind of work). The two were tough protagonists, each the strong-minded leader of a school, and each inclined to give little or no quarter. Mrs. Klein was very much a follower of the early Freud who explored the unconscious with daring and courageous conjecture. She believed the child analyst can know a lot about the preverbal child, and can work with conviction and dispatch to obtain an analytic intimacy with young children not unlike the kind that develops between analysts and their grown-up patients. She was another kind of utopian dreamer, anxious to do prophylactic work with children, and convinced that boys and girls who seem to be doing all right by the ordinary social standards of the neighborhood and the school would nevertheless gain a great deal from analysis. She was not afraid—as a theorist or a clinician—to make deft, penetrating probes toward the innermost part of the mind, and the very earliest experiences became the subject of her confident and suggestive inquiry. In contrast, Miss Freud was constantly inclined to be wary of what she regarded at best as the surmises and guesses of those who followed Mrs. Klein. How is anyone to know, for sure, what is truly taking place in an infant's mind? How is one to do psychoanalytic work with children scarcely able to speak—or, for that matter, those older but right in the middle of tumultuous and necessary psychological developments? Put differently, how can a transference neurosis (a reenactment of childhood attitudes toward parents) get going in children who are only now beginning to develop their *initial*, sustained attitudes toward their parents? How exact is the analogy between children's play with toys, or their drawings, on the one hand, and the "free associations" that adult analysands are asked to produce, on the other? Mrs. Klein was a shrewd, lively interpreter of the play and artistic work her young analysands offered. Miss Freud was no less willing to speculate upon the meaning of what her analysands did or drew—but, one guesses, less inclined to share her thoughts, her guesses, with those young ones. She was also more willing to become, at the start of things, an explicitly nurturing and friendly figure, anxious to be trusted, and to mean something important to the boy or girl she hoped to get to know thoroughly over time.

The intellectual differences between these two forceful leaders were accompanied by a range of personal differences—and, of course, amplified by their followers. This amplification (and often distortion) of the ideas set down by leaders at the hands of their students and colleagues, and (in the case of psychoanalysis) their patients, their (emotional) children, is a subject itself worth psycho-analytic study—although not likely to be taken up by the converted. Mrs. Klein and Miss Freud not only fought on matters of substance, but expressed themselves differently, presented themselves to audi-ences differently, and perhaps connected with different sides of Freud's own personality, and different interests he chose to pursue. These two leaders even divided up, to a certain extent, important parts of the psychoanalytic terrain—America for Anna Freud, and England for Melanie Klein, notwithstanding the emigration of the Freuds to London in 1938.

In a sense, the two child analysts were debating the very nature of childhood. Mrs. Klein was more inclined to see children, even very young ones, as much like adults: propelled by powerful drives; able to convey in their own way the nature of those drives; able to respond to the analyst as grown-ups do—and thereby, eventually, able both to learn about themselves and to change their (troubling) behavior. Miss Freud saw childhood as, to some extent, a world apart. She was inclined to pragmatism, empiricism, skepticism—and was unwilling to be *sure* about what very young children really do feel and wish and fear, inasmuch as they are only learning to talk and unlikely to remain still for long, let alone fifty minutes, and put all their thoughts and associations into words. She worried, too, about the right of the analyst to enter a young life, still very much in flux, at a time when one moment's seeming pathology can soon enough give way to another's great strength. "Normality" in childhood for her was an important focus, and it included "pathology" as a constituent part.

I never was able to prompt much discussion from Anna Freud about her long-ago disagreements with Mrs. Klein. (In print, as well, she was tactful, and at times respectful as she enunciated their differences.) But on the subject of psychoanalytic intervention in childhood, she was willing to speak out with some insistence: "I think it fair to say that Mrs. Klein, and those who have called themselves Kleinians, have always been more willing to do analysis with children [than we were]. I think we have to be rather careful about this—*hesitant*, I'd say, to engage with a child psychoanalytically, and *clear, very clear*, in our minds as to why, exactly why, we are doing so, if we decide to do so. Children quite normally and commonly go in and out of difficulties, and they also gradually build up for themselves ways of dealing with those difficulties. I have always felt that it is wrong to enter a child's life [as a psychoanalyst] unless there is a good reason, a reason that really gives us [a] warrant. Perhaps you could say I was more cautious than Mrs. Klein—and we disagreed on that basis. But you know, much of that is 'old history.' We did work together at times: she and I discussed our views, and agreed to disagree. Perhaps I am now putting the best light on what was not such a good moment. She had enormous energy, and she was—how should I say it?—more imaginative than I was willing to be in my daily analytic work with children, more imaginative, maybe, about what takes place in the minds of young children!"

She went not a step further. I felt certain that her wry (if not sardonic) last sentence was meant to be an important clarification, but not something she then (1972) wanted to discuss at any length. I wondered whether her abiding interest in how much there is to be *learned*, rather than how much is known, and therefore ready and waiting to be "applied," lay behind her more circumspect attitude toward child analysis—when to recommend it, how to pursue it—as compared to what I thought had been the attitude of Mrs. Klein. She smiled, let her face tell me yes, but listened to me with increasing impassivity as I tried to characterize certain differences between them. She seemed to want to let well enough alone, or to keep a respectful distance from children, as they move along in years—to see how the land lies, so to speak, before making what I felt she regarded as a fateful decision: to begin an analysis with a child. Mrs. Klein, on the other hand, was more ready to plunge right in; not that she, too, didn't regard an analysis itself, once begun, as quite fateful, indeed. Finally, Miss Freud spoke briefly, putting the matter to rest. "All of us—thinking about an analysis with a child—would want to stop, look, listen, before making a decision. Maybe some of us [would, as we'd say] in England, 'tarry a bit longer' than others."

As one reads the many forewords, introductions, prefaces, she wrote, the lectures she gave to analysts assembled in institutes or world congresses, the comments she sometimes was asked to give on the occasion of the conferral of an honorary degree, her strong opinions become evident—opinions that as a teacher she did not hesitate to express. At times, as I listened to her speak in a private situation with one or two others, or in a large, public meeting, I felt her becoming somewhat sharp-tongued, even caustic. I felt often that I'd not want to take her on without careful emotional as well as factual preparation: she seemed always ready to stake out her position and defend it well. Several times, hearing her invoke her father ("Freud said . . . ," or "When Freud wrote . . . "), I wondered whether she herself ever tired of such incantory phrases. Sometimes I found myself, driving home from New Haven or sitting in a plane on my way back to America from England, preparing a speech, which I knew I'd never deliver—urging a less "defensive" attitude on her part toward "Freud" and all he'd written, or for that matter *did,* in the course of his life (including the way he behaved as a friend, as a physician, and as a father to her!). I found myself, that is, wishing that she might have broken with the formal leadership she offered so energetically and (for the most part) graciously for so long to organized psychoanalysis: keeper of the keys, custodian of the treasure, loyal daughter to the great man, authoritative interpreter of his every word. I found myself wishing that she had gladly thrown open all the

Freud archives, allowed access to whatever various historians and political scientists and social essayists have wanted to read, to ponder. I even wished that she would have greeted some of the more critical researchers and writers halfway, or more than halfway, acknowledged some of Freud's mistakes as well as those made by his disputants, his onetime colleagues and friends and correspondents who fell by the way, became estranged from him. Surely this great man had faults; and as is the case with everyone, some of those faults were not minor; and some of those faults may well have been responsible for harm done to others. Surely, too, other important analysts had or have faults. If a writer and thinker such as Freud becomes so elevated in the minds of his associates and followers that historians and critics are turned away (or turned into psychological caricatures of themselves in the ad hominem defenses peculiar to some psychiatrists and psychoanalysts), then intellectual idolatry is at work, just as truculent and destructive as any other political warfare.

On the other hand, psychoanalysis has also attracted its fair share of gratuitous snipers. Driven for reasons of their own, they make a mockery of what has been a long, painful, arduous, and honorable effort by thousands of men and women from many countries to search deep within themselves and others for a wide range of psychological truths, and to report what has been observed, discovered, as accurately as possible. Of course, errors of surmise were made along the way; of course, pride and vanity and competitiveness and envy exerted their influence along the way, from the mid-1890's right up to our own time, over a century; and of course, Anna Freud as a person, like all leaders, has had her own failings and faults—in particular a bossy, cranky, combative side. But she also, in her own sometimes understated, sometimes carefully stated manner, tried to avoid turning into a literalist follower, a pietistic leader. The side of her that could be demanding and imperious was also the side of her that could direct a sarcasm at worshipful insiders, for whom her father's texts took on a biblical stature. At times Anna Freud may have restrained or ignored the healthy evolution of analytic theory. Heinz Hartmann may have been right when he told his friends that Anna Freud was his "silent critic"—because, he pushed "ego psychology" not only farther than she did, but farther than her father did. Similarly with Erik Erikson's ideas, which for a long while she chose to ignore—important though they were in helping psychoanalysis become nourished by sociological, anthropological, and historical knowledge. In the end, though, she came around—eloquently in her tribute to Heinz Hartmann, and indirectly with respect to Erikson in the "sincerest kind of flattery," imitation. Her "developmental lines," presented relatively late in her life, bear substantial resemblance to the stages outlined in *Childhood and Society*, and then developed with even more subtly in his later papers on "identity and the life cycle." She had every reason to admire his way of following children, as they grow and change, become adolescents, become adults, and his way of thinking not only about drives and their vicissitudes (oral, anal, genital) but a much wider range of psychological events and developments: the particular manner in which a particular person deals with the many fates (familial, genetic, social, accidental, historical, racial) that combine into the one overall fate called a life.

In a sense, then, Anne Freud's leadership was both restrained and restraining, although with important breakthroughs of resilience and flexibility. At times she was Freud's shy but tough-mindedly loyal daughter. At other times she was more of a rebel—willing to wage her own struggles with orthodoxy, and to embrace, finally, certain earlier brilliant iconoclasts. "I try not to think of myself as a 'leader' at all," she once remarked, with evident displeasure, and perhaps evasively, in response to a question I put to her—perhaps letting me know, at the very least, the constant struggle such a matter must have been for her. She could be opinionated, yet she tried to accommodate the opinions of others—within limits: "I ask myself whether the view [she is trying to evaluate] belongs to psychoanalysis—*as it is evolving*." She hesitated at the brink of those last four words—perhaps a way of emphasizing some internal reminder she had to summon on occasions.

Her own life, of course, was a long and productive one—despite all the challenges to her leadership. After the Second World War, for a decade and more, she rode the crest of a tide of acclaim, only to meet the inevitable scrutiny that history and scholarship bring to any successful ideas or movements, at least in a reasonably open society. At all times in her life, she found her well-known tact and discretion tested—in the early years of leadership by her celebrity, by the almost worshipful stance of many of her (and her father's) admirers, and in later years by the disinterest or disenchantment or exacting (sometimes disparaging and mean-spirited) criticism of various writers, psychiatrists, and even psychoanalysts, who turned to new and different ways of thinking about the mind and dealing with patients. Through it all, she held on to her poise. She both stood and yielded ground. Her life itself offered a kind of honorable leadership: the example of many years spent with children and on behalf of children, an accomplishment all its own, and perhaps the best statement possible, the best standard of behavior to uphold for herself, or any others who cared to take notice.

IDEALIST

*Our dream was the dream of
psychoanalysis—all it had to offer.*
Anna Freud

MUCH HAS BEEN MADE of the confrontation between psycho-analysis, with its emphasis on the importance of sexuality in our lives, and the thick façade of Victorian prudery that prevailed in Freud's turn-of-the-century Vienna, and elsewhere in Europe. Even if nineteenth-century culture was more sensual, or frankly sexual, around the edges and in certain corners, than it appeared, it most certainly proclaimed, loud and clear, its various constraints—a primness, a restriction and reticence with respect to sexuality. Suddenly, with the publication of *The Interpretation of Dreams, The Psychopathology of Every-day Life,* and *Three Essays on Sexuality,* a new way of looking at human behavior became available to the book-reading public, at least those who belonged to the literate bourgeoisie.

While Freud's books, his ideas and speculations, won curiosity, interest, and, finally, adherents, there was immediately plenty of opposition. Proper burghers were shocked, offended; religious authorities were quick to declare their strong disapproval. Little support came from the intellectual or academic or medical or psychiatric world. Freud's isolation from such communities in Vienna is well known, and a number of the analysts who knew him and studied with him also took the heat with him—experienced rebuke and scorn from defenders of the status quo.

I well remember Karl Menninger speaking on this subject during a lecturing stint I did in Topeka.[1] We were offering a seminar together—he spoke of his experiences growing up in the Midwest during the early years of this century, while I presented some moments in the lives of children I had come to know in New Mexico as well as in the South. When I played some tape-recorded interviews I did with white mothers and fathers in New Orleans, enraged that their sons and daughters were ordered to attend an elementary school with one black girl, the Menninger Clinic doctors in the room were dismayed. One after the other, they wondered out loud why it was that a single child's presence stirred such fear and anxiety and hate in so many grown-ups—prompted such agitated outbursts of animus: rage and contempt and alarm and even declarations of vengeance. Suddenly, "Dr. Karl," as he was known, spoke up: "I guess that little girl's 'darkness' reminded them of their own kind of darkness! I sure remember the outrage that psychoanalysis got going in lots of my medical colleagues, and plenty of others, too. They weren't out on the streets shouting and screaming—but they did their own kind of hollering!"

He went on to chronicle the allegations—psychoanalysis as a form of obscenity, as pornography, as a lewd slant on life: such charges from professors and pastors, from journalists and prominent professional people. We were all brought back in time to an earlier age, when what now struck us as widely accepted common sense was regarded, to the contrary, as a degraded and degrading doctrine: minds gone awry and astray.

Yet psychoanalysis was, perhaps, even more subversive than its strongest, most astringent or inflamed critics either realized or declared. Dr. Menninger, at the seminar, discoursed at length on the threat psychoanalysis posed to many—sexuality, kept under wraps for so long, was brought to the attention of influential readers and, eventually, to an entire culture. But even though it was Freud's emphasis on the central role of sexuality in our psychology, on the shaping power of the id's "libidinal cathexes," on our daily lives, that stirred so much controversy and disapproval, his larger view of the mind, its struggles to deal with those sexual drives, went relatively unnoticed.

Freud had shown how we pretend and dissimulate and conceal in order to keep from ourselves, not just others, the urges, wishes, needs, that constantly press upon us, only to be pushed back mightily. In our daily fantasy life, in our dreams and nightmares, in the "slips" we make, of speech and memory, we send signals to ourselves and others about what is happening to us unwittingly or with only a partial measure of awareness. "Now you see it, now you don't," one of my psychoanalytic supervisors would say, referring to that tension between the insight we sometimes have with respect to our mental life and the sleep of sorts in which we walk, at a remove from much that matters within us. But it was Anna Freud who would spell out precisely how we do try to live with all those impulses which her father had described—how the vigilant ego and superego work both to allow and to disallow the id's energies access to expression. The mechanisms of defense become our lifelong habits. We become the people we are largely on the basis of which of those mechanisms we use, with what frequency and persistence.

One person engages in massive repression, turns into Eliot's Prufrock. Another person constantly attributes to others this or that desire, characteristic—*they* are greedy, *they* are pushy, *they* are insensitive, or calculating, or rapacious, or lustful as can be, or inclined to laziness. Yet another person is constantly saying one thing, doing another—acting ever so friendly to people not really liked at all, feared, even hated. So it goes, our novelists and playwrights have always known, the illusions and delusions, the deceits and conceits of everyday life. The exact manner in which such mental maneuvers take place, the psychological rationale for it all, was documented by Anna Freud with great care, and the reader goes through her book once again reminded how devious we can be with ourselves, let alone others. Reading all this, the reader can become a bit cynical about human affairs—always a distinct possibility in the company of a serious psychoanalytic text. Those mechanisms of defense hide so much truth, distort so much in our heads. In that seminar room, Dr. Menninger refused to let us distance ourselves from such deception. He sat silent while we analyzed those poor, benighted, frightened people who screamed their frustrations out at a black girl, and called her all they feared becoming themselves—but then he brought the subject around to us: "The more you learn about the mind, the less you take for granted—not only in New Orleans during a racial crisis! Who is *our* 'them'? We mustn't forget to ask ourselves that every once in a while."

He reminded us of the heated, even hateful, factionalism in some psychoanalytic quarters, reminded us that those mechanisms

Anna Freud described are used by all of us, including those who try to understand how such mechanisms work in others, in our patients. By now, few of us need to be told about the influence that our sexual life has on our interests, activities, commitments, concerns, or that all sorts of impulses continually want to have their say in our day-to-day lives. We are perhaps less willing or able to realize how indirect, oblique, tricky, we are with ourselves as we struggle to keep our balance, pressed by the impulses on one side and the world-at-large with its demands, strictures, limitations, on the other side. Dr. Menninger reminded his audience that "the bigot out there—we understand him [psychologically]; the patient in our office, with a sexual problem—we understand him, too; but you folks and me, trying to get through today and tomorrow, and reacting to each other, hearing what we want [to] from each other, seeing each other as we do—that's an infinitely complex story, and the more you think of it, the more complex it gets, and the less attention [it gets] from us!"

A murmur of nervous amusement—the enormity of the task, and the disheartening vision that can accompany such a project: each sentence and gesture potentially counterfeit or meant as much to mislead as inform! True, there is the so-called "cognitive" side to human interaction, as Heinz Hartmann was anxious for us not to forget—the ego as a learner of facts, as an observer and listener that tries to figure out how the world works and, by God, tries to make it work. But so commonly, as we go about our business with each other, there is an unstated, perhaps hidden, agenda—covert assumptions, undisclosed expectations, unacknowledged resentments, so much of it all a consequence of what we have experienced long before we came to know one another or be together in this particular set of circumstances.

In *The Ego and the Mechanisms of Defense,* after chapters entitled "Identification with the Aggressor," or "Denial in Word and Act," or "Restriction of the Ego," Anna Freud suddenly presents us with a chapter called "A Form of Altruism." Although the subject is surprising, she does not spare it from the knowing, skeptical examination she has given to other forms of human activity. She begins with an erudite discussion of one of the mainstays of human psychology, "the mechanism of projection." She reminds her psychoanalytically sophisticated readers that "writers of the English school" have declared projection a commonplace "in the earliest months of life"— including it in their descriptions of the "first-aggressive impulses." While she does not discuss whether this is so—at least with the babies whose psychology the Kleinians claim to understand—she does maintain that "projection is quite natural to the ego of little children." "It is normal," she tells us, "for it [the child's ego] constantly to get rid of prohibited impulses and wishes in this way, handing them over in full measure to other people." Thus she connects to everyone's childhood a maneuver of the mind that has enormous social, political, and historical significance, a maneuver first described in the Bible (scapegoating), and a maneuver every psychiatrist learns to recognize in connection with his or her patients, and one we see in the way social or racial or international tensions arise: we find "theys" and "thems" to serve our purposes as repositories for everything within ourselves we don't like, have learned to fear, judge wrong or shameful. The worst in us is channeled by this mechanism, which children learn as naturally as they learn to use words, as naturally as they learn to take notice of the world, and themselves.

Hate between groups of people, or individuals, fear and suspicion, bitterness and resentment, are energized by the projective distortions of persons and whole societies otherwise, supposedly, "civilized." At work, behind the scenes, is a disturbed or threatened conscience—a person's intuition, however outside of consciousness, that there is an unspeakable quality, or batch of attributes, of wishes, of remembered actions, to be gotten rid of at all cost. Our eyes and ears soon find the way—we take notice of someone, or some group of people, on whom to unload our contempt. The stronger our sense of right or wrong, or the more vulnerable we feel (morally, socially, economically), the more eager we may be to right things—to right ourselves at the expense of others. No wonder, then, that religious people (so imbued with stern mandates as to what is good and bad, correct and incorrect) have shown themselves capable of being so intolerant of others, so full of hate for rival creeds, factions, faiths; and no wonder fierce secular ideologies of our modern age, political and cultural, psychiatric or psychoanalytic, have shown similar inclinations. A person who calls religion an "opiate," or evidence of a persisting neurosis, can develop a fervent allegiance to a political doctrine or a professional body of literature—and the next step, of course, is the definition of oneself by resort to the exclusion of others, by name-calling.

This kind of gratification, so obvious in nursery-school children, with their shifting cliques, so obvious in elementary- and high-school-age children, with their clubs and gangs, is easily found in distinguished educators or intellectuals, well-known politicians, powerful and oracular church leaders, and, it seems, those who have long training analyses—hence the constant malicious gossip, the intense feuding in universities, political life, religious organizations, and, no less frequently, psychiatric and psychoanalytic institutions. As Miss Freud points out: "The mechanism of projection disturbs our human relations when we project our own jealousy and attribute to other people our aggressive acts." Since all of us are prone to spells of disappointment or anger, to moments in which our confidence in ourselves, our respect for ourselves, has become shaky, the temptation to clean the slate, as it were, in one fell psychological swoop, becomes not so much tempting as irresistible.

When I talked with Miss Freud about the experience I had with such defenses, in interviews I did in the South (some with the sons and daughters of Ku Klux Klan members), and in Northern Ireland with Catholic and Protestant children, their families, their priests and ministers,[2] she was shrewd in the way she distinguished between projection in groups of people, as opposed to particular individuals. "I have been asked for years to give talks on 'the psychology of prejudice,' or 'why people are hateful'—and I always decline! I much prefer talking about what I do all day: work with patients or with analytic candidates, or at the research we're doing. A man came to see me, a journalist, and he wanted me to talk about 'aggression and racism,' a title like that. I told him I didn't know enough to do that, and he didn't believe me, I could tell. I repeated myself after he asked me a second time, and he could see I really meant it. He became quite flattering, and after a bit I felt I had to stop him. I told him, I understand why people turn on other people—but I didn't want to leap from a patient I know doing that (or a colleague!) to the big problems he was bringing up with me.

"As I listened to you I remembered that journalist and his questions, and his offer that I give a lecture. If he were here, and heard you talk, he'd learn something about how psychology becomes the agent of sociology—the way people think of other people, and why that happens. Yes, I agree it is projection at work [when hate gets going between white and black people]. But you must be asking yourself why some become victims of hate, and others resist it. We see quite well-to-do patients who have become quite hateful toward individuals they know, and toward various groups of people. We see quite poor people who can take very little for granted in life, and yet they are—the expression [in England] often is—'of good nature.' They may not have any money, but they haven't turned on people in compensation for their feeling of living, as they do, a hard life.

"I am often asked to explain this—why some people are so distrustful or unfriendly, and use projection to establish *others* as the ones who do bad things, while some people are rather pleasant in their outlook, and don't construct enemies for themselves—don't 'use projection to take a shower,' was the way one of our analytic candidates put it. She was a teacher, and she had a lively sense of humor, and a down-to-earth way of saying things, and once as we talked [in a conference] about all these difficult and worrisome psychological developments, I looked at her and I thought to myself: well, to have a sense of humor, and to be a plainspoken woman, like her, will help any of us feel comfortable enough to resist hate—but her life, her experiences, have enabled her to be the way she is, so we are back to our riddle: what makes people the way they are!

"I do think events in the world can make a difference. [I had pushed hard on that score, asked her repeatedly in the course of a long discussion, only a small part of which is presented here, about that intersection of the public and the private.] We are all *capable* of projection, and we all are tempted to use it, and in small ways, I suspect, we *do* use it, more regularly than we care to admit to ourselves, of course, or [to] others as well. I mean use it as children do, and as the racist people you have described do—though not so frequently, and not in such an organized, consistent way. I am talking here as a psychoanalyst. I mean, I am thinking of my analysands, who will in their 'associations' show plenty of 'projection' at work. If a person isn't doing all he wants to do, or feels he ought to do, he'll find some other group to call pushy or aggressive—rather than face the demanding nature of his own conscience or his ideals, which he got from his parents. The frustration that goes with a feeling of inadequacy, and the self-judgment that goes with that feeling, are addressed by the projection: call Jews or Asians 'pushy' and 'too competitive,' and you feel better yourself. You convert an inner judgment into an outer one, a projection of your own qualities onto others, and then [obtain] the satisfaction that goes with condemning others.

"When things go bad for more and more people, they find projection more and more useful. It is a mechanism made for [a world of] trouble. The whole purpose of projection is to get rid of trouble. Just like that!" She clapped her hands, then went on: "Here one minute, gone the next! It is a wonder, I sometimes think, that more people don't succumb to projection—it offers quick relief, and the world is so used to it. Politicians use it all the time. I've heard it used often by teachers and news commentators—the supposedly harmless ways we all talk about 'those people' who live 'over there'! I remember when the Nazis were getting stronger and stronger. It was a matter of time before they would take over Austria. My father would read what they said about the Jews and shake his head. Once he said, 'Where would they be without us!' I thought of that a lot when I had my 'interviews' with the Nazis. They were so rude and so aggressive—while all the while speaking of the Jews as if they had given the world rudeness and aggressive behavior! It's a small comfort to understand that [how projection works under such circumstances], a very small comfort! I agree, it is a big step from 'the ordinary projections of ordinary people' to 'state-sponsored ones.' That is why we psychoanalysts have to be careful how we talk—we can't talk about the 'dangers of projection' without qualifying our concerns: the dangers that arise when politicians and governments exploit people who are in trouble already [socially, economically] by offering them a series of projections on the radio and the television and in the newspapers. Anyway, projection, in and of itself, need not be such a bad thing!"

In that last sentence, she was repeating what she had declared decades earlier in *The Ego and the Mechanisms of Defense*. In the chapter "A Form of Altruism," she observes that projection "may enable us to form valuable positive attachments and so to consolidate our relations with one another." She adds, "This normal and less conspicuous form of projection might be described as 'altruistic surrender' of our own instinctual impulses in favor of other people." She then offers "an example" to give meaning to an abstract pronouncement—an "example" that stands out noticeably in a book so obviously intended as an addition to a body of theory, and an "example" that has struck some readers as an author's personal statement, if not her autobiographical one, masked as a clinical story. It is a tale of a young governess who lived a relatively selfless life—all of her energies given over to the lives of others. ("Childless herself, she was devoted to other people's children, as was indicated by her choice of a profession.") Miss Freud takes care to let us know through this story that the governess has not repressed her instinctual strivings, or masked them through a series of reaction formations. This is a governess (a young child analyst?) whose "repudiation of her own sexuality did not prevent her from taking an affectionate interest in the love life of her women friends and colleagues." This governess "gratified her instincts by sharing in the gratification of others, employing for this purpose the mechanisms of projection and identification." She amplifies: "The retiring attitude which the prohibition of her impulses caused her to adopt where she herself was concerned vanished when it was a question of fulfilling the same wishes after they had been projected on to someone else. The surrender of her instinctual impulses in favor of other people had thus an egoistic significance, but in her efforts to gratify the impulses of others her behavior could be called altruisitic."

She points out the everyday manifestations of this kind of psychological maneuver—"parents [who] sometimes delegate to their children their projects for their own lives, in a manner at once altruistic and egoistic." To illustrate her point, she calls upon Edmond

Rostand's *Cyrano de Bergerac*, showing the literary side of herself, which some who knew her suspected she had set aside on behalf of her intense commitment to the welfare of children, and of course, her beloved (and her beloved father's) psychoanalysis. Cyrano's sense of his own ugliness ultimately became Cyrano's sacrificing love for Roxanne, a woman he pursues through his friend Christian, whom he assists in many ways: he helps Christian woo Roxanne, and in battle tries to save him, at the risk of his own life. This dedication of Cyrano to Christian, and through him, to Roxanne, is not, of course, as selfless as it may seem. Instincts are being gratified—but vicariously, through an act of renunciation rather than wholesale repression. (Were the latter the case, Cyrano would not be aware of any interest at all in Roxanne, and would not try to get close to her through his apparently idealistic identification with Christian in his capacity as her lover and as a warrior.) This identification carries with it many aspirations, and they are pursued through a surrogate—triumph in love and on the field of battle: under such circumstances, the curious, uncanny calm and bravery and sacrificial generosity of Cyrano become understandable—Cyrano cares about himself, yes, but he has leapt into another's skin, and his apparent indifference to his own fate has to do with his concern for the fate of the person who has, in a way, given him shelter. The playwright, drawing on a historical figure, points out that Cyrano's poems and letters also became fair game for other writers (Corneille, Molière, Swift). Again he lacks interest in his own glory, inasmuch as it seems for him possible only through the triumph of another, with whom he has merged himself.

Anna Freud knows, of course, that there are other pathways to altruism—masochism, which she mentions, and homosexual struggles, and efforts at their resolution, which she also mentions. She is not quite ready, however, to abandon altruism as a possible psychological development in and of itself: "It remains an open question whether there is such a thing as a genuinely altruistic relation to one's fellow men, in which the gratification of one's own instinct plays no part at all, even in some displaced and sublimated form."

This was a question that continued to interest her for the rest of her life. Much of her work with children, obviously, *was* altruistic in the phenomenological sense—long hours given unstintingly to the neediest of boys and girls. She was hardly the determinedly "blank" adult upon whom children or adults fastened their various notions, ideas, fantasies. She gave of herself, as it were, to her patients and her colleagues, both intellectually and emotionally. Yet she was hard put to acknowledge herself, to receive from others. A certain natural physical beauty was partially hidden by a seeming indifference to clothes and the possibilities of hairdressing. She could be at once charming and austerely diffident—not unlike, I sometimes thought, certain wonderfully energetic nuns I have met in Brazil: their potentially quite attractive "femininity" or "maternal loveliness" (when older) submerged into the demanding rhythms of their dedicated working lives, their various commitments to others, and of course, ultimately, to the ideals that supply everyday energy to those commitments.

I certainly remember memorable discussions with her on the subject of altruism as I told her about Dorothy Day and Simone Weil, two idealistic twentieth-century women whom my parents much admired, and whom I tried to understand, the former through a long acquaintance, the latter through her demanding, idiosyncratic, brilliant essays. Miss Freud was always a polite host and listener—and I suppose I asked that of her through my deference and even awe, qualities on which she remarked in her letters to me, as if she was half-asking for a blunter, less inhibited response on my part, a response, perhaps, less dominated by idealization. But when we talked about Simone Weil, in particular, I heard from my New Haven and London host a sharpness of psychological analysis, a heightening of interest, that was itself of great interest to me, to the point where at times I was distracted from our speculations on Simone Weil by my sense that her spirit had, indeed, animated that of Miss Freud.[3]

Once, listening to one idealistic daughter of a European, Jewish physician, born in the nineteenth century, talk of another idealistic daughter of a European, Jewish physician, born in the nineteenth century, I realized full well how various the sources of idealism turn out to be, on close examination, an awareness on my part that merely reflected the keen, vivid, even passionate eloquence of the comments

I was hearing. As she pointed out many times, there is a decided limit to what we can know about someone who is not here among the living, and ready to tell us about himself or herself. Even a dream (Anna Freud reminded us) is a mere beginning of a personal statement, and indeed a dream can obscure and hide a particular psychological subject matter, even lead the listener or the reader down a blind alley. Despite her caution, she was willing to speculate as she tried to make limited sense of Simone Weil's short, strange, mystifying, extraordinary life—this so-called "Red Virgin" who espoused her very own kind of radical, egalitarian politics and who hungered so mightily, thirsted so long and hard for Jesus and all (in her mind) he stood for.

One afternoon, as we talked about Weil's stint as a factory worker (the Renault plant in Paris) and as a farmhand (in the south of France), Miss Freud seemed on the verge of exasperation, an emotion felt by many who have tried to account for the talents and foibles of a woman who could offer the world so very much (the essays that posthumously would be collected as *The Need for Roots, Waiting for God, Gravity and Grace*), yet also be so vehemently self-lacerating, even self-destructive. Simone Weil was determined *not* to be known as a radiant, luminous political and philosophical thinker and essayist, although she surely was all that. Her spiritual search, ultimately, became her consuming passion—a life itself lived in a certain sacrificial way, and ended in such a manner as to baffle and provoke those who still attend her. (She had contracted tuberculosis, and refused to eat amounts of food her doctors suggested—worried about eating more than the amount of food her French countrymen, then under Nazi rule, were allowed each day. If not a suicide, she certainly hastened her death along, forestalling any possibility of a cure or remission.) She died in 1942 at the age of thirty-four in a hospital outside London, only a few miles from Anna Freud's London residence.

"It would be a mistake for us," Miss Freud insisted once, as we talked about Weil's spiritual search, "to try to be psychologically specific with [respect to] her." Her silence then made me think we had reached the end of a road before we'd even begun to travel it. I replied that I was (obviously) in agreement—and didn't add what I was thinking: a bit odd—that expression "psychologically specific." I also was wondering why we couldn't have our guesses, so long as we didn't mistake them for facts, a big qualification, admittedly, given the uninhibited forays of some contemporary so-called "psychohistorians." Eventually, Miss Freud began to make a surmise or two, carefully identified as such, and in time we stumbled into a discussion of "idealism" that had to do (I fully understood only days later, as I went over what was said) with her own life as well as that of Weil, and other lives in which she had taken an interest.

Here, pulled together from different times in our conversation, are some of her thoughts on a subject always hard to discuss in an evenhanded and candid fashion: "It is only fair to ask ourselves why some people want to appear to other people as idealists. I don't like striking a sour note like that, but I had a woman in analysis who gave away a lot of money to someone who presented himself to her as a religious man, devoted to the poor. He told her he was running soup kitchens for poor people—and she believed him. She thought he was 'pure.' I wanted to know right away what she meant by 'pure.' She wasn't 'sure,' she told me. But I felt she *was* 'sure,' and so I persisted. She told me the man had described himself as a 'minister of God,' and said he wanted nothing for himself, only for others—and he looked as if he 'meant it.' I asked her, of course, how she knew. Oh, she was no fool! She looked at his dress, his attire, and observed his car—he dressed as if he was himself down-and-out, and his car was old and full of scratches, and kept breaking down, he told her. You have already guessed [she was reading my face, as I responded to her words, the tone of her voice, and the look on *her* face] that she had been badly tricked. But as we talked, she and I, we discovered a lot about her ideas, and their origins—and so, in a way, that man who pretended to be a good person helped both of us settle a few matters.

"The woman kept telling me that a person who is 'materialistic' can't be 'idealistic.' I knew what she meant, but I didn't say so—because I felt she had constructed a rather naive polarization, especially because she was otherwise rather shrewd about human affairs. After a while it was clear that for her an idealist is an ascetic, someone who denies himself good food, good clothing, a nice apartment or house, a car that is new and works well. When I asked her if the poor are automatically disqualified [from being regarded as idealists] because they don't *deny* themselves a comfortable life, they simply don't have one, she said yes, she didn't think poor people 'have the time' to be idealists. 'Or the money,' I added. She got my point, but didn't like it, I fear. She stopped talking for a while—and meanwhile, I found myself wondering what I thought myself! I remember that certain [psychoanalytic] colleagues came into my mind—people who were quite exceptional in their devotion to others; people who made the rest of us feel a bit selfish, in comparison. I wondered to myself, as I waited for my analysand to speak, whether idealists can sometimes be rather aggressively judgmental people who do their own kind of projection—and I don't mean the kind we were just talking about [altruistic surrender]. Perhaps some idealists *want* others to feel ashamed, or guilty, and try to make them feel that way. The idealist projects his desire to do wrong, or to live quite well, onto others, then acts in such a way as to accuse or shame those others. The basic struggle within that idealist would be that of greed or acquisitiveness, which is judged or confronted secondhand—I mean, through another person, who becomes the one who has to be made to feel worthless, or at a minimum, quite uncomfortable.

"But not all idealists are dishonest pretenders or imposters or overly idealistic so they can make others feel lacking or nervous or ashamed, and so make themselves feel 'superior,' when, in fact, they had been feeling 'inferior.' I have known some idealistic people who don't seem to have anyone else in mind. They are not being show-offs. They are not 'overly' idealistic—so that everyone compares himself to them and feels like a failure. (Narcissism can be a problem for idealists, too. They can be as self-preoccupied, as they do their idealistic good deeds, as others are in their materialistic ways.) I have known several nurses and social workers who haven't elevated them-selves to the status of idealists, and haven't written a single word about anything [she was comparing them with Simone Weil], and yet if one looks at what they quietly do, with no ostentation at all, and no inner torment that is shared with the world, then you can't help but wonder about how they accomplish it. I have never dared ask them about such things—they'd be surprised, I'm sure, to hear me call them idealists, and doubly surprised to hear me ask them questions intended to explore their motives. Their 'goodness' seems to be a natural part of their lives—and doesn't appear to be 'overdone,' or 'exhibitionistic,' or 'driven' in some fashion, so that they have to suffer, or get caught in some neurotic way as they do their work. Do you see what I mean?"

I did, even though she hadn't really told me much about the various individuals she had in mind. She seemed to be struggling for some kind of "normality" of idealism—a variant of it, she had made clear, but one that clearly appealed to her. The longer we pursued that variant, and we did so for over an hour, the more troubled and troubling seemed much of the extreme idealism we both had encountered in certain individuals (by dint of meeting them directly, or reading of them through their own words, or the words of others). I began to chafe at the very word *idealism,* feeling it to be yet another excessively categorical one; life's complexities and ambiguities and ironies and inconsistencies render ineffective such an effort at moral classification. Miss Freud, too, was growing impatient: "Perhaps we are climbing up the wrong tree! If by an idealist you mean someone whose behavior—some of it, some of the time—can be called idealistic, then there is no problem: there are any number [of idealists], and any number of reasons for them being as they are. But I think you and I are trying to find out about 'good,' 'being good'—who is, and why. I think we're trying to find out if there is such a thing as 'being good' that doesn't come from 'other sources'—[from] psychopathology or neurosis or what your friend Simone Weil called 'evil.' ''

I rose to the bait, defensively denied that I was all that "friendly" with Mlle. Weil, whereupon Anna Freud laughed and wondered what I was, with respect to Mlle. Weil, if not a "friend," given all the time I'd put in with her writing, and all the generally favorable writing about her I'd done. I felt myself getting embarrassed, flushed. She quickly resumed talking, as if to spare me further squirming; and also changed tack slightly, perhaps to avoid an impasse: "Maybe our problem [I was grateful for the 'our'] is that we are being too idealistic about idealism! A long time ago I wondered whether altruism can appear in someone 'on its own'—not as a result of drive-induced conflict, and the ego's attempt to mediate between the drives and the superego and the world or society. I still can't answer that question. If I was to guess, I'd say no [altruism doesn't emerge on its own]—there is always some conflict taking place 'behind the scene.' But I mentioned those nurses and social workers—perhaps some of them would prompt us not to say no so firmly, if we got to know them well.

"I have met some people—we're back to the nurses and social workers, and a few teachers, too—who make me think that I am being foolish, or I was quibbling when I talked [wrote] with doubt about a 'genuinely altruistic relation to one's fellow men' [in *The Ego and the Mechanisms of Defense*]. I am glad you mentioned it [the quote, which I read to her from a card I'd brought with me, emphasizing the word *genuinely*]. If you are being a bit puzzled by that word, I can understand why. Maybe I was more skeptical than I should have been—or too demanding. Simone Weil gave herself a terrible time—that woman of great goodness and high honor acted with herself as if she was not to be given an inch, not to be patted on the back and complimented warmly! It is as if she didn't really believe in her own goodness—or anyone else's, either, except for God's. Well, all right, a few ancient Greek philosophers, and the others you mention [her priest friend, and some dead French writers she mentioned in her letters and notebooks]; but mostly, she was skeptical of everyone, that is my impression, and I worry that we are following in her footsteps."

She was speaking for herself, I thought then—although it reminded me that I was, perhaps, more prone to idealization than she. But I also quickly reminded myself that she was no stranger to that inclination herself—given her relationship with her father, and Lou Andreas-Salomé, whom she so much admired, and perhaps others I didn't know whose lives she felt to be wholly worthwhile and impressive. Just as that train of thought crossed my mind, she picked up with a somewhat parallel line of discussion: "Perhaps the best we can do is decide whether we think someone's behavior is worthy on its merits—and be grateful for that outcome in the person's life. Sometimes we are tolerant of others; sometimes we are stern or tough on people. Adolescents can be very idealistic one minute, and the next, give no one the benefit of the doubt, no one—and that [latter way of thinking] isn't being very nice to people, isn't showing 'idealism,' which I think of as being kind to others, and understanding of them: being *forgiving*. Long ago [again, in *The Ego and the Mechanisms of Defense*] I described adolescents going back and forth, and I guess I myself still go back and forth on this subject! But I think I'm more and more inclined to look at what a person *does*, day after day, and if it's good work, and it's work done so that the people affected feel grateful and pleased, and not, as the saying goes, taken for a ride—then I'll try not to be stingy with the word *idealistic*!

"The problem poor Simone Weil had—she wasn't able to 'deliver' her idealism. I'm sure she wanted to do a lot for others, but she couldn't, because she was so caught in her own troubles and suffering. Yes, I agree, her writing has been 'a great gift' for others. But in her lifetime even that was not done much—I mean she kept her writing to herself, and she wanted to destroy it, isn't that right? I don't mean to write her off! You seem worried. But I'm suggesting that idealism—if we are to evaluate it psychologically—has to come to expression in deeds; if not, then we are left with the problem of judging the thoughts of people, and *there*, I'm afraid, we aren't going to accomplish much, that is, if we're going to be talking about people who have idealistic thoughts and those who don't. I've worked with some very difficult people who create a lot of trouble for others—you and I wouldn't want to call them idealistic—and yet as they lie on the couch and say what comes to mind, they can often sound very idealistic, plaintively so! They have tried so hard, they tell me, to do the right thing, the absolutely right thing, but the world has stepped in the way, and so they have not succeeded. Perhaps you and I feel they haven't *really* tried so hard—but you see, we are judging deeds, or the absence of deeds, when we say that, not words and intentions!"

As the discussion wound down, I began to realize that, its substance aside, a good deal of emotion had been generated. Here was an elderly woman, who had certainly seen a lot of life, traveled widely, heard the intimate details of countless lives, young and older, either confided directly to her or told through intermediaries at all those seminars and staff conferences—and she was far from jaded or indifferent to (or the equivalent, smugly sure of herself with respect to) a subject many others simply might not have an interest in taking on. Rather, she had allowed herself to get quite intently involved with the life of Simone Weil, as I related it to her, and she had put a great deal of herself into this difficult and perplexing question of goodness or idealism or altruism—what it is, how one evaluates it in others. She harkened back to her earlier life, to the important thinking and writing she had done in her twenties and thirties; and as she did so, I thought I saw more than a few years slipping off her, or maybe counting for less as she confronted this puzzle with animation and vitality.

As I watched her, I also looked back at her life, at what she had actually done with the time allotted her. She had never proclaimed herself a humanitarian; she had never become involved in important political causes; yet she displayed, at times, a strong sense of herself, and a willingness to take on others in the interests of ideas and professional practices she believed to be threatened. She could be fussy, insistent, exacting, and, some would say, intolerant of others, and all too sure of herself—hardly a "saintly" woman of the kind, at least, that a sentimental tradition would have us believe to be both desirable and a realistic possibility. Of course, as I well know from my time spent with Dorothy Day—a self-sacrificing, highly idealistic person, who was constantly trying to do good—to be good (gutsein) is also to be a human being who is, inevitably, flawed in various respects. Moreover, those who try hardest to implement their idealism, live out its tenets, are often those most strenuously tempted in quite other psychological and, yes, ethical directions—an insight the Hebrew prophets and Christian saints knew long before an obscure nineteenth-century neuropsychiatrist began to take seriously his dreams and those of his patients.

It is interesting, as a matter of fact, that Anna Freud's discussion of altruism hinges exclusively on defense mechanisms as they contend with drives—with no mention of conscience. True, the essay is part of a book on the ego and its contentious life with the ever demanding id; but the ego has another potential ally, and potential enemy, too, in the superego, and surely those for whom idealistic behavior is a real choice or desire must be those for whom the demands of conscience are a constant psychological presence. Freud and his followers could of course take for granted the power of conscience in a way many doctors today simply cannot—many children are now brought up to do as they please, to think all too exclusively of themselves, to "clarify" their values, rather than embrace as an utter bottom line the Ten Commandments, say, or the Sermon on the Mount.[4] Cultural relativism, moral relativism, and, with them, psychological consciousness turned into an almost religious principle—all of those social trends have had their impact on the strength of the superego. Put differently, if Freud were to come alive again today, he'd see a different kind of superego at work among patients—one hardly as powerfully compelling and authoritative as the "agency" he met in his office as he talked with men and women driven to the edge of despair, often enough, by the need to pass the superego's muster.

I raised the issue of conscience by reading words of Dorothy Day: "I often have felt I never had a real choice in the matter. I was tormented by my conscience, even when I was a young girl—I'd do something I knew was wrong (I'd say 'What the hell!') and I'd pay for doing it later: I'd be miserable! I remember, after my conversion, and I'd got our soup kitchen going, I'd say something wrong to someone—be insensitive or thoughtless—and I'd feel as if the world was crashing down on me. The only way I'd feel better was to confess my sins, and try to be better the next day. To tell you the truth, living as I do now—I've *enjoyed* it! People come here, and they look at me as if I'm a martyr, because I'm not living in a Park Avenue duplex. They don't understand who I was long before I came here. I was someone who was hounded by my conscience long before I had to 'flee the hound of heaven.' I'm still not totally convinced that I'll not end up in hell—some last-minute mistake on my part! (I'm only *half* fooling.)"

When I read the above to Miss Freud, she smiled. She contrasted the humor in the statement with some of Simone Weil's devastating self-arraignments, and correctly so—although Weil had her own moments of awareness and ironic distance on herself. A now apocryphal story, relayed to me by her brother André,[5] makes this clear: "My sister spent a long afternoon and evening with a learned Jesuit, discussing philosophy and theology. She could be formidable in arguments, and by the time the two were ready to stop, the Jesuit was seriously confused and troubled—maybe in danger of losing his faith! He asked my sister what *she* believed—since she'd been so effective at pulling out the rug from under him. She told him that she didn't know what she believed for sure, but she wondered whether God did have one big purpose in mind for her, at least so far—that she test the faith of Jesuits by having long and friendly and exhausting philosophical marathons with them! She told me that with a big smile on her face: it was a mix of pride and mock pride. She was serious— she knew how much she liked those arguments and how good she was at them; but she also knew how futile and useless they can be. She had a conscience that told her everything. Everyone emphasizes how serious she was—correctly; but she could be serious in many ways, and one way was to laugh at herself! She knew she was 'odd'— as people would say in our time; but she also knew she was the way she was, and it wasn't as if she could be different, or wanted to be different. It's hard to talk of these matters to people brought up in a different world, with different values!"

Both those women had their own empathic qualities, much summoned in their lives—the projective identifications that enable variants of "altruistic surrender." Certainly both struggled throughout their lives, one long, the other all too short, with the urgent energies of the instincts—which Dorothy Day knew through years of surrender to their demands, and Simone Weil knew in the way that a fierce protagonist, ready even to die in a fight, knows an enemy. Both those women, finally, were quite intent on waging this struggle—saw their lives as useful and worthwhile only if such a struggle *were* waged. As Anna Freud contemplated them, their battles with the world and themselves, she said something of herself: "These were highly conscientious individuals! I've said the obvious—but not everyone can see it, especially today, when even in many religious homes parents aren't likely to bring up children who are that demanding of themselves. There are still plenty of parents who shout and scream at their children—but these two women probably weren't shouted and screamed at. They were probably much loved—yet *conditionally*, by mothers and fathers who had high standards, and knew how to make those standards clear to their children. It is useless to speculate further [on their childhoods], but they both tell us the same thing: they were ill at ease if they didn't try to be 'good'—a definition that they obviously spent their lives trying to make.

"These were women who were given ideals long before they became idealistic. They spent years and years under the spell of those ideals, I suspect, before anyone knew what those ideals were, themselves included. I am thinking of their family life. You've told me that Dorothy Day told you that when she was a little girl she wondered about what she would be, and she worried about others who lacked the advantages her family offered her, and she asked questions constantly about the reasons certain wrongs kept being committed; and we know that Simone Weil as a child was also worried about 'justice,' and her own relative comforts as a doctor's child—that as a girl of five, even, during the First World War, she was cutting back on sugar, so that France's soldiers would have more, or as a gesture of solidarity with them. These are idealists or altruists who had been 'in training' for some time! My hunch is that if you had 'a series' of such people in analysis, you'd find more and more examples. I know both of them [Day and Weil] talked of conversions, but I wonder whether conversions come to those who haven't been seeking them and preparing for them many years in advance. To some extent, 'vocational guidance' begins well before courses in it are given to adolescents!"

I asked her, right then, whether such was the case with her. Did she have any glimmer, as a child, of what she might one day be? She replied, rather abstractly, that children explore a range of fantasies with respect to their future and that only in retrospect do we realize that certain of those fantasies had a larger significance—as prophetic harbingers of what a life would eventually turn out to be. After this predictable argument for a range of variability and possibility in each child, she pulled back, steering clear of a direct answer to my question, and veered in another direction: "I don't believe that idealists are only made in childhood—but I do believe that some people aren't ever going to have the kind of concerns, if not obsessions, that a Simone Weil or a Dorothy Day had, whereas others are at least potential candidates for their kind of life, such as the nurses and social workers we talked about, who give of themselves so unstintingly, to the point of exhaustion and depression at times. If we could somehow look at their childhood, year after year, we'd get some clues about how this kind of person develops—the mixture of moral and emotional and intellectual growth that takes place, and how all of that connects with certain teachers and friends, who may help give shape to a choice of profession or activity. But we don't have the ability to go back in time with people unless they choose to become psychoanalyzed—and my hunch is that many of them won't."

With that last comment, she was alluding to yet another challenging question—the lack of interest in psychoanalysis among many people who live in the tradition of Dorothy Day or Simone Weil. She herself had more than implied, on several occasions, that psychoanalytic candidates themselves are different today from what they once were, and that young social and political activists look elsewhere rather than inward psychoanalytically for their guidance and inspiration. In the past, she had reminded an audience, there were "dreamers"; now there are practical people, anxious to become more effective.

"We had a dream—as Dr. Martin Luther King would say." A pause, a lovely, brief smile, a slight, self-conscious shifting of her weight in her chair, as if to let me know that she did not intend to be self-important or presumptuous. "Our dream was the dream of psychoanalysis—all it had to offer: not only individuals, but schools and universities and hospitals and the courts and the 'reform schools' that worked with 'delinquents,' and social service agencies. We had many dreams then, many hopes—we had ideals we wanted to see realized. But as we all know, dreams come and go, and if some of what is in them becomes realized in the world (there are people who will fight to do that!), plenty of what is in them becomes forgotten. I worry now and then that not all that is forgotten is forgotten in the name of neurosis by our analysands!"

I so much wanted her to continue, but she told me with the look on her face that she would go no farther. This elderly woman, who had given her life to teachers and social workers and nurses, to children of war and concentration camps, to blind children and deeply troubled children, to children caught in divorce and familial antagonisms of all kinds, this quietly idealistic person who on occasion dared look candidly, unnervingly at the blind spots of the profession she loved—she had in her own fashion and in her own life said all that needed saying.

WRITER

The more I became interested in psychoanalysis . . . the more I saw it as a road to the same kind of broad and deep understanding of human nature that writers possess.
Anna Freud

ALL THROUGH HER LIFE, Anna Freud chose to present her ideas, no matter their complexity, or density, in a narrative that was lean and bare and utterly accessible. She used language like a window, through which any reader might see the world being evoked, characterized. This transparency, this clarity of presentation, is all the more remarkable considering the intricate, knotty ideas she is offering, and her ability to accomplish this feat in two languages, her native German, and her adopted English. Moreover, she spoke as she wrote, in the pared-down language of reserve.

"Jargon," William Carlos Williams once insisted, "tells you something, somewhere, is sure as hell wrong with the one using it. . . . How you say what you have to say tells you a lot about who you are. . . . Dammit, I've fallen asleep at the wheel plenty of times—and the snoring is what has gotten published!"

"I try to listen to my patients carefully," Williams said on another occasion, and explained that his reasons were both medical and literary: "Some patients are clear and direct—they make you marvel at what spoken English can be: here is what I have to say, and I'll not clutter it all up! Other patients are hard to understand, hard to figure. I get angry, trying to shake out the meaning from the words! Either way, I try to pay attention—a doctor's job to do it; any sentence can be the clue to the [medical] puzzle before you! When I'm back home and reading those journals and books, the clouds, the fog, the big-shot words and phrases, the bragging and boasting through language—I'm ready to go back to those poor uneducated folks, feinting and stabbing with words, saying it all or trying not to say it all: I'll take them, all of them, to Dr. So-and-so, Professor So-and-so, all these folks who don't want *just* to be understood—hell, that would be a disaster in their book to be caught saying what there is to say, and that's that!"

One of Anna Freud's moral and intellectual and literary master-pieces is *War and Children*—an account, as mentioned earlier, rendered in the most ordinary and restrained language, of the work she and her colleagues (Mrs. Burlingham and others) did with London children who had to go through the Blitz years, sometimes apart from their parents, in one of the nurseries she founded and ran. In a section entitled "Reaction to Evacuation," she writes: "The war acquires comparatively little significance for children so long as it only threatens their lives, disturbs their material comfort or cuts their food rations. It becomes enormously significant the moment it breaks up family life and uproots the first emotional attachments of the child within the family group." This stunning pair of sentences, the first with its ironic "only," the second with its low-key qualification that is meant to upset an entire order of things, spin around our minds, with their firm notions of what matters more and what matters less. Yet, like the good novelist, she uses language and storytelling in such a way that the reader does not feel dragged by the collar into some seminar room, there to be *told* the score, if not *told off*.

A few pages later, she reminds us that "possessiveness of the mother is, as we know, an important factor in the mother-child relationship." That last phrase is about as close as she will let herself come to the heavy clinical expressions she heard used all the time. She then spells out a history of that "relationship"—in such a way that the phrase "as we know" does indeed seem to apply to the reader—a casual, friendly sign telling the reader that the author is ready to assume a lot, is addressing an informed colleague rather than a psychological know-nothing. "The child starts its life as one part of the mother's body," she points out—no startling bit of news for anyone; but she has a reason for stating the obvious: "In so far as the feelings of the mother are concerned it remains just that for several years." This observation, like many she makes, has more to it than may first meet the eye—a way of pointing out how lasting and tight is this variant of human relatedness. "Harm to the child is resented by the mother as if it were harm done to herself"—and then a more general statement that is both obvious and true, yet by the nature of things commonly overlooked: "Every human being normally overestimates his own importance, his own personality and his own body." These days, as the concept of "narcissism" is endlessly discussed by certain psychoanalytic theorists, it is well to read that sentence over a few times, and take it to heart: if we are to understand what happens to mothers and their children, to anyone whose "narcissism" is under investigation, we had best have a look at ourselves, as well—lest, otherwise, we offer up a secular version of the saved and the damned. She now can get closer to the mothers and children whose behavior she has been observing: "This overestimation on the part of the mother also includes the child. This explains why an infant who is neither good-looking nor clever may still seem to possess both qualities in the eyes of its own mother. It is this primitive possessiveness and overestimation at the bottom of motherly love which makes it possible for mothers to stand the strain of work for their children without feeling abused. It is common knowledge that only love for children will prevent their continual demands, the continual noise caused by them, and the continual damage done by them from being considered a nuisance."

The "common knowledge" that she had in mind is, perhaps, not as widespread as she thinks among those of us who are or have been parents—because the very "overestimation" Miss Freud had earlier mentioned deprives us of the detachment required to observe ourselves candidly. In any case, she is not trying to turn unselfconscious parents, thoroughly entranced with their children, into lay therapists examining their parental "narcissism" and in the process becoming less and less enamored of their sons and daughters. She is, rather, trying to prepare her readers for what, in fact, the Blitz did—it caused some children to lose their parents, temporarily or permanently: to the army; to bombs that killed or injured; to factory work on behalf of the war that made it necessary for children to stay in day nurseries, or nurseries out in the country, safe from Messerschmitts and Stuka dive-bombers. Such children will no longer be under the care of mothers and fathers who think the world of them, who will give their all for them for the reasons just described. The jolt to the children is therefore overwhelming, as is the task for those, like Miss Freud, who had to act in loco parentis, but do so without the kind of family dynamics she has just described. "Foster mothers," she points out, "are expected to suffer children whom they neither love nor overestimate." She indicates what happens—some foster parents at heart remain "indifferent outsiders," and some try to become attached to their young charges as if they were their own, only to risk "losing" them with the appearance of their mothers.

All this psychological drama became part of the experience of war for the children Anna Freud worked with—and, of course, what she tried to understand and write about fifty years ago is again of great interest to us, as we ask what it means to send children to day-care centers and nursery schools and head-start programs. Here is Miss Freud, in 1975, reflecting on the unexpected contemporary relevance of her war work—and on the way she came to write about it years before: "I remember sitting with friends and trying to figure out how to set up those 'war nurseries.' We had experience with young children, of course—but we'd never worked with them in the midst of a war that had come right to them: bombs dropping, parents hurt or killed, danger everywhere. We didn't know what might be in store for us. We fell back on ourselves—that's what happened. We asked ourselves what we knew about children, 'the bottom line,' and we came up with those important needs that children everywhere have: attachment to a person, a parent; a climate of emotional stability around them—people who are solid and sensible; and an educational influence that is also solid, and is aimed at helping the child grow both intellectually and emotionally. Now, all that sounds uncontroversial. Who would oppose those aims? It's easier to say what you hope to accomplish than to do it. But it was important for us, first, to say it—and remember, fifty years ago what we said wasn't so much common knowledge or 'common sense' as it is today. When I hear someone say 'Oh, yes, naturally,' to something we say at Hampstead, I smile to myself: I'm glad, and I also feel a little pride—we've managed to expand the 'critical mass' of 'common sense'!

"When we got started, we wanted to make sure that we were all working for the same purposes. We had our informal meetings, and when a child was in trouble—well, we all huddled. We were being supported by good friends in England and in the States, and we wanted them to know how everything was going, so we wrote reports; and besides, we wanted to know *ourselves* how the children were getting along—what to make of some of the things they said and they did. We said to each other: let's learn from all this; let's not be too sure of ourselves.

"Writers will tell you—novelists and poets—that they learn from writing; that they don't know what they think, or they only half-know, until they sit down at a desk and find out by putting words down. In our [psychoanalytic] work, we say the same thing to our patients: speak what comes to mind, and you will learn. I suppose, in a way, the analyst serves a function to the analysand that the writer's ego serves—when he tries to give a shape to his thoughts and ideas as they come from all over his mind to the paper. Many patients are very good listeners of themselves, and so there is less work for us; many need our help more—to point out where they're going as they remember and talk. I remember one writer [whom she had in analysis] telling me that when he came to see me, his mind could 'figure things out,' whether I talked or not, but it couldn't seem to do so anyplace else! Then he told me he could only write in certain places, too. Somehow his 'juices' got going, he told me, if he was in the 'right place.' We explored that thoroughly, of course—but at the end of our explorations there was still a bit of the mystery of artistic productivity. I think my father was right—to 'surrender' to Dostoyevsky's creative genius. But one thing many writers tell us, and I am grateful to them: be prepared to pay attention to your words—they will help clear your head! I am sure some of us have words that aren't very clarifying—but we try. I often have ideas all 'organized' and ready to put into words, but when I actually write, I find there are other things waiting for my pen to put before me.

"I wrote about our wartime nurseries with my colleagues in mind, and with the parents of the children in mind, and with our generous friends in mind. I wrote because we were all excited by what the children were teaching us—the good adjustment some of them made, and the poor adjustment others made, and the reasons we were figuring out. We wanted to share our thoughts with others; and we first wanted to share our thoughts with ourselves. We were nurses and doctors and psychologists and teachers—and I must not forget, about twenty or twenty-five (I forget the exact number) were 'just' young women who helped us, and were trained by us to work with the children. As we taught them, we learned ourselves. We had to learn to speak clear, plain English to communicate with them—and it is always a blessing to be required to think hard about what you have to say, and then to have to say it in a way that others understand. Yes, by 'others' I meant those young women. We called them 'girls' then. Of course, before I wrote about our London war work, I had faced the challenge of talking with parents and teachers, back in Vienna, and that was a big challenge. Once August Aichhorn and I talked about it: how to speak so the 'average' reader will understand—I guess we meant someone who is well educated, but not a 'professional'; and I remember him smiling and saying: 'Your father did a pretty good job at that!'

"I think that if an idea is really important, it can be stated in such a way that a reader who hasn't learned our technical vocabulary can understand it quite well. After all, we're talking about the mind and we're talking about what we've learned from our patients—and ourselves—about the mind. If we can't put all of that in words that others can understand—then maybe we're having trouble ourselves understanding what is happening."

She stopped herself abruptly at that point, and looked down at the floor of the Yale University dormitory where we were sitting. In a moment, she was reconsidering, having some second thoughts: "It is a matter of taste, too—and the personality of the analyst, I should add that: some of us want to learn a new language, and we want to use it. Some of us have put a lot into being a 'professional,' and we don't want to let that slip through our fingers. The universities—even the secondary schools—teach young people all these 'languages'; and I don't mean French or German or Spanish. They teach technical talk—in psychology or sociology, in medicine and law, even in the arts, the humanities. If you are 'educated,' then you are supposed to use that kind of talk—and so you have learned to speak, before you know it, more languages than you ever thought. I remember in Vienna—we'd have our theoretical times, but we'd always sprinkle the discussions with 'examples,' some of them personal and some clinical. Even theoretical talk was conducted in ordinary language— the way my father wrote; though yes, it is true, even then some were more anxious to be 'clear,' and others to be fairly 'dense.' That is why I mentioned 'personality'—different people think in different ways, and choose to express themselves in different ways: this is not a new discovery! I know some analysts who consciously move back and forth—they might have an idea that comes to them as a result of their clinical work, or their research, and then they feel they should express it in technical terms, more so than the idea was, when it came to them. It is an open question whether they are doing that because they want to, or because they think they *should*.

"No, I wouldn't want it to be any one way—how we write or talk. We are a 'field' now—hundreds and hundreds of analysts all over the world, with journals and meetings every month, every week, it seems, somewhere. There should be room for different *styles* of expression, as well as the freedom of expression we must have: that is the fundamental rule within our [psychoanalytic] offices, that we talk openly and hon- estly—in our own manner. For me, writing is a way of examining my thinking, and getting it 'straight'—learning what I think, and then shar- ing it with colleagues and friends and anyone who should happen to read what I've written. I can understand that writing has different pur- poses (and meaning) for others—and that is fine."

She wanted to go no farther, and we soon moved on, to discuss the writing she did on adolescence, some of her finest, most touching, I have thought—and said as much to her. I first came across passages from her chapter "The Ego and the Id at Puberty," in *The Ego and the Mechanisms of Defense*, when I was in my last year of college. I had not read the book, knew little or nothing about psychiatry or psychoanal- ysis, but, as mentioned earlier, was doing volunteer work with "trou- bled young people," as they were called—elementary school children and high-schoolers who had academic and emotional "problems." Our job was to concentrate on the intellectual side of things, do tutoring. The person who ran the program, a college psychology teacher, gave us some reading, mostly articles rather than books, and excerpts from the latter, one of which was (I later learned) taken from a long paragraph of Anna Freud's book: "Adolescents are excessively egoistic, regarding themselves as the center of the universe and the sole object of interest, and yet at no other time in later life are they capable of so much self-sacrifice and devotion. They form the most passionate love relations, only to break them off as abruptly as they began them. On the one hand, they throw themselves enthusiastically into the life of the community and, on the other, they have an overpowering longing for solitude. They oscillate between blind submission to some self-chosen leader and defiant rebellion against any and every authority. They are selfish and materially minded and at the same time full of lofty idealism. They are ascetic but will suddenly plunge into instinctual indulgence of the most primitive character. At times their behavior to other people is rough and inconsiderate, yet they themselves are extremely touchy. Their moods veer between lighthearted optimism and the blackest pessimism. Sometimes they will work with indefatigable enthusiasm and at other times they are sluggish and apathetic."

I can still remember reading those words. It was such a contrast to my textbooks, the articles prescribed in social science courses. At twenty, in the last throes of the kind of delayed adolescence many 1950s college students experienced, I felt the tug of the mirror as I contemplated those apparent contradictions and ironies, so relentlessly stated. Our adviser, who worked both with us and with the students we tutored, told us that he thought that passage would help us deal with some of the tough moments we were bound to keep experiencing—the "back-and-forth side of adolescence," as he put it.

Years later, when I was learning to be a pediatrician, and then a child psychiatrist, that passage constantly came to mind, as I know it has for many men and women—teachers, nurses, doctors, welfare workers—who have tried to make sense of young people in all their bewildering complexity. My wife, Jane, a high-school English teacher, often gave that passage to her class—to accompany the reading they would do: *The Catcher in the Rye*, *The Adventures of Huckleberry Finn*, Willa Cather's *My Antonia*.[1] The point was not to use

Anna Freud as a guide to an understanding of a particular text, but to let an astute observer's evocation of youth be there for the students, a resource as they contemplated the fictional characters, and inevitably, through them, had a thought or two about themselves. I've also used that passage with students—to accompany their reading of, say, James Agee's *Morning Watch*, a novella meant to convey the subjectivity of early adolescence in a Tennessee Episcopal boarding school in the early years of this century, a story drawn, obviously, from Agee's own life. Agee's poignant tale, at once melancholy and lyrical, connects well with Miss Freud's account—it is almost as if she had read the novella, then wrote a commentary based on its rendering of the perplexing contrariness of adolescence. But why wouldn't these two, so unlike in their respective backgrounds, share a common vision of youth's opportunities and its tribulations? Each of them was one of the "odd" ones Miss Freud mentioned in her address at the New York Psychoanalytic Institute in 1966—original and idiosyncratic in the careers they eventually fashioned for themselves, and each was a very individual kind of writer.

Much of Agee's writing, such as *Let Us Now Praise Famous Men* and his last effort, the novel *A Death in the Family*, draws on his personal experience, which he transmuted into both documentary writing and fiction. He was often, with a certain disdain, called "an adolescent" (the word certainly has its pejorative aspect) or, even worse, "an eternal adolescent"—and the descriptions of him by those who knew him are not unlike the more general description of adolescence Miss Freud offered in her book. He was self-centered and self-preoccupied at certain times and in certain ways—yet he had a large heart for others, an enormous interest in how people lived who were brought up under different circumstances from those he had experienced as a child. He became passionately involved with a series of women—and somehow a number of those involvements ended rather suddenly. He was both gregarious and shy—an apparent inconsistency of character that psychiatrists occasionally know how to understand: the former quality, for instance, can be an attempt to master the latter, which, nevertheless, can linger in a person's life. He had his heroes and mentors, whom he adored, and he was hugely rebellious. He certainly had an eye out for money (needed to sustain a Manhattan cosmopolitan life), but he also had his share of the "lofty idealism" Miss Freud mentions—and, indeed, *Let Us Now Praise Famous Men* is a passionate, eloquent expression of that idealism. There was in him the monkish ascetic who figures in *Morning Watch*—at war with the highly sensual man who lived intensely and for the moment. Prickly and as sensitive as can be, he was also rude and even harsh with some people at certain times. He was, finally, a man of large mood swings, and with them came bouts of energetic enthusiasm for life and spells of apathy, even despondency. Most of all, there was in him the melancholy yearning—the constantly vivid seeking—that persisted into his twenties and thirties and forties; indeed, even at the end, when he was suffering from severe coronary heart disease (he died of a heart attack at forty-five), he was, for many who knew him, still the "poet with an adolescent's temperament," as his friend Walker Evans once spoke of him.

I mention this enormously gifted writer in connection with Anna Freud's description of adolescence because we once discussed the connection between her description of that period of life and the descriptions I'd heard of Agee, and the descriptions he himself wrote of youth in his poems ("Permit Me Voyage") as well as his fiction. She had not known of Agee, but by the next time I met her she had been able to read a few poems of his I sent her and some excerpts from *Morning Watch*.[2] She reminded me of a sentence in her book that immediately preceded the excerpt I have presented above: "In nonanalytic writings we find many striking descriptions of the changes which take place in character during these years, of the disturbances in the psychic equilibrium, and, above all, of the uncomprehensible and irreconcilable contradictions then apparent in the psychic life." She said that with respect to the "nonanalytic writings," she had in mind those of Goethe and Rilke, two poets whose work she knew well, each of them very much an influence on her.

We were thrust back into a discussion of adolescence, a conversation that for a while turned fairly technical, even theoretical—adolescence in psychoanalysis as a *second* period of heightened sexuality, whereas in the minds of many people, adolescence brings with it an *initial* sexuality. She indicated that were she writing today she might well stress the differences between adolescence in men and in women, a subject that she did not take up yet has had an evolving intellectual history in psychoanalysis, and of course, in the larger Western culture. She emphasized the "reciprocity" between "drive pressures" and "ego defenses"—the call to arms that can take place on the part of the ego when the sexual or aggressive side of a person becomes urgently felt. All of that was no big news to either of us, but was a way to discuss the tightrope that so many young men and women must walk, as they awaken to the body's power and the mind's (and heart's) interests, while at the same time taking notice of their situation in a community, in a certain country, and the pressures of family and class and culture and society bearing down on them.

Suddenly, I felt my mind wandering—perhaps because we seemed to be going through a slightly didactic and dull recitation of apparently uncontestable psychoanalytic pieties. I found myself wanting to change the subject, lest my eyelids droop, and I end up having to stifle a yawn. Miss Freud, however, had already noticed, and suggested a cup of coffee. As I sipped it, I heard myself asking her if she had been complimented over the years for the passage in her book that I quoted above. She nodded shyly, but did not speak. I asked her if any particular part of that book was a favorite of hers. She shook her head. By then, I realized that she wasn't quite sure what I was trying to say, and so had fallen back on the psychoanalyst's prerogative of silence, while at the same time trying to be reasonably attentive and polite to a guest. Before our exchange sputtered to a halt, she took charge: "I remember writing that passage you mentioned. I don't think it's as 'fine' as you say, but I do remember the time and place of its composition—more than I can say for other writing I've done. I *was* trying hard; I wanted to get across a mood, a feeling of what adolescence is, the ups and downs, the zig and zag! I was closer to it then, and I remembered it vividly: for a while I thought it would never end. When I decided to teach, a friend asked me which [age] children I'd like to be with. I said 'young ones' right away! Of course, I was myself then an adolescent, though we didn't use that word, and we weren't as self-conscious then as we are now [about psychology and matters such as adolescence]. For a long time, I had to argue with some of my colleagues—that we not be in a rush to do analysis with adolescents. It is such a time of change. It is a time of ferment, and that is what I tried to say—that everything is going very fast then, and you can't be sure, when you talk with a young person, whether what you hear and see will last ten minutes or half a day, and be replaced by its opposite. So, it's best to hold on and wait. I wanted to say that even then. I was aware that we were being asked to see people of all ages, and I recall saying to myself: *not* all ages! With elderly people, there is always the question of whether it is worth it—the limited time an older person may have left. With young children, we have tried to establish specific conditions for which an analysis is recommended. With adolescents—I always want to consider whether what I see today will be present a few weeks or months later."

We were interrupted by a phone call, but afterward she was quick to resume, although on a slightly different note. "Before we put this subject to rest, let me tell you that I was most personal in those two chapters, obviously [chapters on altruistic surrender and on adolescence], and perhaps that is why the writing is different. I certainly knew as I wrote those chapters that I was not constructing theory; I was trying to describe part of 'life'—as writers try to do. I don't think of myself as a writer; but I write. Sometimes even someone who isn't a gifted writer tries to do the best possible job—and can come up with a few sentences that stand out. At such moments, I'm sure, the person's experience is being tapped—and so the composition, the paragraphs being written, take on a great deal more significance than otherwise. I know I hoped that those chapters would stay in the minds of those who read them. They stayed in my own mind— because I put a lot of energy into writing them, and they meant a lot to me: I tried hard to write well. Sometimes it is a greater effort to write than other times—perhaps because the 'material' or the 'subject' is difficult, or because you are really giving your 'all' to what you are writing. I think it was *that* [the latter]—when I was writing those two chapters. When I write in that way, I will look at a Rilke book, and realize what a distance separates him and the rest of us."

She read Rilke's poetry all her life, and her modesty with respect to him and other poets and novelists is both understandable and appropriate. On a different occasion, she had once said to me: "I loved his poetry; I still do. If I had gone to university, I would have studied literature, I think. If I could have written *good* poetry, I'd have become a poet. The more I became interested in psychoanalysis, though, the more I saw it as a road to the same kind of broad and deep understanding of human nature that writers possess. My father had taken the Greek playwrights seriously, and look what it meant for all of us."

Anna Freud's poetry—to draw upon Yeats's distinction—was that of the life: the extraordinary service she so unstintingly rendered to children, to teachers, to a profession, although her private life may well have fallen short of the high ideal Yeats had in mind as an alternative to literary distinction. One of Anna Freud's favorite Rilke poems is called "The Poet," and may give a clue about her attitude toward her substantial accomplishments in both her working life and her private life: "I have no beloved or place for home, / no circle where I am center. / The things to which I give myself / grow rich— while I'm impoverished." Although not the center of one primary circle, she was at the center of many circles, and although loneliness may have visited her often in her life, she was an outgoing person with a solid and lasting family life—a host of people with her and attentive to her in various ways until the very end.

Anna Freud's considerable power as an essayist enhances her success within her profession. She had her father's gift for going public, as it were—with plain but strong and lucid prose that could command the interest of a broad range of educated readers, and stay with them for a long time afterward. While she was a tough, tenaciously persistent advocate of her psychoanalytic views with her colleagues, she could also go before the lay public in print and in lectures with a graceful modesty that was both winning and intriguing for its touchingly intimate expression: a writer who knew how to "connect," as in E. M. Forster's often mentioned imperative. "We are all aware that teachers are still very suspicious and doubtful of psychoanalysis," she tells her audience of teachers and parents—a boldly disarming start of her first lecture (on "Infants, Amnesia and the Oedipus Complex"). She continues in that same vein: "When, therefore, in spite of this, you as teachers working at the day-care centers of the city of Vienna decided to have a short course of lectures from me, you must somehow or other have received the impression that a closer acquaintance with this new discipline might be able to afford you some help in your difficult work. After you have listened to the four lectures, you will be able to decide whether you were mistaken in your expectation, or whether I have been able to fulfill at least some of your hopes."

Her modesty also kept the audience in mind: "In one particular direction I have certainly nothing new to offer you. I should fail in my object if I attempted to tell you anything about the behavior of schoolchildren or day-care children, since you are in this respect in the more advantageous position. An immense amount of material passes through your hands in your daily work, and demonstrates very clearly the whole range of the phenomena before you: from the physically and mentally retarded children, the obstinate, cowed, lying, and ill-treated children, to the brutal, aggressive, and delinquent ones. I prefer not to attempt to give you a complete list, for whatever I do you might well point out to me a large number of omissions."

Phrases such as "somehow or other," "at least some," and "might" have a certain relaxed tentativeness at odds with the high-handed self-importance of the experts, from many disciplines, who are wont to address teachers and parents. Moreover, she is frank to acknowledge what she doesn't know, or can't do as well as others. She describes with eloquence the millions of parents and thousands of teachers who struggle (often against great odds) to comprehend and nurture and educate their children, and in general help them move along the years toward those elusive goals of "happiness," of "maturity," of "adulthood." This is a speaker and writer who wants a respect that is earned; who not only has taken the measure of the skepticism her listeners or readers may feel, but may well share some of it herself: "We must not demand too much from one another," she says at the beginning of her last lecture—as if to remind herself and anyone listening that messianic pronouncements are not what she will offer.

Even her very first, so-called "technical lectures," directed at her fellow analysts in 1926, when she was just over thirty (*The Psychoanalytical Treatment of Children*), were peppered with metaphors, with asides at once polite but pointed—a skilled writer with a voice all her own, and one she was not afraid to use both forcefully and calmly. "The child is not," she insists, "like the adult, ready to produce a new edition of its love relationships, because as one might say, the old edition is not yet exhausted." Here she is taking direct issue with Melanie Klein—which she proceeds to do further: "Let us in this connection reconsider Mrs. Klein's method. She maintains that when a child evinces hostility towards her in the first visit, repulsing or even beginning to strike her, one may see in that a proof of the child's ambivalent attitude toward its mother. The hostile components of this ambivalence are merely displaced onto the analyst. But I believe the truth of the matter is different. The more tenderly a little child is attached to its own mother, the fewer friendly impulses it has toward strangers. We see this most clearly with the baby, who shows an anxious rejection towards everyone other than its mother or nurse. Indeed the converse obtains. It is especially with children who are accustomed to little loving treatment at home, and are not used to showing or receiving any strong affection, that a positive relationship is often most quickly established. They obtain from the analyst what they have up to now expected in vain from the original love objects."

Whether one sides with Mrs. Klein or Miss Freud, the latter has, one must acknowledge, the strength of her everyday observations—a response at once clinical and colloquial to didactic assertions. The reader is asked to check out abstract knowledge with a writer's first-hand acquaintance with children in all their variety. It is as if a social scientist is being confronted by a storyteller—and before an audience where such a confrontation would not necessarily get judged in favor of the storyteller. To be sure, Mrs. Klein's argument is not presented in full; rather, it is summarily given, only to be refuted. But the manner of refutation carries with it a second argument, implied rather than stated: it will not do to hand down formulations in a high-handed, unqualified manner; we ought test all that is told us through "direct observation," a phrase readers of Anna Freud would encounter again and again in her writing. She set up a contrast of the aloof theorist and the analyst *engagée*: the former presumably is not looking actively at what takes place in the street, the home, the school, whereas the latter is looking face-to-face at social and psychological reality. This approach risks the smugness of deliberate ordinariness, of false humility, a match, perhaps, for the temptation on the other side of parochial arrogance, if not blindness to the actual evidence.

Anna Freud argued earnestly with Melanie Klein on the matter of transference in analytic work with children. Mrs. Klein believed that a full-fledged transference develops with children, if in a somewhat different manner and at a different pace from that with adults. Anna Freud disagreed. As she develops her side of the controversy, she writes with power and beauty about the phenomenon of transference, at a time when its occurrence was known, but its nature had not been fully described: "We know how we bear ourselves in the analysis of adults for this purpose [to elicit transference responses]. We remain impersonal and shadowy, a blank-page on which the patient can inscribe his transference-fantasies, somewhat after the way in which at the cinema a picture is thrown on an empty screen. We avoid either issuing prohibitions or allowing gratifications. If in spite of this we seem to the patient forbidding or encouraging, it is easy to make it clear to him that he has brought the material for this impression from his own past."

Years later, the simile she develops would seem trite—at the time, however, the middle 1920s, a psychoanalyst with a writer's cast of mind was trying to explain by analogy what happens in one sphere of life (adulthood), only to show what does not happen in another sphere (childhood): "But the children's analyst must be anything but a shadow. We have already remarked that he is a person of interest to the child, endowed with all sorts of interesting and attractive qualities [which the boy or girl gets to know, she pointed out earlier, in the course of playing games with the analyst, sitting and drawing and painting with him or her]. The educational implications which, as you will hear, are involved in the analysis, result in the child knowing very well just what seems to the analyst desirable or undesirable, and what he sanctions or disapproves of. And such a well-defined and in many respects novel personality is unfortunately a bad transference-object, of little use when it comes to interpreting the transference. The difficulty here is, as though, to use our former illustration, the screen on which a film was to be projected already bore another picture. The more elaborate and brightly colored it is, the more will it tend to efface the outlines of what is superimposed."

Miss Freud goes on to point out that those children do not keep their analytic experience separate from the rest of their lives in ways that grown-ups can manage to do: bringing all the details of the day to the analyst, who is deliberately not in touch with the patient's relatives or colleagues the way the child analyst has to be with parents and teachers of a child—because they are the ones who bring the child to the office, who complain about the neurotic behavior in the home or classroom that has prompted a try at analysis in the first place. Miss Freud describes this latter kind of relationship in the following manner: "For these reasons [indicated in her simile of the brightly colored screen], the child forms no transference neurosis. In spite of all its positive and negative impulses towards the analyst it continues to display its abnormal reactions where they were displayed before—in the home circle. Because of this the children's analyst is obliged to take into account not only what happens under his own eye but also what occurs in the real scene of the neurotic reactions, i.e., the child's home. Here we come to an infinity of practical technical difficulties in the analysis of children, which I only lay broadly before you without going into actual detail. Working from this standpoint we are dependent upon a permanent news-service about the child, we must know the people in its environment and be sure to some extent of what their reactions to the child are. In the ideal case, we share our work with the persons who are actually bringing up the child; just as we share with them the child's affection or hostility."

Whether it be the "cinema screen" or the "news-service," she is anxious to liven up her presentations, call upon figures of speech, tell clinical stories; and always, even in the sections where she wages a straightforward argument, she is anxious to use the language of everyday discourse—at times an almost uncanny performance: plain talk put in the service of a fairly intricate line of thinking. A glance at articles in psychoanalytic journals, or at psychoanalytic books, readily reveals the difference between Anna Freud the writer and the others with whom she shares a profession and a technical vocabulary. Several times I made the above point to her, hoping to elicit some explicit explanation or rationale, if not justification, for her way of developing thoughts and ideas in her essays, in her public lectures (which she wrote in advance), prefaces, forewords written for the books of others, not to mention in her own books and her sometimes long and informative letters. She seemed loath to say much—or she would shrug her shoulders, as if to say what many writers say: this is me; this is the way I write, for reasons I don't really know and, maybe, don't care to know!

Once, and in connection with the above quoted paragraphs from her earliest writing, she did talk about her writing: "I fear I have never been best at 'thinking' alone; I always want—I *need*—to connect an idea I have to something that is happening in the world. I was a teacher, remember—of young children. I loved the challenge: to make things clear to them. Several times in addresses at psychoanalytic institutes or congresses I have confessed: What you were early in your career, you'll probably find a way of being again. That's the way it's been for me, at least. When I write, I think the teacher in me comes out: I'm all ready to catch the attention of those I want to reach—ready to do that by the way I present the material to them. Before I write a word down, I talk to myself. I want to know what I'm trying to say—and what I'm trying to (hope to) accomplish by what I'm going to say. No, I don't have anyone's writing in mind as I write. What I have in mind is—well, my question to myself: what is the exact essence of what you're going to write, a sort of bottom-line summary. A précis. When I know that, I can start getting to my destination, step by step. I start at one point, and hope to get to another. I try not to get lost; if J do, imagine what will happen to the reader. If I find myself wandering, or confused by my own words, then I don't assume the reader is going to rescue me. I go back to what seems clear and well defined, and see if I can try another road from there to here.

"A friend of mine—he taught with me—told me a long, long time ago that you should never get too attached to your own pet phrases and your own ways of getting to the children, or else they'll get bored, or they'll become impatient: oh, we've heard this again and again—so, why doesn't she spice things up, and try something new, so we can learn new things! There is plenty to say for routines, and a little boredom never hurt anyone: sometimes that's the way life is. You can't always have 'excitement'! But there are those 'ruts' that our teenagers worry about falling into, and it can happen, and children are often quick to spot it—and readers, too. I am not meaning to compare readers to children—though if some of us, reading, could be as witty and open to things as some children can be while reading (or not reading), that would not be so bad for us. In any event, you asked about my writing, and that is about all I know to say."

As she talked I noticed her face, wide awake, full of activity, her eyes mobile one minute, fixed and piercing the next, a broad smile on occasion, followed by an intent, furrowed brow. I also noticed her hands, now resting on the arms of an ample chair, now roused to action, and once outstretched, both of them, as she talked about her struggle to go from "there to here." Suddenly, I imagined a field, with two posts, a pathway in between, and Anna Freud taking someone's hand, firmly but gently, leading him, leading her, from "there" to "here." This series of people, who, in their variety, as it is put in the *Book of Common Prayer*, are of "all sorts and conditions," constitute her readership, waiting to be edified, or as Walker Percy put it "being handed along, then handing another along."[3]

I think the teacher in her has enabled the writer in her not only to win the attention of her readers, but to hold onto it—so that she can gradually increase the pressure, as it were, in order to get across more and more thoughts, or qualifications of thoughts. She is a master, in that regard, of the semicolon—one phrase added onto the other, until the reader is noting the burden, but also fascinated by the journey, and anxious to see where it leads, to what home territory. In a foreword to *Lest We Forget* by Muriel Gardiner (a psychoanalyst who, while living in Vienna, helped members of the German resistance to the Nazis escape, or to carry their secrets in and out of the country, and the model for Lillian Hellman's story "Julia"), Miss Freud more than proves equal to a high moral occasion—eloquently salutes an old friend whose brave witness, whose courageous day-to-day activities on behalf of others (she who was an American and wealthy, and Aryan, and need have risked nothing for no one), amounted to a remarkable kind of altruism. In one paragraph the use of those semicolons illustrates what a writer intent on making a point, building on it, adding beam after beam of strength to it, can end up doing on behalf of readers—transport them across the barriers of time and place right to the momentous occasion: "Those of us who, at this period, were forced to share the experience of living sleepless in bed in the early morning hours, waiting for the dreaded knock of the Gestapo at our door, find it difficult or even impossible to imagine that anybody could voluntarily choose to face the same anxieties. Every hidden socialist or Jew searched for and found in Muriel Gardiner's apartment would have meant the end, not only for him but also for her; every mad dash to the border escorting refugees could have ended in disaster. Moreover, this was not all. There were all the other accompaniments of an underground existence: the inevitable failures; the disappearances which placed people beyond the possibility of help; the endlessly drawn-out waiting periods when nothing happened; the discomforts and deprivations of daily life; the frightening possibility of being duped by imposters and the humiliating experience of being taken for an imposter herself."

As a writer of a foreword, she knows what her job is, and quite ably accomplishes it. The ideas flow, the sentence builds, a wealth of information is conveyed in a relatively short space, and the reader is introduced to an important story. The drama of an extraordinary time and an extraordinary person doing extraordinary deeds is not lost, buried in inadequate, tumbling prose, but rather given the spirited, alert, energetic narrative introduction it warrants.

Some of the passages in *Normality and Pathology in Childhood* are equally skilled, amounting in their sum to a trenchant and sweeping kind of social and cultural history, for instance in the passages that begin with "when," which I quote in the essay "The Achievement of Anna Freud," to be found in the appendix. At moments in that book she is surveying an entire century of Western bourgeois life—a compact version of the long glance Phillipe Ariès gave us in *Centuries of Childhood*.⁴ A child analyst coming to the end of her life, whose impact on thousands and thousands of parents and children has been enormous, decides to stand back and look at all the dreams that were entertained, all the frustrations and disappointments experienced, in the name of a new "science," a new way for human beings to be with one another, to learn from one another. She is certainly not nihilistic or in despair as she writes, but there is a cumulative skeptical power to those sentences, one like the next in structure—a buildup to an important caveat worthy of George Eliot or Chekhov or Tolstoy: life's inevitably limited nature won't yield to the naive, utopian fantasies and expectations of any of us, regardless of education and background. Even people relentlessly willing and able (that is, who have the time and money as well as the desire) to look inward at great length and with painful scrutiny will not thereby earn automatic entrance to the city of heaven.

In the end, Anna Freud was telling her readers—perhaps after learning the lesson herself, a lesson for each of us to learn in our own particular way—we are left with our humanity: some of its flaws, perhaps, taken away; some of its edges, perhaps, softened; but still with the distinct limitations built into us by our very fate. We are born and we will die. We have dreams, and they are dashed by time, by accidents and incidents, by chance and circumstance. We have good times, but even the luckiest and most gifted of us eventually know bad times. Hope may lead us, as it did Anna Freud, to try to change things for the better. But ours is a guarded hope, a cautionary hope, a hope touched by the melancholy wisdom of all those prophetic figures of ancient Israel and Greece; by all those novelists and playwrights and poets whom Sigmund Freud admired so very much, and Anna Freud after him; it is a hope given shape and qualification by those two, by the father's brooding doubts as he got ready to say goodbye at the end of Auden's "low dishonest decade," and the daughter's apprehensions and reservations as she, too, began to take her leave in the 1970s and early 1980s. A lonely sadness not unlike the kind Rilke evokes in "The Poet" came upon Anna Freud at the end, as happens to so many of us when leave-taking approaches; but she had much to give us, and through her lively, spirited writing, much to leave us: a legacy whose worth will stand the test of time the way that good stories, true to life's nature and complexity, manage to do.

The following essay, mentioned earlier in this book, was written toward the end of 1965, and published in early 1966 in The Massachusetts Review. *I had just come back from years of living in the South, working with black and white children going through school desegregation, and with youths involved in the sit-in movement. Writing the essay was a way of helping me make sense of my research by appeal to the work of someone whose clear vision had long been of help. When Miss Freud read it, she responded with a letter that has meant a lot to me over the years. It is reprinted following the essay. This exchange lead to many others, in letters, meetings, long conversations. I published another essay about her in* The New Yorker, *in 1972, and later, when we met, she elaborated with good humor on my "too good opinion" of her!*

As an additional facet of this portrait, I offer one of her longer letters, a response to a book I wrote that I dedicated to her. I believe that letter tells a lot about her, about where she found the reward in the "very slow, very individual work" that she accomplished over a long and productive life; and about the elation she could feel at the thought that for children "there are ways out, after all."

I also offer two other letters that I feel are of distinct interest—statements that reveal her life-long idealism, as it could be touched, awakened. When she suggests that she ought, perhaps, to have given herself over to an involvement in the world's social and economic and political struggles (as opposed to the clinical work she pursued all her life), she is not, really, outlining an either/or choice, but giving expression, I believe, to what George Eliot would call her "ardent" nature—an unashamedly direct and passionate response to the world's injustices. These caught her attention, as they can sometimes for all of us catch up with us morally, and give us an introspective pause.

When I showed those letters to Erik Erikson, he was himself given a bit of a pause. During a long walk, he pointed out what it meant for Anna Freud to indicate any second thoughts, however momentary, with respect to her life-long work. For her to write down these thoughts was an even more significant gesture. He saw these letters as indirect acknowledgement on her part of the enormous influence exerted by "society" on "childhood," an influence he had certainly stressed, and not always with the support of his psychoanalytical colleagues and former teachers, including Anna Freud. He was, therefore, interested indeed in that letter, pleased with its tone, its implications, although at the same time he, too, had no wish to use this expression of a lively social conscience as a means of undermining the importance of everyday work with patients, an effort that has its own important dignity and worth.

THE ACHIEVEMENT OF ANNA FREUD

In the Newsletter for June, 1965, of the American Psychiatric Association, a brief announcement was made of Anna Freud's 70th birthday, coming at the end of the year. It seems only a short while ago that she was seen beside her aged father, two Viennese exiles lucky to be standing in an English garden after the Anschluss of 1938. The old man had been ailing for a long time, but showed not a sign of it in the last photographs; his set face and piercing eyes hinted at the determination and fire in him to the last. He wrote until the end of his 83 years, starting the *Outline of Psychoanalysis* shortly after arriving in London and only fourteen months before his death—it was to be published posthumously—a brilliant, clear, up-to-date account of the heart of psychoanalytic work.

In his last years his daughter Anna did more than appear with him, holding his arm tactfully, smiling faintly while he looked ever serious (and defiant in the pain he constantly suffered). By 1926, at the age of thirty-one, she was a psychoanalyst specializing in child analysis. That year she gave a series of lectures, later published as *The Psychoanalytical Treatment of Children*, on the special requirements of therapeutic work with young boys and girls: earning their confidence, communicating with them in the absence of words, developing ways to explain their troubles to them, ensuring that what is won in treatment is not lost in the home or school. The following year, at the Tenth International Psychoanalytic Congress, held in Innsbruck, she read a paper rich in its theoretical discussion of the difference between analyzing adults and children. Adults know their suffering, and have developed characteristic styles of dealing with the various demands of the world, the devil, and the flesh. In contrast, children quite often have no idea that they are ill, want no help from an analyst, and are in the midst of growth, so that rather than presenting the fait accompli—that is, the neurosis which represents a "solution" to the various and conflicting demands of the mind—the child offers the challenge of his ongoing development (the symptom may go away in time anyway).

Moreover, the child's mind is much more public property than the adult's. What troubles the child is shared with his family, his teachers, and school-chums. That is to say, the child is going through the educational process of acquiring a "personality" (and, alas, neurosis) while the adult has likely forgotten all the trials—at home or outside—that contributed to the later pain or tension bringing him to analysis. Put differently, the adult is troubled but usually can't "remember" the exact sequence of events that are responsible for the trouble. The child often will describe quite readily what is happening about him, but may well not consider himself suffering or in danger—it is his parents or teachers who are concerned. In any event, he has a problem with the future as well as the past, since he must not only be helped to realize how he feels, but helped to grow, to think, feel, and act coherently and sensibly.

The differences between psychoanalysis of children and adults continued to occupy Anna Freud's thoughts in the next decade. In 1929 she gave a remarkable series of lectures to the Hort teachers in Vienna, later published as *Psychoanalysis for Teachers and Parents*. She was as much concerned with whom she spoke as with what she said. An account of the Hort says that it is ". . . a kind of kindergarten, but particularly for children from six to fourteen years of age. The kindergarten itself takes only children up to six years or until school age. The children who come to the Hort are the children of parents who go out to work. They come daily and return to their parents in the evening. Here, in the Hort, they prepare their school homework, occupy themselves with light work or communal games, and are taken for outings by Hort workers."

The contents of this volume have had a sad time of it over the past thirty years. They have been widely and compulsively acknowledged yet by no means thoroughly understood. As a result while Miss Freud's discussion of the Oedipus complex and the latency period in child development may seem quaintly old-fashioned, it is doubtful whether even now many readers truly realize the complicated nature of her final comments on the problems frequently met up with in raising children and for that matter teaching them in school. What Anna Freud said, she said firmly: no educational technique can really fill in for the absence of a solid, considerate relationship between parents and children; the character of the future citizen is established in his first years, the mother being the first lawgiver; if parent or teacher does not appreciate the essentially understandable purposes and activities of the child they may both regulate and dominate him, but pay the price of his later illness or inadequacy.

While, again, none of that sounds very surprising today, the clinical cases used by the author to fasten down her abstractions are still as unquieting and pedagogically challenging as they ever were. One example after another tells parents and teacher alike not to mistake even psychoanalytic knowledge for the kind of emotional understanding and relationship it means to facilitate (still too subtle a point for many well-educated parents or partisans of this or that "theory" of education). The pain and conflict inevitable in all nurseries and classrooms are scrupulously illustrated, in the hope that no one will walk away with a fixed set of principles, or ultimately worthless expectations, but rather a general willingness to see that the child's behavior *makes sense*. Once that is accomplished the child may rather flexibly be severely scolded or permitted liberty, depending upon the particular transgression at issue. (It is as if right then she foresaw how, in the name of psychoanalysis, rigid indulgence would soon replace automatic harshness as the ruling order of the day.)

Her next labor was an enormously influential one, *The Ego and the Mechanisms of Defense*, published in 1937 by Leonard and Virginia Woolf at the Hogarth Press. It is safe to say that this book marked the most significant turn in psychoanalysis since the heightening of her father's interest in ego psychology twenty-five years earlier. In a real sense this one study conclusively divides two periods of psychoanalysis. At the beginning Freud saw and charted the instinctual segment of the unconscious, and psychoanalytic theory was all taken up with the energy (libido) of the drives and their many vicissitudes. Brill has described these pioneer concerns of Freud and his followers: "We made no scruples, for instance, of asking a man at table why he did not use his spoon in the proper way, or why he did such and such a thing in such and such a manner. . . . We had to explain why we whistled or hummed some particular tune or why we made some slip in talking or some mistake in writing. But we were glad to do this for no other reason than to learn to face 'the truth.' " By "truth" was meant the drive-bound promptings of the unconscious. Some still think so, not only in psychoanalysis but contemporary life in general, where uncovering the drives "deep down" in a person's mind is equated with "really" knowing him. Yet, how he comes to terms—both consciously and unconsciously—with those drives in his mind may well be the larger and more significant truth. In any event, it is the truth that eventually Freud, open-minded and willing to look hard at his own theories, came to seek toward the end of his life.

The workings of the ego, like those of the id, are in large measure unconscious. That is, not only what we think and dream may elude us, but how our minds make a habit of coping with those thoughts and dreams. Anxiety, fear, and a whole range of symptoms come from the encounter of instincts with ego. Ego includes conscience (super-ego); and ego—as Anna Freud demonstrates—is no mere "window" between the impelling drives and the outside world, the kind of word for which "awareness" could be exchanged. The ego has a history. It is what has been learned at home and at school. It is the mind's intellect and skills, its social agent, its eyes and ears. The ego is an intricate style of being, a storehouse of implicit assumptions whose supplies keep us going, not to mention determining the land and distance we choose to travel. If in both nightmares and daydreams we are all mad, all wild and sometimes odd lovers, all murderers and anarchists, then what makes us different is our native gifts, our upbringing, the time and place in which we live, and the manner we have somehow "chosen" (who can ever really settle the problem of free will?) to deal with ourselves.

The ways of the ego are numerous. One person habitually attributes the sources of his problems to others; another is exceedingly deft at converting sadness into joy, or vice versa. I may become fatigued and ache in my head or my stomach, while my neighbor turns *his* tension into a frenzy of rituals. Pride may mask despair, and shyness may call upon arrogance to give it expression. At the heart of these attitudes and postures, these "characteristics," and their attendant states of feeling, there are certain very specific irreducible "mechanisms" that deal with the instincts or drives. The activity of these mechanisms is as endless as the pressures the drives constantly exert. The imagery is either hydraulic or cloak and evil. Thus drives (and the behavior they urge) can be denied and pushed down whence they come; or they can be changed into their apparent opposites, or attributed elsewhere, to other people. They can be disengaged from their energy, the intellect thus presented with a bonus to use "thoughtfully," or they can be rendered weak by turning their original energy into complicated, hardworking so-called obsessions and compulsions that bind so relentlessly one or another aim. More ominously, drives can be otherwise handled, by being permitted to overwhelm the literally defenseless person's mind (psychosis) or compel his retreat (regression) into himself, his past, his very old ways of getting along.

There are names for all this life that goes on in the mind, and Miss Freud supplies them, but not without touching illustrations that enliven the meaning. Talking of the capacity adolescents have for "intellectualization" she observes the "wide and unfettered sweep of their thought . . . the degree of empathy and understanding [they show]." She goes on to observe that the adolescent's "empathy into the mental processes of other people does not prevent him from displaying the most outrageous lack of consideration towards those nearest him. His lofty view of love and the obligations of a lover does not mitigate the infidelity and callousness of which he is repeatedly guilty in his various love affairs."

She saw it her task to demonstrate the consistency of our inconsistencies and to do so she did not shirk facing what are, finally, life's ironies. In the last pages of the book, when the ego lies before us in all its critical significance to our lives (and diagnostic importance to the psychoanalyst), we find comments like this: "In periods of calm in the instinctual life, where there is no danger, the individual can permit himself a degree of stupidity. In this respect instinctual anxiety has the familiar effect of objective anxiety. Objective danger and deprivation spur men on to intellectual feats and ingenious attempts to solve their difficulties, while objective security and superfluity tend to make them comfortably stupid."

So rich is the entire book it is possible to skip by comments like those as interesting but somewhat vague and oracular asides—until, that is, we seek explanation for the most upsetting dilemmas of our time. How, for instance, are we to comprehend many of the richest boys and girls in the richest nation in the world behaving like aimless delinquents? Or how do we account for the incredible survival managed by generations of Negro families in Mississippi, where brutality for centuries seems to have produced people whose alertness, generosity, and integrity quite visibly bewildered those of us who spent the summer of 1964 there? All of us were so free, literate, well fed, and clothed; yet confronted by the civilized, gentle endurance of the people we came to help, many of us wondered—out of no misty sentiment—what we lacked.

For Miss Freud such paradoxes are clearly to be expected, and she doubtless shares the confusion or surprise they generate in us. Indeed, shortly after her masterpiece on ego psychology was finished she herself was to experience unexpected hardship, and from it find the inspiration for a long time of hard and rewarding work.

When the Nazis came to Vienna they were still sensitive enough to world opinion to spare important people, though only after ransom was exacted. Freud thus escaped, to live on a bit over a year, even several weeks into World War II. Before his death he would see the madness he knew possible in individual men given incredible political and institutional structure. Anna was not permitted leave from Austria with her father without a day's arrest and interrogation by the Gestapo, on March 22, 1938. "Anna bei Gestapo," Freud wrote in his diary. Until that day he had hesitated, at eighty-two, to leave a city he had lived in for seventy-nine years. Thereafter, he could not wait to get out.

Anna Freud's arrival in England, her continued stay in London, the enormous variety and productivity of her work there, all fit ironically into *her* earlier life. When the first World War broke out she was a youth of nineteen on a visit to England. It took some weeks for her to return to Austria—she came back on a boat with Austria-Hungary's ambassador to England through the long Mediterranean way rather than over a continent rendered impassable by war. A quarter of a century later she would return to England, this time by land, and just before such a route would again be impassable.

Nor did she return to England a stranger to its language or culture. She had learned English as a youth, and in 1920—at twenty-five—used it fluently in an address to the Sixth International Congress of Psychoanalysis. In those years, the 20's and 30's, her initial profession, that of a schoolteacher, was not properly speaking abandoned, but joined to her interest in the analysis of children. When she talked to teachers about the psychological problems of schoolchildren she spoke not as the theoretician, or even clinician, come to deliver the "consultant's" wisdom, but as a comrade, all too aware of just how complicated a problem it is to teach, and for that matter, to give advice to teachers. "We must not demand too much from one another," was her way of beginning a lecture to teachers, of dampening even in the heady early 30's any inclination of the hungry for more than the lean truth.

Scarcely two years after meeting with the Gestapo she was noting under the title of "Further Observations" the reactions of children to the "big air attack on London on the night of Wednesday, 16 of April (1941)." She described it as follows: "Even for people who had gone through the period of the so-called Blitz in September and October 1940, the events of this night were surprising and alarming. There was more gunfire than ever before, the sound of falling bombs was continuous, the crackling of fires which had been started could be heard in the distance, and again all these sounds were drowned by the incessant droning of airplanes which flew over London, not in successive waves as in former raids, but in one uninterrupted stream from 9 P.M. until 5 A.M."

Her two books *War and Children* and *Infants Without Families* reveal the fate of children exposed to such conditions and their consequences—physical hurt, loss of home and parents, disruption of routine, constant moving about with exposure to all sorts of people and surroundings. With her friend and colleague Dorothy Burlingham, she helped organize and run the Hampstead Nursery, three houses for children of different ages. It was one of many so-called "colonies" of The Foster Parents' Plan for War Children, Inc., which was started in 1936 when Spain's children faced bombardment. Throughout the war she worked in the nursery, dedicating herself to ordinary people up against terrible circumstances, caring for children and seeing to it that their emotional needs were as respected as their hunger and various injuries. During the war England was full of lonely, frightened, confused children; they often had a hard time making sense of a world of sudden explosions, arbitrary departures, shifting scenery, and inconstant grown-ups. Those who came upon Hampstead were fortunate.

Miss Freud's writings about these years turn careful, scientific scrutiny into poetry: "Children are, of course, afraid of air raids, but their fear is neither as universal nor as overwhelming as has been expected. An explanation is required as to why it is present in some cases, absent in others, comparatively mild in most and rather violent in certain types of children." What others might call "case material" is offered as follows:

> One of our mothers, a comfortable and placid Irish woman, the mother of eight children, when asked whether her rooms had been damaged by bombing, answered, with a beaming smile:
> "Oh, no, we were ever so lucky. We had only blast and my husband fixed the window frames again." Blast, which removes the window frames, not to mention the window panes, can be a very uncomfortable experience; but again, we can be certain that for the children of this mother the occurrence of the blast was not a very alarming incident. We had, on the other hand, the opportunity to observe very anxious mothers with very anxious children. There was John's mother. . . . She never went to bed while the alarm lasted, instead stood at the door trembling and insisted on the child not sleeping either. He, a boy of five, had to get dressed, to hold her hand and to stand next to her. He developed extreme nervousness and bed wetting.

Later on she notes that

> . . . the fear of air raids assumes completely different dimensions in those children who have lost their fathers as a result of bombing. In quiet times they turn away from their memories as much as possible and are gay and unconcerned in their play with other children . . . the recurrence of an air raid forces them to remember and repeat their former experience.

Summing up her thoughts about the reactions of children to evacuation (then thought the most humane thing to do for blitzed children) she asserts that

> War acquires comparatively little significance for children so long as it only threatens their lives, disturbs their material comfort or cuts their food rations. It becomes enormously significant the moment it breaks up family life and uproots the first emotional attachments of the child within the family group. London children, therefore, were on the whole much less upset by bombing than by evacuation to the country as a protection against it.

It is hard to overestimate the worth of such information, supplied so quietly yet firmly. Incongruities are not feared, nor prevailing customs and sentiments left unchallenged. The psychoanalyst can at once see clearly, talk sensibly, and work with humor and kindness. It does not always happen that way.

After the war Anna Freud continued her very practical work with children and at the same time tried to fit whatever observations she thereby made into a coherent view of the mind's structure and function. Paper after paper appeared; they were usually short; they were all tightly written; and invariably they contained skillful, even elegant mixtures of the useful and the theoretical. Some of them appeared in scholarly annuals like the *Psychoanalytic Study of the Child*, while others could be found in journals dedicated to service, like "Child Study" or the "Health Education Journal." The titles tell of her broad interests: "Nursery School Education—Its Uses and

Dangers"; "Sublimation as a Factor in Upbringing"; "Sex in Child-hood" and "Difficulties of Sex Enlightenment"; or "Certain Types and Stages of Social Maladjustment." Reading them I always feel her uncanny ability to put a fastidious mind to earthy subjects. Thus, in a classical paper on childhood feeding disturbances (1946) she covers an extremely broad and difficult subject in thirteen well-organized pages. The coverage is both formal and categorical yet appropriately larded with descriptions of the "squashy and smeary foods" disliked by some children or the "sweets, biscuits and cakes" they may be drawn to. Characteristically, when she concludes she is wary of the literal-minded reader: "The various types of eating disturbances, which have been separated off from each other in this paper for the purpose of theoretical evaluation, are invariably mixed and interre-lated when observed clinically."

Now, in her seventieth year, Miss Freud has published a remark-able book, *Normality and Pathology in Childhood*. She has tried to fit together interests and ideas that have run through all her writings, not only the books and the score or so longer articles and lectures, but a number of briefer communications and monographs. She has also managed to provide a uniquely historical view of psychoanalysis as a changing field of inquiry. Someday a social historian will find this book indispensable as he studies psychoanalysis by tracing its emer-gence from a specific medical, intellectual and social climate, show-ing the forces resisting it, those welcoming it, and even those uncritically entranced by it (a development Freud by no means over-looked). Such a history of psychoanalysis would naturally have to come to terms with Freud's mind—its action like a dazzling *pas de deux* between a pragmatic observer of the facts and a theory-bound metapsychologist. Beyond that, however, would be the larger histori-cal task of describing the institutional development of psychoanaly-sis, its spread over the world, the different forms such geographic and cultural dispersal has given to it, and the reasons why.

Moreover, the concerns of analysts have been changing, not always harmoniously. The tug upon psychoanalysis from the doctors and the healers is matched by the pull of those who are much more interested in its intellectual promise, its possible contributions to psychobiography, to the social sciences and philosophy. Even in the clinical psychoanalytic study of children, as specialized a field as one can find in medicine or psychiatry, there are sharp differences in interests and in the interpretation of observations. More significant are the overall differences—they have become severe disagreements on occasion—in matters as basic as how to work with children, what use to make clinically of their day-to-day behavior, and where the actions of children may have relevance to a psychoanalytic theory of adult life. In most of these matters Anna Freud has quietly figured, taking her stand not by rhetoric but by the example of her work.

Her constant emphasis—in this book particularly and through her life—has been upon the importance of direct observation. For a long time psychoanalysts were quite naturally suspicious of what they saw, of the "surface" manifestations of the mind's life. They saw that after weeks and months of listening to a patient they found hidden truths about his feelings that nothing "observable" (his conversation, attitudes, interests, or manner) could reveal. As a consequence, any conscious expression, any kind of behavior that might simply be watched and noticed, seemed at worst an irrelevant distraction or disguise, and at best a mere pathway to a truth that is always hidden and deviously expressed.

In time, prodded by people like Miss Freud, drastic changes have occurred in the view many analysts have of what they can observe directly. The unconscious no longer has to be "proved," it can be seen in its everyday manifestations—slips, symptoms, patterns of thought or action—as well as in the office after a long course of treatment. The unconscious can also be seen in the way people respond to it, by the "mechanisms of defense" they adopt. What is more, in children it can be seen *developing*. Naturally, insofar as the analyst relies upon such observations, and draws conclusions very cautiously on the basis of those observations, his theoretical elbow-room will be rather strictly limited. Whatever he postulates he will want to verify, either by checking on the observations of others, or making more of his own. Even among Freud's writings, he will tend to fall back upon those that grew out of clinical study rather than those that depended too exclusively on speculation. To such analysts the genius of Freud will be precisely those speculations that gave order to the considerable "clinical material" he encountered—and was both "free" and perceptive enough to notice. What he said about Moses, or Leonardo da Vinci, or the "death instinct" is fascinating and stimulating but not in itself the basis for further psychoanalytic research. To those analysts the job ahead is not the further construction of theory—the edifice is already unwieldy, and some would say toppling—but further clinical study, further observations, in hospitals and clinics, in the society and across into other cultures, so that more "hard" facts can support whatever additional generalizations are to be made.

Children, particularly, demand watching. They are so individual, so diverse—not yet molded by society. Their constant activity, their spontaneity, their willingness to share unabashedly what thoughts, wishes, and fears they have, make them ideal candidates for the psychoanalytically trained observer. Since psychoanalysis itself has placed such emphasis on childhood, on its crucial events and enduring significance, one might have expected a rather extensive psychoanalytic child psychology to have developed, that is, a coherent view of normal child development which accounts for how emotional stability and "normal" behavior in infants, children, and youths are either enabled or thwarted.

In point of fact there was an ironic lag—it is only now being filled—between psychoanalytic *interest* in childhood and psychoanalytic *study* of childhood. What happened was that analysts took the observations they made in their office on neurotic adult patients and, in Miss Freud's delicately stated words, "ventured beyond the boundaries of fact finding and began to apply the new knowledge of the upbringing of children." Add to such efforts the inclinations of a nervous, affluent middle-class, no longer interested in the Ten Commandments or the Sermon on the Mount—with enough time and success on its hands to believe that at last "happiness," that is, "mental health," could be spelled out step by step for the child—and a social phenomenon was on its way.

A "psychoanalytic education" for children, one that would "prevent" neurosis, became a fervently sought goal. "The attempts to reach this aim," writes Anna Freud, "have never been abandoned, difficult and bewildering as their results turned out to be at times. When we look back over their history now, after a period of more than forty years, we see them as a long series of trials and errors."

She goes on to make a summary that may well be in itself a cultural document of this century:

> . . . at the time when psychoanalysis laid great emphasis on the seductive influence of sharing the parents' bed and the traumatic consequences of witnessing parental intercourse, parents were warned against bodily intimacy with their children and against performing the sexual act in the presence of even their youngest infants. When it was proved in the analyses of adults that the withholding of sexual knowledge was responsible for many intellectual inhibitions, full sexual enlightenment at an early age was advocated. When hysterical symptoms, frigidity, impotence, etc., were traced back to prohibitions and the subsequent repressions of sex in childhood, psychoanalytic upbringing put on its program a lenient and permissive attitude toward the manifestations of infantile, pregenital sexuality. When the new instinct theory gave aggression the status of a basic drive, tolerance was extended also to the child's early and violent hostilities, his death wishes against parents and siblings, etc. When anxiety was recognized as playing a central part in symptom formation, every effort was made to lessen the children's fear of parental authority. When guilt was shown to correspond to the tension between the inner agencies, this was followed by the ban on all educational measures likely to produce a severe super-ego. When the new structural view of the personality placed the onus for maintaining an inner equilibrium on the ego, this was translated into the need to foster in the child the development of ego forces strong enough to hold their own against the pressure of the drives. Finally, in our time, when analytic investigations have turned to earliest events in the first year of life and highlighted their importance, these specific insights are being translated into new and in some respects revolutionary techniques of infant care.

A little further on she takes note of the great hope and faith that was involved in all this: "In the unceasing search for pathogenic agents and preventive measures, it seemed always the latest analytic discovery which promised a better and more final solution of the problem."

In any event some of the advice given to parents was useful, helping them to feel more open and relaxed with their children, and sparing their children a substantial variety of harsh and senseless practices. There were disappointments, too:

> . . . Above all, to rid the child of anxiety proved an impossible task. Parents did their best to reduce the children's fear of them, merely to find that they were increasing guilt feelings, i.e., fears of the child's own conscience. Where in its turn, the severity of the super-ego was reduced, children produced the deepest of all anxieties, i.e., the fear of human beings who feel unprotected against the pressure of their drives.

All in all, what emerged were children to some extent unlike others before them, but nonetheless human: ". . . It is true that the children who grew up under its influence were in some respects different from earlier generations; but they were not freer from anxiety or from conflicts, and therefore not less exposed to neurotic and other mental illnesses."

Then she emphasizes that "this need not have come as a surprise if optimism and enthusiasm for preventive work had not triumphed with some authors over the strict application of psychoanalytic tenets." After all, she reminds the reader, conflict is built into life, into human development, into the complicated organization of the mind that characterizes "civilized" man. Somehow, to switch into a theological perspective she might not find congenial, the sin of pride permitted many people to forget this.

Even though Miss Freud might not take to such talk, she is clearly worried that the public will expect the impossible from analysis, and even more, that analysts will make unjustified assumptions about what they know and how they ought to do their work. In her new book she begins and ends with a reminder that not only is there a lack of the information needed to insure proper advice to the public on a number of matters connected with child rearing, but even more significant, the same situation holds for the heart of psychiatric and psychoanalytic work with children, its ability to *assess*, to appraise the child's behavior and decide what in it is pathological and what is a part of growth and development. "As our skill in assessment stands today," she concludes, ". . . accuracy of diagnostic judgment seems to me an ideal to be realized not in our present state of knowledge but in the distant future."

However, this book is neither pretentiously humble nor interested in conveying an impression of the widespread ignorance or incompetence of a scientific field of inquiry. On the contrary, it is probably one of the boldest, strongest—and definitely most original—statements to come from an analyst in a long time precisely because its author has the courage and intelligence to face squarely the really formidable and vexing problems in psychoanalysis. What, after all, is normal? Can we child psychiatrists predict the future adult's adjustment on the basis of what we see in him as a toddler or child of six or seven? And if so, can we prevent later illnesses by spotting them and immediately treating them? When, indeed, ought a child's emotional troubles be weighed serious enough for psychiatric evaluation? For that matter, what are the differences between the treatment of children and adults, and would it not be desirable for all children to have some exposure to therapy?

In many ways she demonstrates that the criteria for normality in childhood are topsy-turvy to those in the adult world, thereby giving us the clue that those criteria cannot simply be culled from evaluations made in the office or clinic, but involve social, developmental, and cultural influences—a fact that may be obvious to many outside both hospitals and psychiatric offices but forgotten by those inside who are under daily pressures to make diagnoses and afterwards embark upon various and decisively different courses of treatment. At what point does the "normally rebellious" adolescent become a "sick" one or an "anti-social one"? The medical disposition may vary depending upon which of those three labels are used. With children not yet adolescents food fads vary from culture to culture and sleeping disturbances, clinging behavior, or temper tantrums may upset the parents or people in one neighborhood and not bother those in another. In any event they don't trouble the child: "Where the parents interfere [with such symptoms] their restraining action, not the symptom is blamed by the child for causing distress." Moreover, it is eminently normal for children to be going through a continual series of trials: "In sharp contrast to former conventional beliefs, it is now well known that mental distress is an inevitable by-product of the child's dependency and of the normal developmental processes themselves."

What is normal for children thus varies with age, with culture, with the contemporary problems facing the child, with the relationship of his present troubles to his past achievements and the tasks about to face him, with his evident capacity (or lack of it) to resolve whatever problems confront him. To a large extent each child's strengths and weaknesses have to be evaluated on their own merits, and Miss Freud insists that there is a "wide range" even to the *variations* of normality. A child may be showing a temper or having trouble eating a certain food and be doing so quite appropriately, that is, for his age some such development is understandable, reasonable and common enough. Thus, a child will become anxious and petulant when left alone too long. If he doesn't, if his "patience" seems as plentiful as "ours," as the adult's, it is more rather than less likely that he is disturbed. Again, a child will go through periods of sleeplessness or insomnia that relate to his increasing awareness of the world, hence nervousness about it. When he gets older he will have more tension and misery as his mother, the first judge and referee he knows, sets limits on him. Of course, such *developmental* anxiety varies from family to family, and for that matter, from school situation to school situation. (Even more confusing, a child may be "good" at home and "bad" at school, depending upon a large number of possible considerations.)

Even with clearly disturbed children, there is no way right now to predict their psychological future. In 1951 Ernst Kris called the knowledge of the normal an "underdeveloped" or "distressed" area of psychoanalysis, though Anna Freud's effort to trace general *patterns* of growth has helped in that area. The same holds for the region of diagnostic prediction, even in adult work as well as with children. I can obtain similar clinical histories from two patients, yet find their current problems remarkably different. We daily see the parents of our sickest patients and wonder why *their* children. We meet only mildly troubled people and find their parents, their earlier lives, impossible. We wonder, as we hear of this or that complaint about the child and learn about his family life, how he might *ever* grow up, even given treatment let alone in its absence. In a section dealing with "homosexuality as a diagnostic category in childhood disorders" Miss Freud speaks the facts bluntly as we now know them:

> . . . In other words, that certain childhood elements in given cases have led to a specific homosexual result does not exclude a different or even the opposite outcome in other instances. Obviously, what determines the direction of development are not the major infantile events and constellations in themselves, but a multitude of accompanying circumstances, the consequences of which are difficult to judge both retrospectively in adult analysis and prognostically in the assessment of children. They include external and internal, qualitative factors.

The lesson is clear: human beings are thoroughly individual; and it is a risky business to categorize their complaints or to theorize smugly about their future.

Even the decision whether or not to treat a child is often a hard one to make. In some cases time will clearly "solve" the problem; in other cases there may indeed be a problem, but educational work with the parents and a brief kind of "fact-finding" work with the child may make therapy, or certainly analysis, unnecessary. Some problems classically need analysis, though they are not necessarily those manifesting the most open and troublesome symptoms. In other cases "the analyst is faced by nothing but enigmas, with no certainty about the therapeutic possibilities."

Finally, Miss Freud does not—as do some of her colleagues—recommend analysis for "normal" childhood conflicts: ". . . the child analyst cannot escape the feeling that here a therapeutic method is assigned a task which, by rights, should be carried out on the one hand by the ego and on the other by the parents of the child."

When Ernest Jones asked Anna Freud what she thought her father's most noteworthy characteristic was, she replied instantly: "his simplicity." He was indeed a man of simple personal habits. He wrote simple prose. He made an astonishing number of observations, and quite simply, quite stubbornly, fought for the intactness of their preservation, so that eventually they would survive over the generations and cross into every continent.

Anna Freud has remained fittingly loyal to her father by refusing to stand in useless awe of his accomplishments. She has gone forward where he left off, giving her life to children from unhappy homes, to children in the midst of the terrors of war, to normal children in their puzzling, inspiring variety. All the while she has written the clear, civilized prose of the confident scientist, the warm, good-humored prose of the kind and sensible human being. One can fairly glide along the pages of her latest book, even though it is obviously addressed to professionals. The most complicated idea emerges so effortlessly that it seems to be pure "common-sense." She has never exploited her name or her profession. She has lived discreetly with her doubts, refusing to allow them to make her strident, pedantic, or doctrinaire. She, too, has achieved simplicity.

20, MARESFIELD GARDENS,
LONDON, N.W.3.

HAMPSTEAD 2002.

July 10, 1966.

Dear Dr. Coles,

Thank you very much for your letter and for sending me your article about myself. I have read the latter almost with a feeling of shock that you guessed so precisely the various things which I wanted to accomplish and to be in life. Neither I, nor surely most other people feel that all these wishes have come true. But you seem to think so and for that I am very grateful.

Yours sincerely

Anna Freud

THE HAMPSTEAD CHILD-THERAPY COURSE AND CLINIC

12 & 21, MARESFIELD GARDENS, LONDON, N.W.3

PSYCHIATRIST IN CHARGE:
LISELOTTE FRANKL, M.B., B.S., PH.D.

DIRECTOR: ANNA FREUD, LL.D.
20, MARESFIELD GARDENS,
LONDON, N.W.3.
TEL.: HAMPSTEAD 2002.

June 1, 1968.

Dear Robert Coles,

Thank you so much for sending me your children's book and your poem. I like both very much indeed.

When I was in New Haven for a month recently, I hoped very much that by some chance I would meet you there, or that I would meet you during a brief stay in New York. I wanted to tell you how deeply impressed I was by your "Children of Crisis". But I am sure that you have heard the same feeling expressed by many other people.

I do think that you should visit us here in Hampstead. What we can offer you is a small Nursery School for under-priviledged children; a small nursery group for blind children; a fairly big Clinic for the treatment of all sorts of problem children who fight against adverse external and internal circumstances; and a large group of workers who are passionately interested in child development.

Do let me know whenever you see a chance for a visit. Not August when we are closed; not September when I am on holiday; not April when I am often in Yale; but at all other times of the year.

Very sincerely yours

Anna Freud

20, MARESFIELD GARDENS,

LONDON, N.W.3.

HAMPSTEAD 2002.

July 19, 1969.

Dear Dr. Coles,

It is always a pleasure for me to
hear from you and to receive your books is
a special pleasure. I read both immediately
and with great interest.

The Grass Pipe reads exceedingly well
and wholly understandable for any pre-adoles-
cent. There is one feeling though which it
aroused in me: is it not too optimistic to
believe that finally the youngsters will
apply to the father and accept his opinion?
How many of them do while there is still
time? Or am I too pessimistic in this
respect?

I went wholly and all out on the book
on hunger. It made me feel that perhaps it
is all wrong to work clinically with children
as I do here and not on the much bigger social
problems of real deprivation. What a terrible
indictment for any Society to spend money on
anything else before these extreme needs are
satisfied. And how can one understand it?
Would it not be comparatively easy to come
to the help of these districts and create em-
loyment? Is there any political reason why
it does not happen?

When will you come to London and visit
us here?

Yours sincerely

Anna Freud

20, MARESFIELD GARDENS,

LONDON, N.W.3.

HAMPSTEAD 2002.

Dr.Robert Coles,
Harvard University
Health Services,
75 Mt.Auburn Street,
Cambridge,Mass.02138.

January 20, 1970.

Dear Robert Coles,

I should have thanked you for your two books long
ago when they came in the middle of December. But I felt
that the fact of having one of them dedicated to me was
too big a thing to be answered quickly by saying that
"I looked forward to reading it". Therefore I waited for
the peace of the Christmas holidays to read it very thoroughly
and to think about it. This I have done now.

I feel that "Wages of Neglect" is a wonderful book,
the best of its kind, or, rather, the only constructive
one, to my mind, which has been published on these matters
so far. It shows not only the terrible state of affairs,
which leaves one with a resulting feeling of hopelessness,
but it really shows a way out and throws light on what could
be done, what has been done already and what should be done
in many places. At least it left me with a feeling of elation:
there are ways out, after all, and they are not even so very
difficult to take.

In contrast to what your book shows, I received in the
last days a cutting from the New York Times (12th January),
"Obituary of Heroin Addict who died at 12",written by a
Joseph Lelyveld. I do not know whether you have seen it.
It shows the reverse side, the desperate plight of a ghetto
child and the inadequacy of the social services which dealt
with him. Joe Goldstein of the Yale Law school sent it to me
since we have the plan there to collect such cases and count
up in one or two of them the amounts of public money spent on
them fruitlessly, with absolutely zero result, in absolutely
the wrong way, and to contrast it with what could be done in
more enlightened ways with no increase in expenditure. It is
quite horrifying if looked at closely.

-2-

There is no chapter in the book which I cannot
confirm from personal experience.
About the "Rock-Bottom Poor": Mrs.Burlingham and
I had a Day Nursery for such children, aged between one
and two when we were in Vienna still. Their parents were
those who were what was called "beyond the dole", which means
that they received nothing at all from the community and
begged their livelihood by singing in the Vienna streets.
Vienna was full of beggars at that time. But we were very
struck by the fact that they brought the children to us,
not because we fed and clothed them and kept them for the
length of the day, but because "they learned so much",
i.e. they learned to move freely, to eat independently,
to speak, to express their péreferences, etc. To our own
surprise, the parents valued this beyond everything. This
showed, of course, that they themselves were not quite
hopeless yet. But then Vienna, even then, was not as hopeless a place as the American slums are.
We meet the same in the underpriviledged parents
of our Hampstead Clinic Nursery School now. We have immigrant
children there from Italian or Indian parents, London slums
(usually Irish), and African children. They are immensely
pleased when the children learn to speak English and, altogether learn to speak, and even correct their speech.
But we also have very neglectful parents and very
abnormal parents, where I feel that there is no hope of
changing them and that our role is to provide for the child
a substitute parent in the form of the teacher and the
Nursery community.

There is one point which I did not find in your
book and that is the very high priority of body care.
We find that with many neglected children the first approach
is by way of liking their body and caring for their body,
and having the pride and pleasure in it which the ordinary
middle class mother has in her child's pretty bodily
appearance. Therefore we do a lot of washing of hair,
combing, looking in the mirror, providing something pretty
to wear, admiring whenever the child has something worth
admiring. Recently we had a little Jean who came to us
as a hopeless little waif with stringy hair and dripping
nose and left us some years later as a pretty, attractive little
school-girl. We tried simultaneously to sort out her inner

-3-

confusion in individual treatment and to make her discover
"herself". I have doubts whether this was as successful as
the external appearance but at least she will be better able
to cope with school. Once, in the beginning, she sat peace-
fully next to the teacher who was sawing up a tear in her
teddy-bear and watching that, she said: "He likes being taken
care of by you."

There is one point here which is very important to me.
So much of this work is very slow and very individual. In
contrast, most people in public social work think that, since
the need is urgent, relief has to come quickly, and must not
take years. But it always does. We find that even when children
are in our Nursery School for two years only, this is much too
little; three years or even four are so much better. The
other problem is numbers. Since there are so many neglected
children, many people think in terms of "many". But their
problems are individual ones and, even in a group, they have
to be approached individually. That means that groups have
to be kept very small and the number of teachers large. Whereever
the opposite happens, i.e. where large numbers of young children
are in the charge of very few adults, or for insufficient
periods, it might as well not be done at all. Or rather, the
only effect is then to keep the children in a room instead
of in the street. It does not do anything real for their
inner life.

I was very pleased to find what you wrote about the
interaction between external and internal factors. This is
exactly what I have in mind. What I want to write about next
is one of our small Italian girls, a "newcomer" in England,
with an excellent mother but from a very poor background otherwise and exposed to all sorts of stresses. She brought to
all her tasks an enormous strength of personality and, I believe,
is one of the most "normal" children we ever had.

I hope that I have not bored you with all this.
It is merely to express once more my thanks for the dedication
which pleases me very much and puts me under an obligation.

I shall be in New Haven (Davenport College, Yale) from
April 1st to 24th. I should be very pleased indeed to see you there.

Yours sincerely

Anna Freud

NOTES

PREFACE

1. See, for example, the *Children of Crisis* series, in five volumes, especially *A Study of Courage and Fear* (Boston: Atlantic–Little, Brown, 1967); also, *A Farewell to the South* (Boston: Atlantic–Little, Brown, 1972). I dedicated a book of psychiatric and psychoanalytic essays to Miss Freud: *The Mind's Fate* (Boston: Atlantic–Little, Brown, 1975); and Maria Piers and I dedicated our *Wages of Neglect* (New York: Quadrangle Press, 1969) to her, a book about the psychological struggles of troubled, urban youth. See also *Erik H. Erikson: The Growth of His Work* (Boston: Atlantic–Little, Brown, 1970), in which I write about her as his analyst and teacher.

2. "Neuropsychiatric Aspects of Acute Poliomyelitis," *American Journal of Psychiatry*, vol. 114, no. 1 (July 1957).

3. I discuss Anna Freud's relationship to Erik H. Erikson, of course, in the biography of him (op cit.). I also make repeated mention of Miss Freud in the biography of Simone Weil—*Simone Weil: A Modern Pilgrimage* (Reading, Mass.: Addison-Wesley/Merloyd Lawrence, 1987)—and to a lesser extent in *Dorothy Day: A Radical Devotion* (Reading, Mass.: Addison-Wesley/Merloyd Lawrence, 1987).

4. She read several of Williams's shorter pieces of fiction in *The Doctor Stories* (New York: New Directions, 1984), and a *New Yorker* profile of Walker Percy I sent her. See *Walker Percy: An American Search* (Boston: Atlantic–Little, Brown, 1978).

CHAPTER I

1. I had a half-hour talk with her on that matter one morning in New Haven in 1970. She spoke as many of my college students do who want to work with needy or troubled people, but who don't regard themselves as able or willing to become physicians. "I never really thought of the matter," she said, "until the question of 'lay analysis' became a serious one, because

some wanted to deny psychoanalytic training to those who are not physicians. Then I thought of the matter a lot!"

2. She was at her most winning and touching when she spoke of her teaching days. Her face lit up; her eyes grew brighter. I often wondered whether psychoanalysis, in a way, hadn't become one long detour, of sorts, for her. She was at her warmest when she talked of certain teachers and nurses who had, like her, taken psychoanalytic training with a minimum of earlier, academic experience—individuals who brought to their analytic training the experience and wisdom that come with direct and prolonged contact with children.

3. I felt she was more respectful of Heinz Hartmann than any other psychoanalyst, save the obvious one who founded the field—even a bit in awe of Dr. Hartmann's brilliant, wide-ranging mind. His *Ego Psychology and the Problem of Adaptation* (New York: International Universities Press, 1958), originally published three years after her book *The Ego and the Mechanisms of Defense* (New York: International Universities Press, 1966), provided a second major study of the ego. Together, the two books prompted a major shift in psychoanalytic thinking. Several times I talked with her about another of Dr. Hartmann's books, *Psychoanalysis and Moral Values* (New York: International Universities Press, 1960)—an extremely valuable and thoughtful exposition of the relationship of the moral life not only to the superego, but to the ego as well.

4. I remember well the appearance of those remarks, made upon the conferral of an honorary degree upon her by Jefferson Medical College—in *The Journal of the American Psychoanalytic Association* 15 (1967): 833–840: a beam of personal candor and a contribution to the social and cultural history of a profession.

5. See Edwardo Weiss, *Sigmund Freud as a Consultant: Recollections of a Pioneer in Psychoanalysis* (New York: Intercontinental Medical Books, 1970).

6. Anna Freud knew Milton's *Areopagitica*, and its rational optimism fitted well with the more hopeful side of psychoanalysis, to which she belonged, despite a guarded and reserved side of her personality.

7. I've struggled for a long time with the question of psychiatric interpretation of men and women who earn a place in history by virtue of their singular achievements. When does important and clarifying psychological interpretation give way to crudely reductionist explanations that do scant justice to what a particular person has accomplished, against whatever odds of anxiety, fear, moodiness, even craziness? See my essays on "psychohistory" in *The Mind's Fate* (op cit.).

8. See her long letter to me in the appendix, with a description of that nursery.

9. See Max Schur, *Living and Dying* (New York: International Universities Press, 1972).

10. Auden's lovely tribute to Freud, "In Memory of Sigmund Freud," can be found in his *Collected Shorter Poems* (1927–1957) (New York: Random House, 1966).

CHAPTER II

1. Her educational writing is part of a tradition we still cherish in the West—from Rousseau to observers such as Paul Goodman, Edgar Z. Friedenberg, Jonathan Kozol, and Tracy Kidder: essayists who want to emphasize and celebrate the importance of schools, as well as criticize their sometimes serious flaws.
2. In fact, she offered much help to me as I tried to interpret the drawings and paintings of the children I knew. See the discussions of those artistic productions in the five volumes of *Children of Crisis* (Boston: Atlantic–Little, Brown, 1967, 1972, 1978), as well as *The Moral Life of Children* (Boston: Atlantic Monthly Press, 1986), *The Political Life of Children* (Boston: Atlantic Monthly Press, 1986), and *The Spiritual Life of Children* (Boston: Houghton Mifflin/Peter Davison, 1990.)

CHAPTER III

1. August Aichhorn, the hugely flexible, imaginative, resourceful clinician, ever ready to reach out toward the most troubled and provocative of youth—see his extraordinary accounts, his stories, in *Wayward Youth* (New York: Viking, 1935); Otto Fenichel, a most learned theorist—especially known for *Psychoanalytic Theory of Neurosis* (New York: W. W. Norton, 1945).
2. Freud the dour skeptic—and theorist quite taken with his "discovery," the id—was often challenged by Freud the nineteenth- and twentieth-century scientist who placed great hope in a growing knowledge as increasingly influential in human affairs, although never, of course, redemptive. As for Freud's religious views, I struggled hard with them in a chapter, "Psychoanalysis and Religion," in *The Spiritual Life of Children* (op. cit.).
3. The best account of this episode can be found in *The Moral Life of Children* (op. cit.).

CHAPTER IV

1. Jane was, frankly, far less inclined than I to be in awe of Miss Freud—or intimidated by her; in fact, she (a teacher) could be quite blunt with a person

over forty years older than she, and earn thereby not annoyance or irritation, but an almost deferential friendliness—perhaps a sincere nod on the
part of a onetime Viennese teacher toward a young American one who had
done noteworthy and impressive work with black children in Louisiana and
Georgia schools under the worst of segregationist authority.

2. In recent years the implacable resistance of the American Psychoanalytic
Association to nonmedical analysts has softened—perhaps because fewer
psychiatrists have been interested in taking psychoanalytic training than was
the case in the 1940s, 1950s, and 1960s. Psychoanalysis now hasn't quite the
appeal it formerly had—as compared, for instance, to the neuro-psycho-
pharmacological side of psychiatry.

3. She was always available to Maria Piers and to me as we tried to understand the difficult problems of poor and ghetto children. We were glad to
dedicate our book on that subject, *The Wages of Neglect* (op cit.) to her; and
the dedication was not only an act of admiration, but one of gratitude for
hours of consultation. (See appendix for her letter with respect to that
book.)

4. That work is described in *The Moral Life of Children* (op cit.) and *The
Political Life of Children* (op. cit.).

5. See a "study" I attempted of Dorothy Day's social and spiritual efforts: *A
Spectacle Unto the World: The Catholic Worker Movement* (New York: Viking,
1973).

CHAPTER V

1. I heard Williams discuss psychoanalysis many times—as he saw it take
root among the New York intelligentsia during the 1930s. His blunt, earthy
descriptions were (are) sui generis. I have described the luck and privilege of
knowing him in *William Carlos Williams: The Knack of Survival in America*
(New Brunswick: Rutgers University Press, 1975).

2. No question, many civil rights activists we knew in the 1960s South were
profoundly distrustful of psychoanalysis—called it both "reductionist" and
"bourgeois." I found some of the criticism both unfair and wrongheaded—
although I also could see why many of those young men and women felt at
such a remove from the world of psychoanalysis I had come to know. I
labored over this question in "Serpents and Doves: Non-Violent Youth in
the South," originally published in *Youth: Change and Challenge*, edited by
Erik H. Erikson (New York: Basic Books, 1963).

3. See Miller's *Errand Into the Wilderness* (Cambridge: Harvard University
Press, 1956), and his anthology entitled *The Transcendentalists* (Cambridge:
Harvard University Press, 1950).

4. See the next to last paragraph of *Childhood and Society* (New York: W. W. Norton, 1950).

CHAPTER VI

1. I had come to Topeka from Albuquerque, where we were then working on a study of Indian and Spanish-speaking children. Dr. Menninger had fired off many a letter, in response to articles I'd written, and we did a memorable series of seminars together—he sharing his firsthand knowledge of the history of psychoanalysis, while I presented some tape-recorded Hopi children's voices, quite a contrast in subject matter!
2. Later to appear in *The Political Life of Children* (op cit.), published four years after her death.
3. Miss Freud's voice is a prominent part of my book on Weil (op cit.).
4. Heinz Hartmann is excellent in his analysis of Freud's moral assumptions in *Psychoanalysis and Moral Values* (op cit.), as is Philip Rieff in his *Freud: The Mind of the Moralist* (New York: Viking, 1959), and, too, both Peter Gay and Paul Roazen (see Selected Bibliography).
5. In a public symposium, entitled "Simone Weil: Live Like Her?" at the Massachusetts Institute of Technology, October 1975.

CHAPTER VII

1. I have discussed the moral power of such novels in *The Call of Stories: Teaching and the Moral Imagination* (Boston: Houghton Mifflin/Peter Davison, 1988).
2. Eventually I sent her some essays I wrote on Agee, trying to connect his literary evocation of childhood with the kind of descriptions she favors: see *Irony in the Mind's Life* (New York: New Directions, 1974), and later, with Ross Spears, *Agee* (New York: Holt, Rinehart, 1985).
3. His final moral, philosophical, and psychological exhortation in *The Moviegoer* (New York: Knopf, 1961).
4. Ariès's book (New York: Vintage, 1962) deserves a wider readership among us in pediatrics, psychiatry, psychoanalysis—a historical context for notions of childhood some of us ground rather uncritically in biology or in an all-too-ahistorical verson of "culture."

I know of at least three full biographical studies of Anna Freud—
one by Elisabeth Young-Bruehl, written with the permission of those
who worked closely with her and have the right to grant or deny
access to her papers: *Anna Freud: A Biography* (New York: Summit,
1988). Of the other two, the one by Uwe Henrik Peters was published
in German (1979), before Miss Freud's death, and in English after she
died: *Anna Freud: A Life Dedicated to Children* (New York: Schocken
Books, 1985). Raymond Dyer's *Her Father's Daughter: The Work of
Anna Freud* (New York: Jason Aronson, 1983) appeared immediately
after Miss Freud died. Each of these books has its strengths, and in
certain ways they complement one another. The Peters book follows
her life chronologically, helps the reader realize how busy she was for
so many years, and how much travel she learned to undertake. The
Dyer book surveys her work and discusses especially well her efforts
in Vienna as a child psychoanalyst, and her later struggle, in London,
to use analytic theory as a means of thinking about normal growth as
well as psychopathology. The biography by Elisabeth Young-Bruehl
is a more ambitious attempt to understand both her personal and her
professional life. For me, the Dyer book conveys best Miss Freud's
work with children; the Peters book glimpses best the everyday
nature of her working life; the Young-Bruehl book gets the reader
closest to a figure of international renown all too shadowed by her
father's name and achievements.

Needless to say, any reader who wishes to be acquainted with
the breadth and depth of Miss Freud's writing life ought look at *The
Writings of Anna Freud*, which are available in eight volumes, all published by International Universities Press in New York. Volume one
(1964) offers the writings she did from 1922 to 1935—her lectures on

child analysis, and her "lectures on psychoanalysis for teachers and parents." Four of her early papers are also included, and they foretell a lot about her later interests—at once clinical and social or cultural in the sense that she always wanted to make a connection between what analysts know and what parents can do (if anything) with such knowledge, as they try, day after day, to bring up their children.

The second volume of Miss Freud's *Writings* (1966) is devoted to *The Ego and the Mechanisms of Defense*, originally published thirty years earlier; and the third volume takes up work done between 1939 and 1945—*Infants Without Families* and the reports she wrote on the wartime Hampstead Nurseries: detailed monthly accounts of particular moments, happenings in the lives of various children, and collectively in the institutional life of the nurseries founded by Miss Freud. The reports were not necessarily written with publication in mind; they were offered to a legion of English and American supporters and friends—and so are all the more affecting and compelling: unselfconscious descriptions of children trying to get their daily emotional bearings, and with them, their caretakers and observers.

The fourth volume of *Writings* encompasses the decade that followed the Second World War (1945–1956). The book was published in 1968, with the subtitle, *Indications for Child Analysis and Other Papers*—a wonderfully rich array of theoretical essays, book introductions, descriptions of research done, and, not least, a touching remembrance of her longtime colleague and friend, August Aichhorn, who died in October 1949. The spirit of the fourth volume persists in the fifth, which covers another decade, from 1956 to 1965, and was published in 1969. This latter volume, with its essays on "direct observation" and on the assessment of pathology in childhood, foreshadows the book *Normality and Pathology in Childhood*, which was originally published in 1965 by International Universities Press and would ultimately become volume six in Miss Freud's collected *Writings*. In the fifth volume she struggles, as always, with the question of "child development": what makes for a reasonably "healthy," "normal" child; what causes detours, or outright impasses, on the child's road toward adulthood. In the fifth volume, too, she sets down in several places her growing interest in the relationship between psychoanalysis and law; and she pays respectful tribute to two distinguished analysts, Heinz Hartmann and Herman Nunberg. There are, again, prefaces written for the books of others, as she becomes a leader, and increasingly, an elder, laying on the hands, so to speak, linking arms with others, and "handing them along." She is both a teacher reaching out to her many students as well as the great man's daughter speaking with his authority.

The seventh volume of the *Writings* includes the years between 1966 and 1970, and is subtitled *Problems of Psychoanalytic Training, Diagnosis and the Technique of Therapy* (1971). It is a book rich with candid discussions of what child analysis offers and doesn't offer—a specialty's growing body of knowledge, but also continuing difficulties as its practitioners try to decide when to intervene in the lives of boys and girls, and when to stay at a remove as watchful observers. She allows herself in some essays to dream about "the Ideal Psychoanalytic Institute"; to speculate on the value of psychoanalysis as a personal experience, as well as a body of knowledge useful for those who don't choose to become analysts. She also shows in several essays (including the commencement address she gave in 1968 at Yale Law School) her continuing interest in the question of when the law (through the state and its various agencies) ought to connect with the lives of children, and in which way.

A final eighth volume to the *Writings* is subtitled *Psychoanalytic Psychology of Normal Development*. The book covers Miss Freud's published work from 1970 to 1980, and appeared in 1981, a year before she died. As always, she is refining her conceptual notions with respect to a field she certainly helped build into its present-day significance: the purposes of analytic work with children, the training of would-be analysts, the importance of "insight" in analytic work, the help psychoanalysis can offer to pediatricians. As in earlier volumes, she salutes other writers with her brief but strong and suggestive forewords, and she salutes analysts now gone (Ernest Jones and, again, August Aichhorn) with memoirs. She also becomes a guide to her father's writing, in an essay that gives an appreciative, yet scrutinizing look at his life's work. In that regard, the twenty-four volumes of *The Complete Psychological Works of Sigmund Freud*, published by the Hogarth Press (London) between 1966 and 1974, are well worth having at hand as one reads not only Anna Freud's response to her father's essays and books, but her response (in all her *Writings*) to his ideas as they went through various transformations. (The first eight volumes contain introductions by Miss Freud, and valuable bibliographies.)

Biographers of Freud have not ignored the one child who followed in his professional footsteps. Ernest Jones's three-volume *The Life and Work of Sigmund Freud* was dedicated to Anna Freud, "true daughter of an immortal sire." The three volumes, published in New York by Basic Books in 1953, 1955, and 1957, give the reader a good idea of the role Anna Freud occupied in the life of her father, especially in the last two decades of his life, as does Peter Gay's more recent biography, *Freud: A Life for Our Time* (New York: W. W. Norton, 1988). The latter offers a luminous section entitled "Anna"—a fine portrait of father and daughter as companions and intellectual colleagues. Another interesting version of Anna Freud is given in her niece Sophie Freud's *My Three Mothers and Other Passions* (New York: New York University Press, 1988). There are references to Anna Freud in various parts of the book, but the chapter "The Legacy of Anna Freud" is a special appreciation, one, however, with a critical side. Another interesting book for the information it supplies about both Anna Freud and her longtime friend and companion and co-worker Dorothy Burlingham is *The Last Tiffany: A Biography of Dorothy Tiffany Burlingham*, by her grandson Michael John Burlingham (New York: Atheneum, 1989). This book explores the complex relationship over decades of time between Anna Freud and Dorothy Burlingham, and gives a valuable glimpse as well of the 1920s Vienna world where child analysis grew so vigorously. I had heard about much of that world when I worked with Erik Erikson, and when I was interviewing him for a profile in *The New Yorker* (later a book: *Erik Erikson: The Growth of His Work* [Boston: Atlantic–Little, Brown, 1970]), but found the Burlingham biography especially helpful in characterizing the small community of men and women, so full of intellectual and moral energy, that developed in Vienna during the middle and late 1920s. In that same regard, Peter Heller's *A Child Analysis with Anna Freud* (New York: International Universities Press, 1990), mentioned earlier in this book, is also quite instructive.

Two books in particular serve as useful background reading for one who wants to learn of the Viennese society in which young Anna Freud lived: *Vienna and the Jews, 1867–1938: A Cultural History* (New York: Cambridge University Press, 1989), by Steven Beller, and Carl Schorske's extraordinary *Fin-de-Siècle Vienna: Politics and Culture* (New York: Knopf, 1980).

Two books that will help the reader who wants to understand Anna Freud from the vantage point of those who took issue with her—an important perspective—are Phyllis Grosskurth's biography, *Melanie Klein: Her World and Her Work* (New York: Knopf, 1986); and *Reshaping the Psycho-Analytic Domain: The Work of Melanie Klein, W. R. Fairbairn and D. W. Winnicott*, by Judith M. Hughes (Berkeley: University of California Press, 1989). I also recommend Winnicott's writing about children and their family life—a valuable body of work, indeed, and one that complements in important ways the studies of Miss Freud: *The Child, The Family and the Outside World* (Reading, Mass.: Addison-Wesley/Merloyd Lawrence, 1987); *The Family and Individual Development* (London: Tavistock, 1965); and *Babies and Their Mothers* (Reading, Mass.: Addison-Wesley/Merloyd Lawrence, 1986).

Also of interest, of course, is the work of Erik Erikson, perhaps Miss Freud's most distinguished analysand, especially *Childhood and Society* (New York: W. W. Norton, 1950). In *Erik Erikson: The Growth of His Work* (Boston: Atlantic–Little, Brown, 1970), I reported Erikson's memories of what he kept calling "The Freud Circle"—a world of hope and idealism soon shattered by marching storm troopers. I have written further essays on Erikson and Anna Freud in *The Mind's Fate: Ways of Seeing Psychiatry and Psychoanalysis* (Boston: Atlantic–Little, Brown, 1975).

Psychoanalysis in recent years has not been without its critics. Philip Rieff's *Freud: The Mind of the Moralist* (Chicago: University of Chicago Press, 1979) is one such important look at Freud, and much of what Rieff says about him applies to his daughter—neither was long on self-indulgence. Paul Roazen has been a vigorous critic of Freud and Anna Freud both—and she certainly knew of his strong-minded and often brilliant (and well-researched) writing in her final years. I recommend all of Roazen's books on various aspects of psychoanalysis, especially *Freud: Political and Social Thought* (New York: Knopf, 1968); *Brother Animal: The Story of Freud and Tausk* (New York: Knopf, 1969); and *Freud: The Politics and Histories of Psychoanalysis* (New Brunswick, N.J.: Transaction, 1990). Roazen pushed hard against psychoanalytic orthodoxy (and its cultural power), thereby more than annoying many of the elders of psychoanalysis, including Anna Freud. Still, his voice, his reason and reasons deserve to be heard and pondered hard.

I close with a few books that are, I believe, spiritual kin: Miss Freud's *Difficulties in the Path of Psychoanalysis* (New York: New York Psychoanalytic Institute, 1969), also part of volume seven of her *Writings*, but well worth publication as a separate small book—a lovely statement, as I have tried to show, about not only her profession's history, but her own life, its character and purposes; *The Technique of Child Psychoanalysis: Discussions with Anna Freud* (Cambridge: Harvard University Press, 1980), a marvelous series of clinical exchanges with Joseph Sandler, Hansi Kennedy, and Robert L. Tyson; *Psychoanalysis and Psychotherapy*, by Frieda Fromm-Reichmann (Chicago: University of Chicago Press, 1959), the clinical essays of a talented analyst—whose discussions of loneliness connect affectingly with those of Miss Freud in such papers of hers as "About Losing and Being Lost," in volume four of her *Writings*; and two books that offer the touching and memorable voices of children—*A Child's War: World War II Through the Eyes of Children*, by Kati David (New York: Four Walls Eight Windows Press, 1989), and the poignant voice of an adolescent, *A Young Girl's Diary*, with a (very brief) preface by Sigmund Freud, edited and introduced by Daniel Gunn and Patrick Gayomard (London: Hyman, 1990). This "diary," shown to Sigmund Freud by one of the first child analysts, Dr. Hermine Von Hug-Hellmuth, may well have been her very own, or that of a friend, a patient; no matter, some general truths of adolescence come across in the book's pages—truths Anna Freud surely knew and felt as she struggled clinically (and theoretically) with the hold "adolescence" has on us not only in the second decade of our lives but, as a consequence of memory, all through the time allotted to us.

Abraham, Karl, 105
"Achievement of Anna Freud,
    The" (Coles), 177, 179–97
Adler, Alfred, 105, 109
Agee, James, 165, 166
Aichhorn, August, 13, 32, 40,
    58–60, 162; remembrances
    of, 45–47, 57, 210, 211
American Psychoanalytic
    Association, 206 n. 2
American Psychiatric
    Association, 180
Andreas-Salomé, Lou, 10, 43,
    55, 146
Ariès, Phillipe, 177
Auden, W. H., 177

Balint, Alice, 13
Bernfeld, Siegfried, 113
Bibring, Grete, 4, 11–12, 66–67,
    103; on analysts' abilities as
    therapists, 87; on rebellion,
    114
Bibring, Edward, 67
Blos, Peter, 13, 14
Book of Common Prayer, 175
Bornstein, Berta, 13

Boston Psychoanalytic
    Institute, 87
Breuer, Josef, 105, 106
Bridges, Ruby, 73, 74, 75
Brill, A. A., 182–83
Burlingham, Dorothy, 10–11, 16,
    20, 84, 100–101, 158, 187, 200

Cather, Willa, 164
Centuries of Childhood (Ariès),
    177
Chekhov, Anton, 177
Child Analysis with Anna Freud,
    A (Peter Heller), 96–97
Childhood and Society (Erikson),
    76, 77, 126, 213
Coles, Jane, 81–83, 97, 164–65,
    205 n. 1
Cyrano de Bergerac (Rostand),
    140

Dann, Gertrud, 21, 23
Dann, Sophie, 21, 23
Day, Dorothy, 102, 141, 148,
    150–52
Death in the Family, A (Agee),
    165

Deutsch, Helene, 4
Dostoyevsky, Fyodor, 161

Ego and the Id, The (Freud),
　64–65
*Ego and the Mechanisms of
　Defense, The* (Anna Freud),
　12, 16, 61, 67–69, 109, 210;
　adolescence in, 147; altruism
　in, 146; comment about
　"tedious and detailed
　theoretical discussions" in,
　64; "The Ego and the Id at
　Puberty" chapter in, 163–64;
　"A Form of Altruism"
　chapter in, 134–35, 139–40;
　and two periods of
　psychoanalysis, 182
Eliot, T. S., 118, 133, 177
Emerson, Ralph Waldo, 115
Erikson, Erik H., 8, 12–15, 109,
　117, 126; biographical study
　of, 105; *Childhood and Society,*
　76, 77, 126, 213; nurture in,
　72; and self-righteousness,
　118
Evans, Walker, 166
"Experiment in Group
　Upbringing, An" (Anna
　Freud), 21

Fenichel, Otto, 59
Ferenczi, Sandor, 105
Field Foundation, 25
Fliess, Wilhelm, 4–5, 105
Forster, E. M., 169

Foster Parents' Plan for War
　Children, Inc., 187
Freud, Sigmund, 3–4, 6, 16, 19,
　122; adulation of, 67, 110–12;
　analysis of Anna Freud, 8,
　12, 117; "circle" of, 11, 66–67,
　108, 213; *The Ego and the Id,*
　64–65; eightieth birthday of,
　16; Eros and Thanatos in,
　65–66; *The Future of an
　Illusion,* 111; and the Grafs,
　13; and the Hartmanns,
　106–8; and the history of
　psychoanalysis, 189; id, ego,
　and superego, 16, 64–65, 69,
　149, 182–83, 205 n. 2; and
　idealism, 146; and intense
　friendships, 4–5, 105; *The
　Interpretation of Dreams,* 4,
　24, 131; and Nazism, 15,
　17–19, 138, 185; *New
　Introductory Lectures,* 9;
　Outline of Psychoanalysis,
　180; as a pragmatic
　physician, 77; *The
　Psychopathology of Everyday
　Life,* 131; and speculation vs.
　clinical study, 190–91;
　quarrels with Jung and
　Adler, 109, 110; repression in,
　132–33; *Three Essays on
　Sexuality,* 131; transference in,
　37–38; unconscious in, 70;
　William Carlos Williams on,
　109–10; writers admired by,
　177; writing of, clarity of, 62

Freud, Martha (Bernays), 4–5
Freud Anniversary Lecture, 112
Future of an Illusion, The
 (Freud), 111

Gardiner, Muriel, 175–76
Goethe, Johann Wolfgang
 von, 166
Goldstein, Joseph, 84, 199
Graf, Max, 13

Hampstead Nurseries, 21,
 23–25, 52, 75, 187, 200, 210
Hartmann, Dora, 105–6, 107–8
Hartmann, Heinz, 6, 105–9,
 125–26, 134, 211
Heller, Peter, 96–98, 212
Hellman, Lillian, 176
Hitler, Adolph, 4, 15–16, 66,
 109
Hort centers, 32–35, 40,
 44–46, 48, 49, 52, 181

"Ideal Psychoanalytic
 Institute: A Utopia, The"
 (Anna Freud), 118–19, 120
Infants Without Families (Anna
 Freud), 101, 186–87
*International Journal of
 Psychoanalysis*, 45
Interpretation of Dreams, The
 (Freud), 4, 24, 131

James, William, 71
Jones, Ernest, 105, 197, 211, 212
Jung, C. G., 6, 105, 109, 110

Katz, Jay, 84
Kennedy, Robert, 115
King, Martin Luther, Jr., 115,
 152
Klein, Melanie, 121–24, 135,
 171–72
Kohut, Heinz, 119
Kris, Ernst, 195–96
Kris, Marianne, 4

Lest We Forget (Gardiner),
 175–76
*Let Us Now Praise Famous
 Men* (Agee), 165, 166

Menninger, Karl, 131–34, 207
 n. 1
Miller, Perry, 115, 116
Milton, John, 9
Montessori, Maria, 12, 32
Morning Watch (Agee), 165,
 166
Mussolini, Benito, 15, 66

New Introductory Lectures
 (Freud), 9
New Orleans Psychoanalytic
 Institute, 72–75
New York Psychoanalytic
 Institute, 111–12
New York Times, 199
Nietzsche, Friedrich, 97
*Normality and Pathology in
 Childhood* (Anna Freud),
 75–76, 176–77, 189, 210

Outline of Psychoanalysis
(Freud), 180

Percy, Walker, 175
Psychoanalysis for Teachers and Parents (Anna Freud), 32, 35–36, 39, 181
Psychoanalytic Association at Budapest, 96
Psychoanalytic Study of the Child, 188–89
Psychoanalytic Treatment of Children, The (Anna Freud), 171, 180
Psychopathology of Everyday Life, The (Freud), 131

Question of Lay Analysis, The (Freud), 88–89

Reik, Theodore, 105
Rilke, Rainer Maria, 43, 166, 168–69, 178
Rostand, Edmond, 139–40

Sachs, Hanns, 105
Schilder, Paul, 6
Schur, Max, 19
Sixth International Congress of Psychoanalysis, 186
Solnit, Albert, 84
Stalin, Josef, 66

Tenth International Psychoanalytic Congress, 180
Thoreau, Henry David, 115
Three Essays on Sexuality (Freud), 131
Tolstoy, Leo, 177

Vienna General Hospital, 6
Vienna Psychoanalytic Institute, 105

War and Children (Anna Freud), 85–87, 158, 186–87
Weil, Simone, 141–45, 147–48, 149–52
Weiss, Eduardo, 7
Williams, William Carlos, 109–10, 157, 206 n. 1
Winnicott, D. W., 77
Woolf, Leonard, 182
Woolf, Virginia, 182
Writings of Anna Freud, The (Anna Freud), 29, 84, 209–12, 214

Yale Law School, 84, 199
Yale University, 161
Yeats, William Butler, 169

ROBERT COLES, M.D., is Professor of Psychiatry and Medical Humanities at Harvard Medical School and research psychiatrist for the University Health Services. Among his many books are biographies of Dorothy Day and Simone Weil, and the *Children of Crisis* series, for which he won the Pulitzer Prize. The much-acclaimed work *The Spiritual Life of Children* is a continuation of Dr. Coles's thirty-year inquiry into the inner lives of children all around the world.